Eunice
Be blessed in
your reading Dorothy x

Emma R Shelly

God Bless x
RN R

Rosanna Gunner

What a fun
project –
Fran x

Eeu Sam Lucy

THE FAITH LIVES OF WOMEN AND GIRLS

Identifying, illuminating and enhancing understanding of key aspects of women's and girls' faith lives, *The Faith Lives of Women and Girls* represents a significant body of original qualitative research from practitioners and researchers across the UK. Contributors include new and upcoming researchers as well as more established feminist practical theologians. Chapters provide perspectives on different ages and stages of faith across the life cycle, from a range of different cultural and religious contexts.

Diverse spiritual practices, beliefs and attachments are explored, including a variety of experiences of liminality in women's faith lives. A range of approaches – ethnographic, oral history, action research, interview studies, case studies and documentary analysis – combine to offer a deeper understanding of women's and girls' faith lives. As well as being of interest to researchers, this book presents resources to enhance ministry to and with women and girls in a variety of settings.

Explorations in Practical, Pastoral and Empirical Theology

Series Editors

Leslie J. Francis, University of Warwick, UK
Jeff Astley, St Chad's College, Durham University, UK
Martyn Percy, Ripon College Cuddesdon and The Oxford
Ministry Course, Oxford, UK

Theological reflection on the church's practice is now recognized as a significant element in theological studies in the academy and seminary. Ashgate's series in practical, pastoral and empirical theology seeks to foster this resurgence of interest and encourage new developments in practical and applied aspects of theology worldwide. This timely series draws together a wide range of disciplinary approaches and empirical studies to embrace contemporary developments including: the expansion of research in empirical theology, psychological theology, ministry studies, public theology, Christian education and faith development; key issues of contemporary society such as health, ethics and the environment; and more traditional areas of concern such as pastoral care and counselling.

Other titles in the series include:

Using the Bible in Practical Theology
Historical and Contemporary Perspectives
Zoë Bennett

Military Chaplaincy in Contention
Chaplains, Churches and the Morality of Conflict
Edited by Andrew Todd

Exploring Ordinary Theology
Everyday Christian Believing and the Church
Edited by Jeff Astley and Leslie J. Francis

Asylum-Seeking, Migration and Church
Susanna Snyder

How Survivors of Abuse Relate to God
The Authentic Spirituality of the Annihilated Soul
Susan Shooter

The Faith Lives of Women and Girls
Qualitative Research Perspectives

Edited by

NICOLA SLEE
The Queen's Foundation, Birmingham, UK

FRAN PORTER
Independent Scholar

ANNE PHILLIPS
Northern Baptist Learning Community, Manchester, UK

ASHGATE

© Nicola Slee, Fran Porter, Anne Phillips and the contributors 2013

All rights reserved. No part of this publication may be reproduced, stored in a retrieval system or transmitted in any form or by any means, electronic, mechanical, photocopying, recording or otherwise without the prior permission of the publisher.

Nicola Slee, Fran Porter and Anne Phillips have asserted their right under the Copyright, Designs and Patents Act, 1988, to be identified as the editors of this work.

Published by
Ashgate Publishing Limited
Wey Court East
Union Road
Farnham
Surrey, GU9 7PT
England

Ashgate Publishing Company
110 Cherry Street
Suite 3–1
Burlington, VT 05401–3818
USA

www.ashgate.com

British Library Cataloguing in Publication Data
A catalogue record for this book is available from the British Library

The Library of Congress has cataloged the printed edition as follows:
The faith lives of women and girls : qualitative research perspectives / edited by Nicola Slee, Fran Porter, and Anne Phillips.
    pages cm – (Explorations in practical, pastoral, and empirical theology)
    Includes index.
    ISBN 978–1–4094–4618–7 (hardcover : alk. paper) – ISBN 978–1–4094–4619–4 (ebook) – ISBN 978–1–4724–0296–7 (epub) 1. Women in Christianity. 2. Women – Religious life. 3. Feminist theology.
    I. Slee, Nicola, editor of compilation.
    BV639.W7F33 2016
    230.082–dc23   2013012959

ISBN 9781409446187 (hbk)
ISBN 9781409446194 (ebk – PDF)
ISBN 9781472402967 (ebk – ePUB)

Printed in the United Kingdom by Henry Ling Limited, at the Dorset Press, Dorchester, DT1 1HD

Contents

List of Contributors   ix

Introduction   1
Anne Phillips, Fran Porter and Nicola Slee

PART I: FEMINIST RESEARCH PERSPECTIVES

1   Feminist Qualitative Research as Spiritual Practice: Reflections on the Process of Doing Qualitative Research   13
Nicola Slee

2   From Privacy to Prophecy: Public and Private in Researching Women's Faith and Spirituality   25
Jan Berry

PART II: NEGLECTED AGES, STAGES AND STYLES IN WOMEN'S AND GIRLS' FAITH LIVES

3   Understanding the Work of Women in Religion   39
Abby Day

4   Feminist Faith Lives? Exploring Perceptions of Feminism Among Two Anglican Cohorts   51
Sarah-Jane Page

5   Being in Communion: Patterns of Inclusion and Exclusion in Young Lay Women's Experiences of Eucharist in the Church of England   65
Kim Wasey

6   God Talk/Girl Talk: A Study of Girls' Lives and Faith in Early Adolescence, with Reflections on Those of their Biblical Fore-sisters   77
Anne Phillips

PART III: FEMALE FAITH IN DIVERSE ECCLESIAL AND GEOGRAPHICAL CONTEXTS

7   The 'In-the-Middle' God: Women, Community Conflict and Power in Northern Ireland   91
    Fran Porter

8   Fat Chicks, Blue Books and Green Valleys: Identity, Women and Religion in Wales   103
    Manon Ceridwen James

9   Searching for Sisters: The Influence of Biblical Role Models on Young Women from Mainstream and Charismatic Evangelical Traditions   111
    Ruth Perrin

10 The Use of Patriarchal Language in the Church of God of Prophecy: A Case Study   121
    Deseta Davis

PART IV: WOMEN'S SPIRITUAL PRACTICES, BELIEFS AND ATTACHMENTS

11 *Broken Silence*: Researching with Women to Find a Voice   131
    Emma Rothwell

12 Integrating Ritual: An Exploration of Women's Responses to *Woman-Cross*   139
    Susanna Gunner

13 Silent Gifts: An Exploration of Relationality in Contemporary Christian Women's Chosen Practices of Silence   147
    Alison Woolley

14 Patterns of Women's Religious Attachments   161
    Eun Sim Joung

15 Boundaries and Beyond: Weaving Women's Experiences of Spiritual Accompaniment   173
    Caroline Kitcatt

| 16 | Understanding Jesus Christ: Women Explore Liberating and Empowering Christologies
Francesca Rhys | 185 |

PART V: EXPERIENCES OF LIMINALITY IN WOMEN'S FAITH LIVES

17	The Relevance of a Theology of Natality for a Theology of Death and Dying and Pastoral Care: Some Initial Reflections *Jennifer Hurd*	195
18	The Liminal Space in Motherhood: Spiritual Experiences of First-time Mothers *Noelia Molina*	207
19	How Survivors of Abuse Relate to God: A Qualitative Study *Susan Shooter*	221

Bibliography	*233*
Index	*253*

List of Contributors

Jan Berry teaches practical theology at Luther King House in Manchester, where she is Programme Leader for the MA in Contextual Theology, a research supervisor, and Principal of Open College. Her doctoral research into women creating their own rituals of transition was published as *Ritual Making Women* by Equinox in 2009. Many of her prayers and hymns have appeared in anthologies, and she has also published a collection of her liturgical work entitled *Naming God* (London: URC Granary Press/Magnet, 2011). Her research interests are in feminist spirituality and liturgy, and pastoral theology. She is a minister of the United Reformed Church, with a commitment to exploring creative forms of liturgy; in addition to her academic work, she is involved in leading workshops, quiet days and retreats exploring feminist and embodied spirituality, and creative writing for worship and prayer.

Deseta Davis currently works as a tutor in the Centre for Black Ministries and Leadership at the Queen's Foundation for Ecumenical Theological Education, Birmingham. She also serves as Pastor and administrator at the Church of God of Prophecy in Birmingham. She has served in many capacities in her local church, including minister and worship leader and she now heads the worship division. She is also a member of the National Music and Worship Development Team where her main task is to help to develop worship throughout the Church of God of Prophecy in the UK. She is also active within prison ministries and goes into prisons on a regular basis to teach about God's love and the hope of salvation. She has recently completed an MA in Applied Theological Studies from the University of Birmingham, which she found very insightful. Through her role at the Queen's Foundation, she is able to bring the study of theology to a range of people who may never have considered such study.

Abby Day has researched belief and belonging across three generations for more than ten years, first at the universities of Lancaster and Sussex, and now as Senior Research Fellow at the University of Kent. She is currently Principal Investigator of a two-year ESRC-funded research project into the lives, beliefs and practices of elderly Christian women. She is Chair of the Sociology of Religion group in the British Sociological Association.

Susanna Gunner has a background in education – as school teacher, Cathedral Education Officer and freelance consultant. As part of her training for ordination, she studied for an MA in Pastoral Theology and found herself engaging seriously with feminist theology for the first time. The research which led to her dissertation and which informs the chapter offered here, enabled her to bring feminist perspectives to a long-standing enthusiasm for devising fresh and imaginative liturgy. Ordained in 2008, Susanna served her curacy in a market town in northeast Norfolk where she still lives and helps out when she can, but her principal role is now Lay Development Co-ordinator for the Diocese of Norwich. As she puts together a range of courses and resources to enrich and enable lay Christians in their discipleship, she finds lots of scope for exploring a particular interest in the relationships between theology, spirituality and the arts.

Jennifer Hurd trained for ministry in the Methodist Church at the Queen's College in Birmingham (now the Queen's Foundation) during 1990–93. She was ordained as a presbyter in 1995. Having served in three circuit appointments in England and Wales, she undertook a period of full-time study at the Queen's Foundation during 2009–13, working towards a PhD validated by the University of Birmingham entitled 'From Cradle to Grave: The Relevance of a Theology of Natality for a Theology of Death and Dying and Pastoral Care in the Church', under the supervision of Dr Nicola Slee. In 2013, she returned to full-time ministry in the Cymru Synod of the Methodist Church.

Manon Ceridwen James was amongst the first women to be ordained priest in the Church in Wales. She is the Bishop's Adviser for Ministry in the diocese of St Asaph, as well as Rector of Llanddulas and Llysfaen outside Colwyn Bay. She is currently undertaking a part-time PhD at Birmingham University, researching the impact of religion on Welsh women's identities. She has had several poems published in literary magazines, including *Poetry Wales*, and school assemblies published by SPCK on <www.assemblies.org> and in *SEAL Assemblies for Primary Schools* and *Primary School Assemblies for Religious Festivals* (London: SPCK, 2011, 2012). She is involved in ministry training for St Michael's College, Llandaff, and teaches ministry skills, particularly adult education. She has two daughters and a stepson and is married to Dylan. She keeps an occasional blog and tweets under Manon Ceridwen.

Eun Sim Joung is a Research Scholar at the Queen's Foundation for Ecumenical Theological Education, Birmingham, where she is involved in the training and supervision of research. She holds a PhD from Birmingham University, UK, published as *Religious Attachment: Women's Faith Development in Psychodynamic Perspective* (Newcastle upon Tyne: Cambridge Scholars, 2008). Her research articles on Korean women's faith experience and its implications on Christian education and pastoral practice were published in various journals in Korean and English, including the *Journal of Beliefs and Values*. She has also translated books from English to Korean, including *Shaping the Journey of Emerging Adults* by Richard R. Dunn and Jana L. Sundene (Downers Grove, IL: IVP, 2012) and

Cultivating Wholeness by Margaret Z. Kornfeld (New York: Continuum, 1998), both to be published by Christian Literature Crusade, Seoul, Korea.

She has been a contributor of Bible notes to *Words for Today* (Birmingham: International Bible Reading Association) for several years and a visiting lecturer teaching women's studies and leadership at a number of universities in Korea. She is involved in the lay ministry of and to international women in Birmingham.

Caroline Kitcatt is a spiritual seeker, a person-centred counsellor, trainer, supervisor and manager. She is a BACP Senior Accredited Counsellor, and is the Centre Director of the Norwich Centre for Personal, Professional and Spiritual Development. She works as a trainer on the Norwich Centre training course for spiritual directors, and accompanies seekers herself. She successfully completed her doctoral research into women's experience of the spiritual direction relationship in 2010, for which she was awarded the Terry Phillips Prize. This is awarded to the research student studying in the Centre for Applied Research in Education at the University of East Anglia (UEA) who presents their findings in the most creative written form. She taught for many years on the Post-Graduate Diploma in Counselling at UEA with particular responsibility for the module on spirituality and counselling. Since completing her doctorate, she has been developing her skills in the area of creativity and spirituality.

Noelia Molina is a psychotherapist, lecturer and researcher. She holds a BSc and MSc from Trinity College, Dublin, and a Higher Diploma in Applied Spirituality from the Milltown Theology and Philosophy Institute. She has been working in private practice since 2004 on an individual, couple and group therapy basis. She lectures on the degree and Masters programmes at the Irish College of Humanities and Applied Science. She is also a visiting lecturer on the MA in Applied Christian Spirituality at All Hallows College, Dublin City University. Her recent and forthcoming publications include the article, 'Stay at Home Mums: The Economics of Motherhood', to be published in *Stay at Home Mums: An International Perspective* (Toronto: Demeter Press, 2014). Currently, she is completing her doctorate on the transition to motherhood as a spiritual process. Noelia has a deep academic and professional commitment to the area of spirituality, gender and motherhood studies.

Sarah-Jane Page is a lecturer in Sociology at Aston University, Birmingham, UK. She completed her PhD at the University of Nottingham in 2009, which focused on the experiences of clergy mothers and male clergy spouses in the Church of England. She has undertaken a number of post-doctoral research posts (for example, a project on clergy fatherhood in the contemporary context at Durham University, and a research study on religion, youth and sexuality, undertaken at the University of Nottingham <http://www.nottingham.ac.uk/sociology/rys>). Her research interests include the study of religion in relation to clergy and clergy families, gender, sexuality, embodiment, feminism, young people and parenthood.

Articles specifically pertaining to her work on clergy have been published in journals such as *Feminist Theology*, *Feminist Review* and *Travail, Genre et Sociétés*. Chapters of her research on religion, youth and sexuality have appeared books such as *Religion, Gender and Sexuality in Everyday Life* (Ashgate, 2012, edited by Peter Nynäs and Andrew Kam-Tuck Yip) and *The Ashgate Companion to Contemporary Religion and Sexuality* (Ashgate, 2012, edited by Stephen J. Hunt and Andrew Kam-Tuck Yip). She is also co-authoring a book with Andrew Kam-Tuck Yip entitled *Religious and Sexual Identities: A Multi-faith Exploration of Young Adults* (Ashgate, forthcoming 2013).

Ruth Perrin currently works as the Director of Training at King's Church, Durham, where she oversees a church-based internship for young adults. She regularly preaches and teaches in evangelical contexts about 'Generation Y', biblical literacy and inspiring the faith of women. Her Grove booklet, *Inspiring Women*, was published in 2007 and she is a consultant on the Bible Society's 'H+' project. Ruth's current doctoral research at the University of Durham explores the hermeneutical development of young evangelical adults, including a chapter on gender-related issues.

Anne Phillips is a Baptist minister and formerly Co-Principal of Northern Baptist Learning Community, Manchester where she and her male colleague modelled gender equality in a fully collaborative style of leadership. Anne taught Christian education and faith development, theological reflection, and pastoral studies with an emphasis on women and children. She also oversaw the work of the Learning Community's Regional Tutors, and the dispersed learning they deliver. She continues to be active in research, and lectures widely on issues around spirituality, and children in the church.

Anne's first career both in Ghana and in different parts of the UK combined secondary and FE teaching, mainly of RE, with bringing up two children. She came into Baptist ministry via an ecumenical route, taking the Diploma in Pastoral Studies at St John's College, Nottingham. As Chair of the Baptist Union's Children's Working Group, she was their representative on several ecumenical bodies responsible for publications relating to children. At the same time, her interest in the marginalization and victimization of women and children was growing and she wrote, and pioneered the implementation of, the first child protection policy for the Baptist Union, *Safe to Grow* (Didcot, BUGB, 1994, 1st edition), followed by '*Breaking the Silence*', a study pack on domestic violence. She has a PhD from Manchester University, and her book based on her doctoral research, *The Faith of Girls: Children's Spirituality and the Transition to Adulthood*, was published by Ashgate in 2011.

Fran Porter is a freelance social and theological researcher, writer and teacher with particular interests in women's Christian faith experience, socially engaged theology, equality and feminist engagement with theology, church culture, biblical studies and hermeneutics. Born and raised in England, Fran lived in Belfast for 27 years and was involved in church, voluntary and academic sectors in Northern Ireland. Since 2008, she has been living in the Midlands. She is an Associate of Coventry University's Applied Research Centre in Sustainable Regeneration and is a Research Scholar at the Queen's Foundation for Ecumenical Theological Education, Birmingham.

Her publications include *Changing Women, Changing Worlds: Evangelical Women in Church, Community and Politics* (Belfast: Blackstaff, 2002), *It Will Not Be Taken Away From Her: A feminist engagement with women's Christian experience* (London: DLT, 2004) and *Faith in a Plural Society: The Values, Attitudes and Practices of Churches in Protecting Minority Participation* (Belfast: Centre for Contemporary Christianity in Ireland, 2008). She is currently writing *Women and Men After Christendom: The Dis-ordering of Gender Relationships* for the Paternoster *After Christendom* series. Fran has a BA in Theology from the London School of Theology, and an MSc and PhD in Women's Studies from the University of Ulster.

Francesca Rhys is a Methodist minister based in Leeds. She has contributed to *Words for Today* (Birmingham: International Bible Reading Association) in 2012 and 2013, and co-edited *And It Can Be – Lgbt Methodists moving towards an inclusive Church* (Manchester: Outcome, 2009). She was assistant editor and translator for *The China Study Journal* (London: Churches Together in Britain and Ireland, 1987–92). She is sustained in ministry by painting and recording the fruits of Ignatian-style scriptural meditations, as well as by co-ordinating Messy Church events based on progressive theology.

Emma Rothwell is currently Assistant Director of the MA in Pastoral Theology at the Cambridge Theological Federation and completing her curacy in a large team ministry in Cambridgeshire. Prior to ordination, Emma spent 15 years in education, as a teacher and in school management, developing fast-track with the DfES and working as a teaching associate and lecturer at the Faculty of Education, Cambridge University. Her research interests covered gender differences in education, proximal and peer-led learning, reflexivity and action research. Emma's current research interests are pastoral education in the community context and higher education. Emma enjoys life with her husband, Steve, also a priest, and two sons, Isaac and Leo.

Susan Shooter completed her doctorate in Theology and Ministry at Kings College, London, and a book adaptation of her thesis was published in 2012 by Ashgate: *How Survivors of Abuse Relate to God: The Authentic Spirituality of the Annihilated Soul.* Before ordination, she taught languages in a comprehensive school in Derbyshire and at the University of Nottingham Language Centre. She was parish priest for 13 years in Rochester Diocese, serving as Biblical Strand Leader for Canterbury Christchurch University's Certificate in Theology and

Ministry. She now lives in north Cornwall where she has the Bishop of Truro's permission to officiate, and undertakes work for South West Ministry Training Course as consultant for curates and training incumbents. She continues to write and her article 'How Feminine Participation in the Divine Might Renew the Church and Its Leadership' is forthcoming (*Feminist Theology*, 2013). Currently she is working on a creative piece about Marguerite Porete.

Nicola Slee is Research Fellow at the Queen's Foundation for Ecumenical Theological Education, Birmingham, where, amongst other roles, she supervises Masters level and doctoral research in feminist practical theology, co-ordinates research support and training, and teaches courses on gender, theology and spirituality on the MA in Theology and Transformative Practice. Since 2010, she has convened the Symposium on the Faith Lives of Women and Girls, out of which this book has emerged. Alongside her half-time role at Queen's, she has a varied freelance portfolio of editing, writing, speaking engagements, retreat work and spiritual direction. She has been actively involved in a number of campaigning groups and is currently an honorary Vice-President of WATCH (Women and the Church). She regards herself as a feminist practical theologian and a poet, and has wide-ranging research interests in feminist and practical theology, including spirituality, liturgy, ministry, education and pastoral care, as well as creative writing and poetry.

Her publications include *Faith and Feminism: An Introduction to Christian Feminist Theology* (London: DLT, 2003), *Praying Like a Woman* (London: SPCK, 2004), *Women's Faith Development: Patterns and Processes* (Aldershot: Ashgate, 2004), *Doing December Differently: An Alternative Christmas Handbook* (co-edited with Rosie Miles; Glasgow: Wild Goose Publications, 2006), *The Book of Mary* (London: SPCK, 2007), *The Edge of God: New Liturgical Texts and Contexts in Conversation* (co-edited with Michael Jagessar and Stephen Burns; Peterborough: Epworth Press, 2008), *Presiding Like a Woman* (co-edited with Stephen Burns, London: SPCK, 2010) and *Seeking the Risen Christa* (London: SPCK, 2011). From 2001 to 2012, she edited the International Bible Reading Association's annual series of daily Bible reading notes, 'Words for Today'. She is currently working on a collaborative venture with Gavin D'Costa, Eleanor Nesbitt, Mark Pryce and Ruth Shelton, entitled *Making Nothing Happen: Five poets explore faith and spirituality* (Farnham: Ashgate, forthcoming).

Kim Wasey is Church of England Chaplain at Salford University and Assistant Priest at St Chrysostom's, an inner-city parish in Manchester. She is also the mother of three young children. Kim has worked in various church and higher education chaplaincy settings, contexts which prompted her doctoral research into young women's relationships with the Eucharist. She completed her doctorate at Birmingham University, through the Queen's Foundation for Ecumenical Theological Education, in 2012. Prior to this, she read Theology at Manchester

University and also has an MPhil by research at Birmingham University on the ministry of Anglo-Catholic slum priests in the nineteenth century.

Alison Woolley is a PhD student at the University of Birmingham where she is researching the use of chosen practices of silence as a spiritual discipline in the faith lives of contemporary Christian women. She combines her explorations of the value of silence with her part-time work as a Music Therapist in Yorkshire, where she works alongside young people with severe or profound and multiple learning difficulties.

Introduction

Anne Phillips, Fran Porter and Nicola Slee

The Nature, Contexts and Aims of the Text

The Faith Lives of Women and Girls is a collection of essays based on recent, original field research conducted by a range of contributors and informed by a variety of theoretical perspectives, into the faith lives of women and girls – broadly from within a Christian context. The main focus of the book is on original qualitative research that identifies, illuminates and enhances understanding of key aspects of women's and girls' faith lives. Offered as a contribution to feminist practical and pastoral theology, the essays arise out of and feed back into a range of pastoral and practical contexts in the United Kingdom and Ireland – whilst also drawing on and related to other contexts – offering a significant resource to practical theologians, researchers and practitioners. As well as seeking to offer new research into the faith lives of women and girls, an accompanying theme throughout the book is on the research process itself, understood from feminist and practical theological perspectives – we are concerned particularly to ask and explore how the research process enshrines fundamental principles of faith and feminism such as liberation, empowerment, respect for the other, collaborative forms of knowledge, and so on.

We hope that this text makes a significant contribution to feminist practical theology, to the social scientific study of religion, and particularly to feminist-inspired qualitative research on religion. We anticipate that it will be a valuable text for students in theological education (those preparing for various forms of ministry in the churches), for those working in the field of practical/pastoral theology, particularly at Masters and doctoral level, and for researchers in the field. Whilst located primarily in a UK context, we believe that the research here may speak to a wider international readership.

Despite the flourishing of Christian feminist theology over the past three or four decades, represented in a vast scholarly as well as popular literature, feminist practical theology has been much slower to emerge as a distinct discipline, particularly in the UK. Whilst this is now changing and one can point to significant work by pioneers such as Elaine Graham, Heather Walton and Zoë Bennett Moore,[1] their work is largely theoretical and speculative, rooted in various forms of praxis but not directly based on field research. This is a fundamental lack in the

---

[1] Elaine Graham, *Making the Difference: Gender, Personhood and Theology* (London, 1995); Elaine Graham, *Words Made Flesh: Writings in Pastoral and Practical Theology*

field of the newly emerging discipline of feminist practical theology. In the UK, apart from our own qualitative research, and a few other rare texts,[2] such research as exists is to be found scattered throughout academic journals and as occasional contributions to edited collections. Elaine Graham and Margaret Halsey's *Life Cycles: Women and Pastoral Care*[3] is the only collection of essays of which we are aware that explores women's lives from a feminist practical theology perspective, but this text is not based on field research and is now twenty years old. Similarly, the series of texts edited by Jeanne Stevenson-Moessner over a ten-year period,[4] whilst overlapping to some degree with this text in their coverage of topics, are not focused on qualitative research in the way that this book is, and come out of the North American context – a very different one from our own. Our book represents the first significant gathering of a body of feminist qualitative research on the faith lives of women and girls within the British context.

Whilst we recognize the value of quantitative research perspectives, and they are not altogether absent from the book, the particular focus of our volume is on qualitative research. The book offers a range of research approaches – ethnographic, oral history, action research, interview studies, case studies and documentary analysis – which, together, represents a rich and significant body of research with the potential to make a serious contribution towards the understanding of women's and girls' faith lives and to enhance ministry to and with women and girls. At the same time, quantitative approaches do feature: a number of the contributors have used quantitative methods alongside qualitative to investigate their chosen topics and, where relevant, these are included in the discussion, but they do not receive sustained attention.

(London, 2009); Heather Walton, *Imagining Theology: Women, writing and God* (2007); Zoë Bennett Moore, *Introducing Feminist Perspectives on Pastoral Theology* (London, 2002).

[2] Anne Phillips, *The Faith of Girls: Children's Spirituality and Transition to Adulthood* (Farnham, 2011); Fran Porter, *Changing Women, Changing Worlds: Evangelical Women in Church, Community and Politics* (Belfast, 2002), and *It Will Not Be Taken Away From Her: A feminist engagement with women's Christian experience* (London, 2004); Nicola Slee, *Women's Faith Development: Patterns and Processes* (Aldershot, 2004); Jan Berry, *Ritual Making Women: Shaping Rites for Changing Lives* (London, 2009); Susan Shooter, *The Authentic Spirituality of the Annihilated Soul: How Survivors of Abuse Relate to God* (Farnham, 2012), and Alison R. Webster, *Found Wanting: Women, Christianity and Sexuality* (London/New York, 1995).

[3] Elaine Graham and Margaret Halsey, *Life Cycles: Women and Pastoral Care* (London, 1993).

[4] Jeanne Stevenson-Moessner (ed.), *Through the Eyes of Women: Insights for Pastoral Care* (Minneapolis, MN, 1996), and *In Her Own Time: Women and Development Issues in Pastoral Care* (Minneapolis, MN, 2000); Maxine Glaz and Jeanne Stevenson-Moessner (eds), *Women in Travail and Transition: A New Pastoral Care* (Minneapolis, MN, 1991), and Teresa Snorton and Jeanne Stevenson-Moessner (eds), *Women Out of Order: Risking Change and Creating Care in a Multicultural World* (Minneapolis, MN, 2009).

A Synopsis of the Book

As with any collection of essays, their arrangement in some kind of linear progression represented a challenge for the editors, aware as we were that there are a number of different ways we could have chosen to categorize them. Inevitably, our final decision about where to place each essay has been constrained by practical as well as theoretical factors and is, to a degree, an oversimplification, a more or less arbitrary schematization. Nevertheless, we hope that their present arrangement offers the reader something of a way through the variety of offerings.

In Part I, we attempt to contextualize what follows in the rest of the book by two essays which offer broad perspectives on the kinds of research this volume brings together. Nicola Slee seeks to suggest ways in which qualitative research represents for many feminist women not only a scholarly, ethical and personal quest for meaning, but also a spiritual practice or process enshrining core religious or spiritual values. Jan Berry offers a robust critique of so-called 'public' theology, challenging a simplistic binary between private and public and demonstrating how this is particularly problematic for women. Much of the research in this book might look at first sight as if it is addressing the so-called 'private' religious lives of women and girls, but read in the light of Berry's discussion, it may quickly be seen that this is not the case. The most intensely personal religious experiences and aspirations of women and girls both emerge out of and feed back into public contexts in many and varied ways.

In Part II, a variety of research into different ages, stages and styles of female faith is offered. If women's lives have been neglected generally in research and in theology, this applies even more to the lives of girls, young women and older women; the chapters in this section focus on these neglected sites. Abby Day considers the values, beliefs and experiences of 'generation A', a group of Anglican women born in the 1920s and 1930s. As well as providing fascinating insight into the neglected experience of this group of women, Day challenges a number of simplistic notions about women's faith that continue to operate in the sociology of religion – namely that women are 'more religious' than men and that their faith is less active and 'serious' than men's – while at the same time exposing the gender bias that is still prevalent in some academic discourse. Sarah-Jane Page contributes a comparative study of two cohorts of Anglican women from different generations – one generation of clergy women in middle age with dependent children, the other a group of younger lay women aged between 18 and 25 – to consider their differing attitudes towards feminism, and how feminism has impacted on their faith and ministry. She shows how both groups negotiate feminism and gender issues in a variety of ways, tracing shifts in both academic and popular understandings of feminism and demonstrating how complex patterns of inclusion and exclusion are realities for both groups, albeit differently experienced. Next, Kim Wasey shares and reflects on some of her findings from a doctoral study into young Anglican lay women's experiences of communion, seeking to articulate their 'ordinary theology'[5] in contrast to 'official' church theologies of the Eucharist and highlighting the horizontal and relational perceptions of communion found among the young women. Finally in this section, Anne Phillips reflects on her research into the faith lives of girls in a British Baptist context, focusing both on the challenges of research with a vulnerable group and how she attempted to shape the research process in ways that would be empowering for the girls, as well as on some of her key findings of the different forms of 'faithing' practised by the girls. She develops the image of the womb as a holding environment, offered to churches which seek to nurture the faith of girls.

In Part III, a variety of geographical and ecclesial contexts provide stimulating comparisons of how the faith of women and girls is context-specific and responds to particular cultural, political and social challenges. Fran Porter considers how women's faith has been both shaped by, and contributed to, the context of Northern Ireland, tracing the variety of ways in which Protestant and Catholic women have responded to 'the troubles' and how their notions of God have been shaped by the conflictual context in which they seek to live out faith. Manon Ceridwen James traces the identity of women in Wales in terms of how the dominant religious tradition in that land has shaped religious, personal and cultural identity. Highlighting the variety of expectations placed upon women by religion, particularly in terms of sexual morality, as well as some resources within Welsh women's poetry which could inform a more honest and robust ethical sensibility, James also draws attention to how Welsh women's identities are shaped in contrast to a powerful and normative Englishness and maleness. The two following essays focus on evangelical and Pentecostal cultures respectively within differing British church settings, showing how these ecclesial cultures may continue to be antithetical to women's faith development and challenging those responsible for teaching and worship in these settings to take account of women's needs. Ruth Perrin considers the attitudes of young evangelical women to role models, highlighting the lack of positive female biblical role models offered to young women in an evangelical setting, even though the same women identify real-life women role models as important to them. Deseta Davis examines preaching in the Black Pentecostal tradition, analysing a sample of sermon texts from a local Church of God of Prophecy for their usage of gender imagery and assumptions. Her findings are salutary and reveal the largely androcentric context within which preaching in this tradition continues to operate, in which women are mostly invisible in preaching and, when included, often presented in stereotypical or negative ways. Davis challenges preachers within her tradition to offer more positive nourishment for women hearers, and suggests ways in which change might begin.

Part IV brings together studies that illuminate a variety of women's spiritual practices, beliefs and attachments. There is an emphasis in this section on the lived

---

[5] Jeff Astley, *Ordinary Theology: Looking, Listening and Learning in Theology* (Aldershot, 2002) and Jeff Astley and Leslie J. Francis (eds), *Exploring Ordinary Theology: Everyday Christian Believing and the Church* (Aldershot, 2013).

quality of women's faith, its strong rooting in relationality and connectedness, and on the differing meanings and value of silence and silencing in women's religious experience. Emma Rothwell describes a piece of action research in which she worked with a small cohort of women in an Anglican parish to share faith journeys, consider women's treatment in both church and society, and create a collaborative record of the research process. Key themes identified in this project are the common sensibility of being silenced by religion and other powerful social forces, alongside the search for alternative images and experiences. Susanna Gunner recounts another participatory research project conducted in a rural Anglican parish with a small group of women, but her study is focused more explicitly on the development of feminist ritual. Describing how she created *Woman-Cross*, a feminist reworking of the traditional Stations of the Cross, and enacted this with the group, Gunner reflects on and asserts the significance of 'ritual faithing' in women's faith lives. In contrast to the dominant use of 'silencing' as an image of disempowerment, Alison Woolley focuses on women's chosen practices of silence, in prayer and meditation, and gives a rich account of the meanings women identify in such practices. In particular, she highlights how women both perceive and experience relationality, not only to self and God but also to others, in their practices of silence, demonstrating how silence is full of presence for these women, and is a place of nourishment and encounter. Eun Sim Joung brings the theoretical perspective of attachment theory to bear on an analysis of the faith narratives of a group of UK-based Korean Christian women, showing how attachment theory can illuminate and discriminate between different kinds of religious attachment held by women. Her work offers a helpful development and nuancing of the common assertion of the relational character of women's faith, suggesting that not all forms of relationality are equally valuable, and that there are more or less functional forms of religious attachment. Each of these studies emphasizes, in different ways, the importance of pastoral support, mentoring and role modelling for women. Caroline Kitcatt considers in detail the significance of women's experiences of spiritual accompaniment, its importance for the support and maturation of women's faith, but also the challenges it can present if there is a confusion between spiritual accompaniment and other forms of relationship. The women in her study highlighted the difficulties that can occur if the boundary between a professional relationship and friendship becomes blurred. For women who have primary roles as carers or nurturers of others, it is imperative that they have access to relationships where their own needs are the focus of the other and where they do not have to exercise responsibility for care of the accompanist. In the context of a number of considerations of attachment and relationality, Francesca Rhys recounts the 'ordinary Christologies'[6] of a small group of women from a range of denominations and traditions, exploring to what extent these women found their relationship to Jesus Christ liberatory. Documenting the range

---

[6] Ann Christie, *Ordinary Christology: Who Do You Say I Am? Answers from the Pews* (Farnham, 2012).

of ways in which the women thought of Jesus/Christ, and their diverse theological understandings, she reflects on the paradox that, whilst Christology has received a huge amount of attention in feminist theology, so little empirical research has explored ordinary women's thinking about and experience of Christ. Her study, whilst small-scale, is an important corrective to this neglect.

Finally, Part V offers three rich accounts of various kinds of liminal experience commonly encountered by women, and their significance in women's faith lives. Jennifer Hurd investigates the encounter with death and bereavement of those diagnosed with terminal illness, and their carers and relatives, bringing to bear the notion of natality as developed by Grace Jantzen in order to explore how such a biophilic perspective might inform pastoral care of those who are dying and those who accompany them. She reports on early findings from four pilot interviews, interpreting the data in the light of features of natality proposed by Jantzen. Noelia Molina offers early findings from her interviews with women who have given birth, exploring the ways in which this experience of liminality may be considered a profoundly spiritual one. She draws out key themes in the women's narratives, particularly the notion of crisis in the early period of motherhood, the significance of embodiment in the relationship between mother and infant, and the ways in which motherhood enacts transformation for the woman in terms of her understanding of her self and her relationship with others, the world and the divine. Finally, Susan Shooter reflects on her research into a liminal experience that one would wish were *not* common for women but unfortunately is: the experience of abuse. Analysis of her interviews with survivors of abuse reveals the theological richness, creativity and generosity of women who, despite having undergone the most appalling experiences, maintain a profound conviction of the timeless presence of God which saves. Shooter challenges the churches not only to recognize the depth of the faith as well as the suffering of women who have experienced abuse, but to affirm and support the ministry of those who have survived abuse – something she shows is severely lacking in terms of how churches respond to women who have been abused.

The Context and Ethos of the Book

The present volume has its genesis in an ongoing research Symposium first convened by Nicola at the Queen's Foundation, Birmingham, in November 2010, whose aim was to bring together women (and, on occasions, men) working at Masters, doctoral and post-doctoral level on the faith lives of women and girls, using qualitative research approaches. In distinction from other feminist theological research gatherings on the one hand,[7] which tend to have wide theoretical and

---

[7] Such as the Society for the Study of Theology's Feminism and Gender <http://www.theologysociety.org.uk/seminar.asp> accessed 1 February 2013.

theological agendas, and practical theological networks on the other,[8] which might attend to questions of gender within a wider framework of other concerns, the remit of the Symposium is intentionally focused in two ways: on research into the faith lives of women and girls, and on qualitative research. The present volume offers a snapshot of papers given at early meetings of the Symposium, and reflects both the subject focus and the culture and ethos of the Symposium.

Since completing her own doctoral work on women's faith development,[9] Nicola had become aware of other women around the UK doing research on women's and girls' faith lives (some of it in dialogue with her work). Through supervising research students at the Queen's Foundation, and being invited to act as external examiner to doctoral candidates elsewhere, as well as through feminist and practical theology networks, she was increasingly coming into contact with many of these women (Anne and Fran amongst them), and a few men who are also researching the faith of women and girls.[10] Most of these researchers have been working in isolation from others with similar interests, often not even aware that there are others undertaking comparable research, since much of this work has been, until now, unpublished, in the form of Masters and doctoral dissertations. Part of the aim of the Symposium has been to offer a forum where researchers could meet, become aware of others working in a common field and share the problems, struggles, frustrations and triumphs of research, particularly some of the specific challenges of conducting field work, thus breaking the isolation of research. One of the issues that quickly became apparent was the difficulties experienced by many members of the Symposium in locating literature that relates specifically to women's and girls' faith lives, which is grounded in empirical research. Hence, one key aim in publishing this volume of research essays is that future researchers will be able to access such studies and gain a sense of a developing field of research into which their own work may speak. Members of the Symposium have said, 'If only there had been a book like this when we were beginning our research, we would have felt far less isolated and had far more of a sense of what it was we were trying to do.'

The present volume reflects the nature and ethos of the Symposium in a number of ways. There is a clear intention within the Symposium to create a forum in which women researchers working at different levels of experience and competence can come together and learn from, as well as support, each other in a collaborative and constructively critical fashion. (This collaborative style has been very much in evidence in the shared editorial work of this volume.) The Symposium brings together women engaging on their first piece of small-scale qualitative research as part of a Masters degree, those working at doctoral level, and more established

---

[8] Such as the British and Irish Association for Practical Theology <http://www.biapt.org.uk/index.shtml> accessed 1 February 2013.

[9] Published as Slee, *Women's Faith Development*.

[10] Men are not represented in the present volume, but a few men have or are due to give papers at the Symposium, for example, reporting research on the experience of transgender and faith, and women's faith in a prison context.

post-doctoral researchers who bring considerable experience both of conducting their own research and supervising others, as well as a significant record of publications. Whilst it is obvious that such a forum offers first-time researchers much valuable experience and expertise to draw upon, this is also a forum in which more established researchers have much to gain and learn. Newer, younger scholars bring their own fresh knowledge of the field, of emerging literature and issues, and contacts with practical contexts which can enrich as well as challenge, on occasion, the assumptions of those of us who have been in the field for longer. One of the real values of the Symposium is the conversational method of learning and sharing. Those who have never presented a paper before are supported in doing so, and constructive feedback is offered in a safe and affirming space which allows women to gain confidence and grow in stature as young scholars. This sense of valuing the work of researchers working at different levels and stages of their career is reflected in this volume, which brings together essays by established writers with those who are just beginning to publish and many for whom this is their first research publication. At the same time, the range and scale of the research is varied. Work at Masters level is clearly much smaller-scale, often exploratory in nature and cannot achieve the depth or sophistication of doctoral or post-doctoral work. Nevertheless and without denying the small-scale and exploratory nature of some of the research represented here, we consider that there is value in such work being more widely disseminated, particularly in a newly emerging field.

Whilst small-scale, some of these research studies are nevertheless pioneering, representing the breaking of new ground in the empirical study of women's and girls' faith lives. Whatever their limitations, they are worthy of publication for that reason alone. Yet the whole is greater than the sum of the parts, and some of the smaller-scale pieces take on greater significance by their contextualization in a volume that brings together larger-scale and more theoretically developed research. Threads that are started in one study but cannot be developed due to limitations of time or expertise are picked up by a more experienced practitioner and woven into something larger and more comprehensive. These essays speak to each other, as do the women who have written them and conducted the research on which they are based, and in so doing, a body of work begins to emerge which possesses its own organic shape and significance.

Without wishing to smooth out the very considerable differences represented in this volume, a common characteristic of these feminist-inspired research studies, whether small- or larger-scale, whether more or less developed, is the way in which they challenge, critique, subvert, or nuance the taken-for-granted assumptions about the nature of female faith which continue to operate in both academia and 'ordinary life' contexts. From Jan Berry's challenge to public theology's limited notions of 'public/private' to Abby Day's challenge of the generally accepted notion (within the social sciences) that women are more religious than men; from Kim Wasey's challenge to the assumption that women's priesthood is a key factor in the empowerment of young lay women to Alison Woolley's challenge to feminist discourse which ignores the positive role of silence in women's lives;

from Francesca Rhys' critique of Christology from the perspective of ordinary women's understandings of Jesus to Deseta Davis' challenge to the androcentrism of Black British Pentecostal church worship; from Ruth Perrin's challenge to evangelical culture that fails to provide biblical role models for young women to Susan Shooter's critique of a church that cannot move beyond a model of ministry *to* those who have been abused to embrace the ministry *of* the abused – the challenges are multiple and aimed in various directions. There are challenges to church practice and theology from a range of different ecclesial contexts, including challenges to theological orthodoxies or conventions; but equally, there are challenges to theoretical perspectives, including feminist perspectives and earlier work on women's faith lives. There are challenges to existing models and understandings of research practice in the light of our own diverse experiences of conducting research.

As well as challenge and critique, many of the research studies represented here offer new knowledge on the faith lives of women and girls, illuminating what have been neglected sites of women's and girls' faith lives. Anne Phillips' pioneering work on the faith of girls sits alongside revealing studies of young women by Ruth Perrin and Kim Wasey; Abby Day's research into older Anglican women offers a rare glimpse into the faith of those who, as she points out, often make up the backbone of local churches yet are very largely ignored as serious theological subjects in their own right. Set in dialogue with Sarah-Jane Page's fascinating comparison of two generational cohorts of Anglican women, these studies between them begin to map out something of the different ages and stages of women's Christian faith. Fran Porter, Manon Ceridwen James and Eun Sim Joung chart some of the faith struggles and gifts of women in diverse geographical contexts, illustrating the ways in which social, political and cultural, as well as ecclesial, contexts significantly shape faith. Alison Woolley illuminates the richness of women's chosen practices of silence, an area which has received very little in-depth research attention, whilst Caroline Kitcatt offers fresh insight into women's experience of spiritual direction. The action research studies of Emma Rothwell and Susanna Gunner bring to life the faith lives of small groups of women working and sharing together as well as demonstrating how qualitative research can, itself, become a tool of empowerment not only for the researcher but for those with whom she works, in this case in local churches. Jennifer Hurd, Noelia Molina and Susan Shooter offer nuanced insight into women's faith in the context of challenging personal and pastoral situations: whether facing death/bereavement, birth or recovery from abuse, their studies demonstrate the depth and resilience of women's faith in contexts which might be expected to crush or occlude it.

The book as a whole also seeks to model the real-life experience of research, its messiness, twists and turns, dead-ends and unexpected avenues. It is a characteristic of qualitative research that researchers situate themselves explicitly within their own research, write in the first person and practise self-reflexivity throughout the research process – often in the form of notes in a research journal, reflection with a supervisor or mentor, or encouraging participants in the research to share candid feedback on the impact of the researcher in the field – and this is something we have encouraged our contributors to write into their chapters. For women of faith who are conducting research into the faith of other women and girls, the overlap between personal and professional, between research and the rest of life, is inevitably blurred in the extreme, and it is obvious that such research will be highly influenced by the personal faith experience and convictions of the researcher. This is not to be deemed a 'failure' of research so long as it is acknowledged and made visible for self-scrutiny as well as the critical scrutiny of others. This brings us to where we begin the book: in her opening essay, Nicola traces the common threads she has discerned in women's research practices, situating our enmeshment in our research activity as a form of spiritual practice. As editors, too, the process of working together on this book and helping to bring to light what might otherwise remain the hidden work of women of faith (the hiddenness extending both to those who have conducted the research and to the women and girls who form the subjects of their research), has been a process of enrichment and enlargement of our own faith.

PART I
Feminist Research Perspectives

Chapter 1
Feminist Qualitative Research as Spiritual Practice: Reflections on the Process of Doing Qualitative Research

Nicola Slee

Introduction

In this chapter, I seek to reflect on some of the characteristic features of qualitative research, as represented in the work of feminist practitioners – including the work of the women contributing to this book – and consider how the practice of research both arises out of and feeds back into women's own ethical and spiritual lives. Both qualitative and feminist researchers are fundamentally concerned with the process(es) of research as an integral aspect of the work. We researchers understand that process and content are integrally interconnected; that feminists are after new ways of knowing – in our case, new ways of doing theology – as much as they are after new knowledge; that, as Audre Lorde famously put it, 'the master's tools will never dismantle the master's house',[1] or, as qualitative researchers might say, positivist perspectives which assume objectivity, neutrality and detachment on the part of the researcher in the interests of control are not likely to yield liberating results for oppressed groups.

Yet even in qualitative and feminist research paradigms that pay explicit attention to the process and to the importance of method, much of the concern is focused on methodology per se, the ethics of research enquiry and the effects of the process on participants – all right and proper concerns. There is much less in the literature about the significance of the research process for the researcher herself, about research as a means of transformation for the researcher – and even less about the research process understood in essentially religious or spiritual terms. There are exceptions. Within the literature of pastoral theology, the notion of scholarship as part of the vocation of the pastor/priest offers some scope for reflecting on the significance of learning, broadly conceived, in the formation

---

[1] Audre Lorde, 'The Master's Tools Will Never Dismantle the Master's House', *Sister Outsider*, in *The Audre Lorde Compendium: Essays, Speeches and Journals* (London, 1996), pp.158–61.

of the believer.[2] The literatures of heuristic or organic research, as well as that of auto-ethnography, are also helpful, in which the use of the self in research is acknowledged and explored, and research is perceived as a vehicle for personal growth and development. Thus, Kim Etherington explores the role of feelings, personal stories, creative processes such as painting and poetry, as well as body work, as legitimate and significant features of the research process, affirming that the recognition and conscious working with the self in research can lead to insight and transformation.[3] Although she does not speak of this process in explicitly spiritual terms, others do. Robert Pazmiño speaks of doing theological research as 'a spiritual practice', a 'form of worship that seeks to glorify and enjoy God through the exercise of one's mind and skill in expression and dialogue',[4] and Mary Clark Moschella acknowledges and explores 'the research process itself as a potential means of spiritual growth and social transformation'.[5]

For myself and for other women researchers I know, the pursuit of research using qualitative methods has been a transformational process – not only in the way that it has contributed to our knowledge and understanding of women's and girls' faith lives, but also in the ways in which the research process itself has embodied and enacted core ethical and spiritual values. I do not intend here to discuss the many definitions of spirituality and feminist spirituality in particular.[6] Instead, I want to take a more experiential, narrative and analogical approach. By comparing the ways in which feminist researchers use qualitative methods to research women's lives (in our case, women's faith lives) with some of the classic ways in which religious traditions enshrine spirituality, I hope to illuminate some of the ways in which the research process may be both experienced and perceived as spiritual practice. I seek to describe the research process as I have experienced it, and as I have witnessed other women researchers experience it, in such a way as to evoke the lived experience of research and to bring to light some of its core personal, ethical and spiritual characteristics and values. I want to suggest ways in which the research process itself forms and shapes us as women

---

[2] See, for example, Mary Clark Moschella, *Ethnography as a Pastoral Practice: An Introduction* (Cleveland, 2008); Robert W. Pazmiño, *Doing Theological Research: An introductory guide for survival in theological education* (Eugene, OR, 2009); John Piper and D.A. Carson, *The Pastor as Scholar & The Scholar as Pastor* (Nottingham, 2011) and Simone Weil's classic essay, 'Reflections on the right use of school studies with a view to the love of God', in *Waiting on God* (Glasgow, 1977), pp. 66–76.

[3] Kim Etherington, *Becoming a Reflexive Researcher: Using Our Selves in Research* (London and Philadelphia, PA, 2004) provides a helpful overview of heuristic and auto-ethnographic approaches.

[4] Pazmiño, *Doing Theological Research*, p. 18.

[5] Moschella, *Ethnography*, p. 12.

[6] See my essay, 'The Holy Spirit and spirituality', in Susan Frank Parsons (ed.), *The Cambridge Companion to Feminist Theology* (Cambridge, 2002), pp. 171–89.

of faith (however we understand that term),[7] challenges us to dig deep within our own spiritual resources (as well as calling on the support and resources of others), teaches us how to discern the sacred in other women's and in our own lives, and enables us to grow in spiritual stature and wisdom. I shall attempt to do this, first, by describing some of the features of the context in which many of us perceive ourselves to be doing research, and then to go on to outline the various stages of qualitative research, trying to show how each discrete aspect of the research process presents its own spiritual challenges and, if we respond faithfully, gifts us with its own particular spiritual graces.

The practice of research, I want to suggest, is one which can, when conducted within the theological framework of a faith perspective, not only reflect but enact and enshrine core values of the faith community. Where Elaine Graham speaks of pastoral theology in broad terms as 'transforming practice',[8] I want to focus in particular on ethnographic and qualitative research and show how they can be such transformative practices. Graham articulates an understanding of praxis as a form of practical wisdom mediated and embodied in the Church's activities of care, worship, social action, formation and initiation, as much as in its formal theology. Although we do not normally think of research as a fundamental characteristic of the life of the Church, perhaps we should. Moschella argues powerfully for *Ethnography as a Pastoral Practice*, as the title of her book puts it, in which the process of ethnographic research, undertaken with intentionality, care and skill, can be a form of pastoral care, prophetic critique and spiritual discernment within the life of the Church. She draws on doctoral work by David Mellott who describes the ethnographic encounter as 'an act of primary theology', a means of being in relationship with God and practising the core values of the faith community.[9] More broadly, Robert Pazmiño argues that theological research can be a form of worship, a practice through which the student learns to love God with mind, heart, soul and strength, and the neighbour as the self.[10]

---

[7] The use of the collective personal pronoun is deliberate, as a way of acknowledging my own situatedness in this account, but also drawing on my experience of working closely with other feminist researchers and the collective context of the Symposium. Although I am focusing on women researchers, I do not wish to imply that *only* women can or do work in the kinds of ways I describe, or understand their research in spiritual terms.

[8] Elaine Graham, *Transforming Practice: Pastoral Theology in an Age of Uncertainty* (London, 1996).

[9] David Mellott, 'Ethnography as Theology: Encountering the Penitentes of Arroyo Seco, New Mexico', (unpublished PhD thesis, Emory University, 2005), in Moschella, *Ethnography*, pp. 90–91.

[10] Pazmiño, *Doing Theological Research*.

Our Location as Researchers

Before looking at the research process per se, it is important to acknowledge the context(s) in which researchers of women's and girls' faith lives find ourselves and the ways in which we experience our location, for this impacts significantly on our experience of the research process and the personal/spiritual challenges it offers us. Without wanting to suggest that we are all positioned in precisely the same location – clearly we are not, and we need to acknowledge our different contexts, whether academic or pastoral, whether as lay women or ordained, as white, black or Asian, as younger or older, as more or less established in the Church or academy – my experience is that many of us describe our location as researchers in similar terms. Rosalind Edwards and Jane Ribbens describe feminist qualitative research into women's so-called 'private' lives as being on the edges of the social sciences,[11] a perception widely shared by those of us conducting research into women's and girls' faith lives. Many of us perceive ourselves and our research to be located on a liminal margin, a location that boasts little status, recognition, or understanding from other theologians or social scientists. We may experience a variety of margins. Theology exists somewhere on the edges of the social sciences or the humanities, hardly considered mainstream by larger, secular disciplines. Within theology, both feminist theology in general and feminist practical theology more specifically, are marginalized discourses. Even within the small world of feminist practical theology, we may experience ourselves as marginal as those who are choosing to use qualitative methods to research women's and girls' faith lives. Then there are other margins for each of us – for Anne Phillips researching the experience of girls, or Abby Day, focusing on older women, or Deseta Davis and Eun Sim Joung,[12] concerned with the faith lives of ethnic minority women and traditions. It is not surprising if we experience ourselves as 'resident aliens', outsiders in an insiders' world, 'internal leavers' as Gwen Henderson tellingly describes the subjects of her research.[13]

This is the location in which we experience ourselves doing research, and it is a spiritual landscape every bit as much as it is an intellectual or professional one: a landscape which might be named in a wide variety of metaphors,[14] but which requires us to exercise courage, self-belief and tenacity. From such a location, we

---

[11] Rosalind Edwards and Jane Ribbens, 'Living on the Edges: Public Knowledge, Private Lives, Personal Experience' in Jane Ribbens and Rosalind Edwards (eds), *Feminist Dilemmas in Qualitative Research: Public Knowledge and Private Lives* (London, 1998), pp. 1–23.

[12] See Chapters 6, 3, 10 and 14.

[13] Gwen D. Henderson, 'Evangelical Women Negotiating Faith in Contemporary Scotland' (unpublished PhD dissertation, University of Glasgow, 2008).

[14] See the wide range of metaphors used by the women I interviewed to describe their experiences of alienation, including landscape imagery, in Nicola Slee, *Women's Faith Development: Patterns and Processes* (Aldershot, 2004), Chapter 5.

conduct our research, drawing on inner resources of conviction, justice-seeking compassion and prophetic daring.

Women's and Girls' Lives as Holy Ground

Whatever the precise focus of our respective research studies, we share an approach to the lives of women and girls as holy ground, a place where we expect to discern the presence and activity of the divine, however we name that reality. Moschella describes the reverence that undergirds all ethnographic research as 'profound respect and regard for the dignity of the persons and communities who allow us to see so much of themselves'.[15] Whilst this attitude of reverence may be required of all ethnographic research, in studying the faith lives of women and girls researchers are aware of approaching a neglected site. We are cartographers of neglected landscapes, charting maps that have not been made, until now.

I am talking here, of course, about the fundamental feminist principle of women's experience(s).[16] We deliberately privilege women and girls as the focus of our study, and whilst we need to face the myriad complex theoretical questions about the legitimacy of such a stance – what do we mean by 'women'? which women and why? how far is gender a stable category and why focus on gender over and above other variables? – we continue to operate a strategic feminism that insists on the prioritizing of women's lives. We do so because we want to hold up the holiness of ordinary women's and girls' lives, to say that their lives are sacred, worthy of painstaking study, that their lives are revelatory of God. To put this theologically, our research becomes a praxis of the communion of saints,[17] a way of insisting on the participation of ordinary women and girls within the life of the people of God and holding up their lives, amongst the company of the faithful, as worthy of narration, visibility and reverence.

This sense of the holiness of our research territory connects also to the profound sense of vocation and mission which many feminist theological researchers profess in relation to their research (something one might hope to find in theological research generally). There is a common desire, not only to witness to the neglected experiences of women and girls but, by bringing that experience to light, to empower the research participants[18] and to challenge and transform the ecclesial

---

[15] Moschella, *Ethnography*, p. 85.

[16] A much contested term, of course. For a useful brief discussion, see Ada María Isasi-Díaz, 'Experiences', in Letty M. Russell and J. Shannon Clarkson (eds), *Dictionary of Feminist Theologies* (London and Westminster, 1996), pp. 95–6.

[17] For feminist theological exploration of the notion of the communion of saints, see Elizabeth Johnson, *Friends of God and Prophets: A Feminist Theological Reading of the Communion of Saints* (London, 1998).

[18] However, this notion of empowerment of research participants has been challenged and nuanced by some feminist accounts. As J. Acker, K. Barry and J. Essenelt suggest,

and other communities to which the participants belong. This sense of vocation may be particularly evident at the start of the research process, in the framing of a research proposal, but is also evident as a motivating force throughout.

Listening to Women's and Girls' Lives as a Practice of Prayer

Much has been written about the importance of listening within practical and pastoral theology, within the practice of ethnography, as well as within feminist theology. Nelle Morton's work on 'hearing into speech'[19] has become a classic text which enshrines a core value of listening to women's lives. Listening is key at every stage of the research process. Long before the formal beginning of research, we are listening to our own lives and the lives of others we know and hearing stories, questions, ideas and hunches, which shape themselves up into our research proposals. We listen to the literature, bringing our own lives and the lives of the women and girls we know into dialogue with it. We listen to our supervisor and to peers and colleagues who may shed valuable light on our research. We listen with acute attentiveness to our participants in interviews or other settings. We listen again, over and over, when transcribing and analysing data. We listen when we present our research to others and when we hear back from them. All the time we are listening at many different levels: to self, to the other, to the literature, to the Spirit at work in each of these. Moschella, borrowing a phrase from Dave Isay, speaks of such ethnographic listening as a profound 'act of love'.[20]

The way we listen as women researchers is, I suggest, a form of spiritual practice that has many of the qualities of prayer understood as the most attentive listening to self, other and God we can manage.[21] We listen with our lives. We bring our whole selves to the act of listening. Our listening is informed by scholarly reading, certainly, but it is also shaped by our own hunger to be listened to, by positive experiences of what it is to be listened to well and also by the painful reality of not being heard, of having our voices and lives silenced. We listen with our bodies, paying attention to feeling, memory, desire. We listen with emotional as well as

---

'an emancipatory intent is no guarantee of an emancipatory outcome', in 'Objectivity and truth: problems in doing feminist research', *Women's Studies International Forum* 6 (1983): 423–35. For a detailed discussion and qualitative data exploring how far feminist research empowered female participants, see June Lennie, 'Troubling Empowerment: An Evaluation and Critique of a Feminist Action Research Project Involving Rural Women and Interactive Communication Technologies' (unpublished PhD thesis, Queensland University of Technology, 2001). Available at <http://eprints.qut.edu.au/18365> accessed 20 December 2012.

[19] Nelle Morton, *The Journey is Home* (Boston, MA, 1985), pp. 202–10.

[20] Moschella, *Ethnography*, p. 254.

[21] Simone Weil, in a much-quoted text, speaks of prayer as, fundamentally, attention. See 'Reflections' in *Waiting on God*, pp. 66–76.

intellectual intelligence, on the look-out for patterns, resonances, allusions. Such listening, as the essays in *Feminist Dilemmas in Qualitative Research* explore, is complex and difficult, as we seek to bring into dialogue public, semi-public, private and personal voices, requiring the 'hearing of my [own] feeling voice' alongside the many competing voices present.[22] We listen to what is explicit in what we read or hear, to what is implicit but not directly said, and to what is null or absent – the inconceivable, unsayable, or not yet capable of being articulated.[23] We listen to tone of voice, sighs, stutters, laughter, tears, pauses, silences, body language, facial expression, the mood of the encounter, how it starts, shifts, changes, moves, circles, ends; how we feel as it's going on and after it's ended; using our feelings as a clue to how the other may be feeling.

As in prayer, so in research, the discipline of waiting is a core gift and skill. We have to learn to focus all our attention on the other and to get ourselves and our egos out of the way. At the same time, we need to know how to use ourselves – feelings, body, intelligence, intuition – to assist our listening. We learn how to wait with, wait on, wait for the other, putting ourselves at their disposal, letting them speak as and when and where they will, sitting with them as they search for what it is they want to say, or remain silent, or stumble and stutter.

Transcribing as a Practice of Holy Writ

The process of transcribing is often regarded as something of a chore (best avoided, if possible, or passed on to someone else) or as a technical challenge of research (how do you turn verbal discourse into text?), but I have never come across transcription described as spiritual practice or indeed, paid much attention at all in practical or pastoral theology.[24] I want to suggest it is, or can be, part of spiritual practice for the researcher.

The act of transcribing is a painstaking, slow, laborious one, part of the ethnographer's craft, which can only be learned by practice. It requires the paying of minute attention to every word spoken by research participants, to the inflection, nuance, timing and timbre of voice, as well as to the researcher's own part in the interchange. While there are different methods of transcribing and different levels of detail required according to the purpose of the research, the search for accuracy and authenticity is at the heart of all transcribing, and requires enormous effort. We

---

[22] Jane Ribbens, 'Hearing my Feeling Voice? An Autobiographical Discussion of Motherhood', in Ribbens and Edwards (eds), *Feminist Dilemmas*, pp. 24–38.

[23] I owe this threefold distinction between the explicit, the implicit and the null, to Maria Harris, *Teaching as Religious Imagination: An Essay in the Theology of Teaching* (San Francisco, CA, 1987), pp. 100–101.

[24] Even Moschella's very careful attention to each stage of the research process misses out transcription entirely. See Etherington, *Becoming a Reflexive Researcher*, pp.78–80, for a brief consideration of transcription.

have to play the recording again and again, going back to places where we can't make out the words or can't make sense of what seems to be being said. Finding a way for words on the page to bring alive the sound of a voice is an art. I want to say it is holy and costly work, a way of enacting the giving of reverence to our subjects' lives as described above. We may be unable to do our own transcription for various reasons, or may work on projects where we are not required to do it, but in any case, we do not regard transcription as an unnecessary burden that gets in the way of the 'real' research.

Transcribing is a way of embodied, visceral listening. As we listen and transcribe, we are employing ear, eye, hand (and foot, too, if we are using a transcribing machine) in a co-ordinated manner to listen with every fibre of our being. We imbibe and ingest the words of the interview, they enter our bodies and live inside us, where the voices continue to talk, to each other, as well as to us, generating their own internal conversations and meanings. Thus transcription becomes a kind of act of communion, a Eucharist in which we take into our own bodies the stuff of other women's lives; an intermingling of lives that leaves us profoundly changed by the process. When doing my own transcribing for my study of women's faith lives,[25] I had the sense of my participants taking up residence within my body, becoming enfleshed within me as a kind of community, an internalized ekklesia of wo/men, as Fiorenza might describe it,[26] an expression of Womenchurch[27] – and this internalized community of research participants not only generated the research but profoundly transformed my own sense of self and belonging. The combined pain, struggle, wisdom, lived faith, insight and so on, of each of our participants, becomes a part of our lives, and we enter into an implicit covenant with them through the act of research. The formal procedures of consent and the conduct of the interview may be the obvious expression of this covenant, but it is the act of transcribing (followed up by the work of data analysis) that seals and ratifies it.

Handling Transcripts as Sacred Texts

Having turned our subjects' lives into texts that are amenable to analysis, we go on to read the texts of our subjects' lives with the same attention, reverence and expectation as characterized the earlier processes of the research. We pore over the pages of our transcripts like scholars poring over the pages of holy writ. We bring the kind of attitude to the transcripts that monks, nuns and lay folk bring to scripture in *lectio divina*, the ancient practice of meditative, ruminative reading of

---

[25] Slee, *Women's Faith Development*.

[26] See, for example, Elisabeth Schüssler Fiorenza, *Jesus: Miriam's Child, Sophia's Prophet: Critical Issues in Feminist Christology* (London, 1995), Chapter 1.

[27] For a definition and discussion of Womenchurch, see Natalie K. Watson, *Introducing Feminist Ecclesiology* (Sheffield, 2002), Chapter 4.

scripture in which the believer seeks to go beyond a mere cognitive or analytical reading of the text to a profound inhabiting of the scriptures in such a way that they form the heart, mind and will.[28] We read and re-read the transcripts, searching beneath the surface for what is going on. We look for signs, patterns, repetitions, as well as gaps, contradictions, difference. We are like priests or preachers who break open the dense word of our subjects' lives and proclaim a liberating word that others can hear.

Data Analysis as Apophatic Practice

We move to the stage of analysing our data, a stage of research which can be at the same time the most exhilarating and the most daunting. We work with our data in such a way that we can begin to come up with categories, themes and concepts that will lay the foundations for our research findings and conclusions. We do this in several stages, each one of which generates more data in addition to the data we already have from the transcripts. We make notes on each transcript, maybe equalling in quantity the data from the transcript itself. We start to compare transcripts and make more general notes from a broader perspective. We may use charts or graphs as a way of mapping some of the key patterns of the data. We code data, using more or less sophisticated methods of coding. We may also use computer software to process and organize our data and to enable the efficient and accurate mapping of interrelationships and patterns, but computer analysis is itself dependent on careful and intelligent coding, and is not a shortcut. All of this is preliminary to the writing up 'proper' of our findings, and can take many months. Research journals, where much of this work may be done, are akin to an artist's sketchbook where many preliminary studies are made before a final painting is executed, or a poet's or musician's notebook, where many different compositions are practised as foundational to the completion of the finished work.

At this stage, we may experience something akin to a spiritual crisis. We may feel completely overwhelmed by the sheer amount of data we have gathered and our own detailed notes. We can no longer see the wood for the trees. We recognize that our field is so much more complex, nuanced and intricate than we ever imagined. We doubt our ability to handle the complexity of the data. We wish we could go back to our participants and ask them five more questions that would really give us what we need to make sense of what we have. While in some cases this may be possible, often for practical reasons it is not.

The landscape of our research at this stage may become akin to the inner landscape of the dark night of the soul or the wilderness of unknowing. It is a place

---

[28] For accounts of *lectio divina*, see Basil Pennington, *Lectio Divina: Renewing the Ancient Practice of Praying the Scriptures* (New York, 1998); David Foster, *Reading with God* (London, 2005), and Christine Valters Painter, *Lectio Divina: The Sacred Art* (London, 2012).

where the landmarks disappear and everything looks the same. The only thing to be done is to submit to the confusion and walk by faith in the way of unknowing. The undoing of our own certainties and the falling apart of our original ideas is probably a necessary part of any creative project, as well as of any spiritual commitment. It is a test of resolve and trust, and many a research project founders at this stage.

At this point, the role of the supervisor or mentor may be crucial, acting as an accompanist who can stand by the researcher and reassure them, 'It's ok. This is all part of the process. Stay with it. Don't panic.' My experience, both of research and of prayer, is that if I don't lose nerve, if I can hold on and, at the same time, let go and submit to the confusion, wait patiently for I know not what, then, at a point and in a way that cannot be predicted, a turning-point will come when a new direction begins to emerge out of the chaos and I can act again. It must emerge organically, in its own time and way; it will not be coerced – and this is precisely what is scary and lonely about the process. It requires of the researcher qualities of courage, faith and resilience to remain in the place of confusion without despairing or pushing to a hasty and unsatisfactory resolution; or, if it is not entirely possible to resist the forces of panic and anxiety, at least to recognize them for what they are – temporary moments within a larger process of creativity – and to refuse to grant them the final word.

Writing up as a Practice of Proclamation

The challenge of converting the entire research process into something that can be communicated to others – whether in the form of a conventional thesis or in other forms – is another praxis through which we enact our faith. Fundamental to our work as feminist practical theologians and social scientists is the conviction that our work is not just for us, but for others: first and foremost, our research participants, but also for a wider audience, however we identify that constituency. Behind this sense of our responsibility and accountability to a wider community lies another conviction, namely that feminist research is not only a matter of interpreting the world but of changing it. At this point, our research practice is akin to the work of a preacher or an evangelist in a faith community, a witness who gives testimony to what they know, who takes the core message of the community out to others, in the hope of convincing and converting others to her worldview, and of changing both individual behaviours and social structures.

Out of our research is distilled a vision, a conviction, usually in continuity with the hopes and ideals that inspired the research in the first place but considerably refined, chastened and honed as a result of doing the research, more robustly rooted in the evidence we have gathered and the literature we have drawn upon. We usually have a passion to communicate that vision to others (although we can also experience a sense of boredom with the research, a kind of burn-out, that can be another challenge of research at this point, compelling us to dig deep and find a new energy for material that we may well have been working with for many years).

One of the key spiritual challenges at this final stage of research is that of completion itself: of committing to an end-point and actually finishing the work. This can be difficult for some of us. As long as we are still writing the thesis, the book, the article, we can fool ourselves that perfection is possible, that we will manage comprehensive coverage or full systemization, we will say all that needs to be said. Yet in the end, we realize we have to settle for 'as good as we can get it' – the imperfect provisional to which we're willing to commit. The more of a visionary we are, the higher the ideals we have for ourselves and our research, the harder this part of the process is likely to be. It requires confronting our own limitations, inadequacies and frailties. We'll always be the most severe critics of our own work because we'll know at first hand its flaws and we'll know only too well to what it was we aspired – and didn't quite manage. (Is there a writer or artist alive who feels they fully achieved their ambitions?) In theological terms, we might express this in terms of an eschatological tension between the 'now' and the 'not yet' of the *basilea*. In research, as in life, we face the spiritual challenge of living with our own, and the world's, imperfections, without losing the vision of what we strive for.

There's a sense, too, at this stage of completion that, as soon as we finish the work, it becomes something else: it separates from us, becomes something external, objective, 'out there', available for others' critical scrutiny, indifference, or applause – rather than our own 'private' possession, rooted in our internal psychic world. And, of course, as soon as we finish it, the research is out of date, obsolete in one sense. The final challenge of completion is to negotiate this transition from internal to external, from 'my' research to something that has a life of its own in the external, public world (however small a world this may, in reality, be), from the ideal fantasy of the piece of work as it could be when unfinished to the reality of what it is, for good and for ill, in its finished state.

Yet it is essential to let the work go and to let it be what it will. We must learn to trust the completed research to do its own work in the world, separate from us. It is a strange relationship we have with our own work, akin to the relationship of parent to child, perhaps. It is our work, yet not ours. We no longer own it, we discover, once we have finished it (if we ever did). It came from others, was fed by others, motivated by them, and now we offer it back to them, in the hope of instigating 'mutual learning, growth and transformation'.[29] In doing so, we must let the work go, and risk it into the world. This is part of the research process as spiritual practice: learning to stand by our work, stand up for it, be willing to be visible and accountable for what we have done; but also not being defensive about it, trusting it will do its own work. This is part of a process of claiming our power and visibility as women, claiming our place in the public arena and demanding that our voices be heard – and being ready to take the flak alongside the praise and be thrown by neither.

---

[29] Moschella, *Ethnography*, p. 214.

Conclusion: The Research Process as Transformative Spiritual Practice

The research journey itself, then, is a kind of paschal process into which we enter: a sharing in the passion of God to make and remake the world.[30] To this process of justice making and the seeking of right relation, we are willing to offer ourselves, our time, our skills, our bodies, our hearts and minds, our whole selves. In the process, we are formed and transformed: losing and finding ourselves countless times in the messy, confusing, uncertain processes of research; labouring and struggling and suffering, as well as knowing elation, joy and excitement. We are chastened and humbled by our research, discovering that we know much less than we thought we did. Yet we are also emboldened and empowered by it, and by the others with whom we share the process, to claim the truth of what we do know and to proclaim it where it can be heard and where it can make a difference to the world. So we move towards our own risenness as women,[31] claiming an authentic authority to witness to what we have discovered, speaking into both academy and Church (as well as other communities we represent) with conviction and without apology. As we do so, we discover we are not alone, but travel with others towards the elusive goal of a world in which each person is enabled to be all that they have it in them to be and where research is for the mutual wisdom, empowerment and liberation of all.

---

[30] The phrase comes from Adrienne Rich, 'Natural Resources', in *The Dream of a Common Language: Poems 1974–1977* (New York, 1978), p. 64, and is used by Mary Grey in her feminist reworking of atonement theology in *Redeeming the Dream: Feminism, Redemption and Christian Tradition* (London, 1989).

[31] See my poem, 'A risen woman', in Nicola Slee, *Seeking the Risen Christa* (London, 2011), p. 132.

Chapter 2
From Privacy to Prophecy: Public and Private in Researching Women's Faith and Spirituality

Jan Berry

Introduction

Research into the faith and spirituality of women explores and interprets women's experience and spiritual practice and brings them into the framework of current theological discourse. The experiences and stories which feminist theological research investigates are often deeply personal; they frequently involve strong emotions and intimate relationships, which are not easily shared, and which many women would prefer to keep private. Yet if feminist research is to add to the store of knowledge, and if, as many of us hope, it is undertaken with the hope of making some kind of difference to women's lives, then such private experiences need to be brought into the public sphere.[1] In their book on ethical issues involved in feminist research, Rosalind Edwards and Jane Ribbens explore the ways in which such research often explores areas which have previously been invisible and marginalized, bringing them into academic and public discourse in a way which could easily become intrusive or exploitative: are we extending the dominance of publicly based knowledge and expertise, and colluding into its intrusion into every nook and cranny of social life?[2]

In this chapter, I analyse the implications of this for my own research, and the ways in which feminist research brings women's private lives and experience into public theological discourse. I look more closely at this issue of private and public, using some theoretical explorations, reflecting on contemporary instances of the blurring of the dichotomy and asking, what does research into women's faith, theology and spirituality have to offer?

---

[1] See Caroline Ramazanoglu and Janet Holland, *Feminist Methodology: Challenges and Choices* on the need for feminist research to 'tell better stories of gendered lives' (London, 2002), p.106.

[2] Rosalind Edwards and Jane Ribbens, 'Living on the Edges: Public Knowledge, Private Lives, Personal Experience', in Jane Ribbens and Rosalind Edwards (eds), *Feminist Dilemmas in Qualitative Research: Public Knowledge and Private Lives* (London, 1998), p. 13.

Researching Women's Ritual Making

My research explored women's practices of ritual making in which, inspired by my work with women's groups over the years and the work of other feminist liturgists such as Diann Neu, Janet Morley and Nicola Slee,[3] I looked at the rituals and liturgies which women constructed to mark and negotiate significant changes in their lives. Whilst these rituals, and the events and experiences which prompted them, were deeply personal and private, they often had wider implications, and public and political dimensions.

My doctoral research was interwoven with my own spirituality and my faith journey. It was qualitative research, drawing on feminist methodologies in social studies and ethnography,[4] using interviews, participant observation and with a strong reflexive and auto-ethnographic element. Whilst all research has its moments of drudgery and tedium, what kept this alive through five years of part-time researching was the opportunity to listen to women's stories and share with them in their rituals. During this process, I heard many deeply moving and personal stories – of loss and grief, of the breakdown of relationships, of celebration of the body, of pride in academic achievement, of growing self-worth and empowerment. On some occasions, I had the privilege of participating in the rituals themselves, sharing with small groups of women in intimate gatherings in the privacy of homes, listening and re-enacting their stories with transformative power.

During this I became aware of, and engaged with, issues of private and public at a number of different levels. The research itself was engaging with private, personal areas of women's lives and making them public, initially perhaps just to the restricted readership of a doctoral thesis, but also in spoken and written papers, and eventually in a book.[5] Whilst I offered research participants the safeguards of confidentiality and the use of pseudonyms, some preferred to be named, seeing that as a vital part of telling their stories.

Therefore, in the initial research processes of hearing, transcribing and writing about women's stories, there was a tension between private and public – the private, personal emotions and events being made accessible to a wider audience. This was potentially liberating and empowering, as women's voices were heard and their stories told, but could also make women and their intimate experiences

---

[3] Diann Neu, *Women's Rites: Feminist Liturgies for Life's Journey* (Cleveland, OH, 2003); Janet Morley, *All Desires Known*, 2nd edn (London, 1992); Nicola Slee, *Praying Like a Woman* (London, 2004).

[4] See Liz Stanley and Sue Wise, *Breaking Out Again: Feminist Ontology and Epistemology* (London, 1993) for one of the earliest arguments for reflexivity in feminist research; also Ramazanoglu and Holland, *Feminist Methodology*, and Amanda Coffey, *The Ethnographic Self: Fieldwork and the Representation of Identity* (London, 1999).

[5] Jan Berry, 'Transforming Rites: the practice of women's ritual making' (unpublished PhD thesis, University of Glasgow, 2006), later published as Jan Berry, *Ritual Making Women: Shaping Rites for Changing Lives* (London, 2009).

vulnerable to the scrutiny of public debate and critique. I was aware of a sense of privilege in hearing the stories, of responsibility in retelling them, and in the trust that research participants placed in me as we travelled together.

As the research progressed, it became clear that some of the same tensions were present in the ritual practice itself. Most of the rituals were semi-private occasions, shared with an invited group. In the safe space of a small group in a private home, women cried, laughed, created symbolic meaning and moved into a transformative space. Such ritual was intentionally private, exclusive in the sense that there was no general or public invitation, and designed to create a sacred space for the participants to mark, negotiate and construct life-changing events.

But if such ritual remains private, there is a possibility that it is no more than a safe outlet for emotions of loss, anger, or hope which has no impact on the wider world or the actual lives of women. Such a therapeutic expression may be helpful to the participants, but if it has no broader implications, it may weaken the concern for social justice that is at the heart of feminist theology. If ritual is actually to be empowering and life-changing, then it needs to speak with a wider voice to the concrete and material realities of the public world.

In reviewing literature on goddess spirituality, Pam Lunn raises similar issues, arguing that whilst some forms of ritual can have an emotional impact on the participants, changing their feelings and perceptions, unless it leads to concrete action and change in the external world then 'this whole movement may be nothing but an emotional opiate, a consolation prize for women who are powerless in the rest of their lives.'[6] This is a timely warning about the way in which liturgy and ritual can act as a kind of safety-valve for powerful emotions; but many of the rituals which I researched had wider, more public and political implications. Rituals associated with work and redundancy spoke to public concerns, and rituals of renaming had implications for women's public identities. In renaming rituals, the women spoke about both the public and private aspects – the legal aspects of changing names, altering documentation and so on, and the more personal aspects of what it meant in terms of their own sense of identity. They were clear, however, that changing one's name was a public matter: it was to do with how they were known by others in the world.[7]

Feminist Theorizing of Private and Public

One way of interpreting the private/public divide is to argue that nothing should be confined to the private sphere. In Hannah Arendt's writing, there seems to be an almost complete breakdown of the public/private dualism.[8] For her, it seems that

---

[6] Pam Lunn, 'Do Women Need the GODDESS? Some Phenomenological and Sociological Reflections', *Feminist Theology* 4 (1993): 30.

[7] Berry, *Ritual Making Women*, pp. 182–5.

[8] Hannah Arendt, *The Human Condition*, 2nd edn (Chicago, IL, 1998 [1958]).

the public realm is the realm of freedom and individuality, expressed in the power to act; the private realm is the realm of deprivation. She does acknowledge the richness of the modern concept of privacy, with its emphasis on subjectivity and intimacy, but argues that even the most personal experiences take on a new reality or substance when they emerge into the public realm. Ultimately, to be confined to the private realm is to be deprived of what it means to be fully human; as soon as an idea or thought is given voice in relationship with others, it emerges into the public realm. Only then can our living and being have any chance of making a difference in the realm of human affairs; and a totally private life means 'to be deprived of the possibility of achieving something more permanent than life itself'.[9] Arendt has a strong sense of the interconnectedness of human life and action: human society is a web, in which any word or action has its effects.[10]

Arendt's concept of public and private is useful in that she begins to break down the sense of a rigid separation into two realms, and to challenge the relegation of certain forms of human activity to a private realm. It seems that in her thinking almost anything can be seen as public, and indeed needs to be, if it to have a significant reality in human activity. For feminists, there is a strength in this argument, in that experiences and realities formerly dismissed or marginalized as belonging to the private sphere, take their place in public debate. Research into women's lives, their faith and spirituality, has a legitimate place in the public discourse of theology. However, it raises the questions: if everything is public, does it become such a loose, 'umbrella' concept that it loses all distinctive meaning; and what happens to those experiences, emotions and perceptions which an individual wishes to designate as private?

There needs, therefore, to be the possibility of designating some realities as private. Iris Young attempts to build on Arendt's work, acknowledging the challenge to the idea of two separate realms, but arguing that the distinction needs to be maintained. It needs redefining, however, so that the two are no longer seen in hierarchical opposition, in which the public is privileged or seen as superior over the private.[11] Young argues that the primary meaning of public relates to what is open and accessible, a matter of debate and accountability. She picks up on Arendt's understanding of private as related to deprivation, and argues that the notion of private must not be used in an exclusionary way. Whilst she acknowledges the right of individuals to choose to keep parts of their lives out of public scrutiny, the use of privacy must not be used to exclude people or topics from consideration and debate. Therefore whilst she retains the distinction between two separate spheres, nothing must be forced into privacy – no social institutions or practices are excluded. Her understanding originates in the challenge of feminists to traditional political theory, in which previously personal issues, ranging from the usage of exclusive language and acts of masculine good manners (such as

---

[9] Ibid., p. 58.
[10] Ibid., pp. 183–4.
[11] Iris Marion Young, *Justice and the Politics of Difference* (Princeton, NJ, 1990), p. 119.

opening doors for women) through to sexual assault and domestic violence, are seen as having political resonances and dimensions:

> The feminist slogan 'the personal is political' expresses the principle that no social practices or activities should be excluded as improper subjects for public discussion, expression, or collective choice.[12]

Young's view challenges us to examine carefully the agenda and themes of what is public, so that we do not fall into the old stereotypical and hierarchical dualisms. These dualisms, particularly if they are used with a hierarchical sense, can be used to confine women, and so-called 'women's issues', from public debate about what is just and good. Research into subjects such as sexual abuse and domestic violence, normally considered 'private' matters, has a part to play in the public arena.

Seyla Benhabib[13] traces the distinction between public and private in modern western thought, and argues that the way in which this distinction has been upheld has served to remove from the public agenda and debate such so-called 'female issues' as housework, reproduction, and the care of others who are vulnerable, whether because of youth or age, sickness or disability.

Benhabib argues that the concept of privacy, or the private sphere, has included three distinct dimensions: moral and religious conscience, freedom of economic choice, and the intimate sphere of family, household and sexuality. But in identifying these areas as belonging to the private sphere, questions of power dynamics and injustice within them have been excluded from public debate and ethical challenge. She argues for a model of the public sphere based upon the discourse theory of Jürgen Habermas,[14] but claims that his model takes for granted certain norms and assumptions about what constitutes justice, and so fails to acknowledge the way in which the opposition of private and public has been used to reinforce the dynamics of power and oppression. What is needed is the challenge of a feminist critique which is not gender-blind but recognizes both the differences of gender, and the existence of power relations within the intimate, or 'private' sphere.

> Such feminization of practical discourse will mean first and foremost challenging unexamined normative dualisms as between justice and the good life, norms and values, interests and needs, from the standpoint of their gender context and subtext.[15]

---

[12] Ibid., pp.120–21.

[13] Seyla Benhabib, 'Models of Public Space: Hannah Arendt, the Liberal Tradition and Jürgen Habermas', in Seyla Benhabib (ed.), *Situating the Self: Gender, Community and Postmodernism in Contemporary Ethics* (Cambridge, 1992), pp. 89–120.

[14] Jürgen Habermas, *Structural Transformation of the Public Sphere* (Boston, MA, 1989), cited in Benhabib, 'Models', p. 118.

[15] Benhabib, 'Models', p. 113.

Benhabib's work challenges us to examine more closely the ways in which the terms 'public' and 'private' are used in contemporary discourse, and to ensure that 'privacy' is not abused to silence a feminist critique of justice or oppression, or to marginalize research into the everyday, domestic realities of women's lives.

Public Theology and Women's Voice

This critique of the dualism between public and private needs to be applied to the current emphasis on public theology. In recent years, we have seen a growing development of 'public theology', an attempt to make a theological contribution to debates on public issues of economics and social justice.[16] This is an important and laudable development, but it seems that much of the agenda of public theology is still dominated by a traditional male understanding of what is contained within the public sphere. Traditionally, in modern western society, there has been a dualism embedded in our discourse of public and private: the public realm of business, finance and economics was associated with maleness, whilst the female sphere was that of the domestic, the private world of home and family, the Victorian 'angel in the home'. Whilst many would argue that those days have gone, and that women are now equally active and engaged in the realms of politics, business and economics, there is plenty of evidence that this is not universally so. Boards of directors are predominantly male; there is still a minority of women in government and cabinet positions, and church leadership in the public arena still tends to be male.

This dualism has also been reflected in theology, particularly in the recent emphasis on public theology. There are two ways in which feminist theology has a contribution to make here. First, there is the ongoing challenge of ensuring that the public sphere does not remain a male one; women are equally capable of speaking on matters of finance, economics and social justice (see, for example, Elaine Graham's contribution to the Commission on Urban Life and Faith[17] and the subsequent book *What Makes a Good City?*[18]). But secondly, and perhaps more importantly, feminist theology needs to resist the traditional dichotomy between public and private, and argue for a rigorous examination of what should come under public debate and accountability.

---

[16] See, for example, Duncan Forrester, *Truthful Action: Explorations in Practical Theology* (Edinburgh, 2000); Bonnie Miller-McLemore, 'Pastoral Theology as Practical Theology', in *Christian Theology in Practice: Discovering a Discipline* (Grand Rapids, MI, 2012). The International Academy of Practical Theology made public theology the subject of its conference in Manchester in 2002; it was also the subject of the British and Irish Association for Practical Theology conference in 2009.

[17] Archbishops' Commission on Urban Life and Faith, *Faithful Cities: A Call for Celebration, Vision and Justice* (Peterborough, 2006).

[18] Elaine Graham and Stephen Lowe, *What Makes a Good City: Public Theology and the Urban Church* (London, 2009).

The recent attempts of theologians to find a prophetic voice in the public sphere are important and necessary, but need to engage with a critique of gender and power. Duncan Forrester talks of two ways of doing public theology, the 'magisterial' and the liberationist,[19] and Elaine Graham[20] identifies two approaches, the neutral and universal, and the preferential or particular. Certainly public theology has included a liberationist and preferential approach in relation to economic poverty and social exclusion; but it may need to take more seriously differences of gender and sexuality if it is fully to overcome the old dichotomy and become a public voice on issues which have traditionally been considered private matters. In the rest of this section I want to examine two such issues, violence and abuse against women, and sexuality.

Violence against Women

In recent years, there has been increased awareness and attention paid to issues of violence against women.[21] It is no longer acceptable for incidents of violence and assault in the home to be treated simply as 'domestic' issues; the reality of rape within marriage is recognized; procedures are put in place to try to ensure that there is adequate protection and care for victims of rape and sexual assault. Matters which once would have been seen as belonging to the private spheres of home or sexual intimacy are now matters of public awareness, knowledge and debate. Ken Plummer looks at the telling of sexual stories as 'social actions embedded in social worlds',[22] and shows how stories are constructed in a culture that is both ready to hear and partially shapes them. One of the examples he uses is that of women's stories of rape, which he argues have changed dramatically in the telling since the 1970s. He shows how the ways in which these stories have been shaped have been led by a concern to deconstruct the myths around rape, to create a history of violence against women, and to build a political platform which exposes the damage done by violence and aggression. What was once regarded as a matter for private shame has become a challenge to public perception; and the same is true of other sexual stories, such as recovery from abuse, and LGBT (lesbian, gay, bisexual and transgender) coming-out stories.

In the area of violence against women, there is much valuable research in the fields of feminist pastoral and practical theology that needs to be part of public debate and accountability. There is a constant danger that the discipline of pastoral care, in particular, can be seen as being concerned only with the private lives of

---

[19] Forrester, *Truthful Action*, pp. 118–25

[20] Elaine Graham, *Words Made Flesh: Writings in Pastoral and Practical Theology* (London, 2009), pp. 218–20

[21] Pamela Cooper-White, *The Cry of Tamar: Violence Against Women and the Church's Response* (Minneapolis, MN, 1995).

[22] Ken Plummer, *Telling Sexual Stories: Power, Change, and Social Worlds* (London and New York, 1995), p. 17.

individuals. Zoë Bennett Moore's book[23] helpfully surveys recent developments in this field in both Britain and the United States. She picks up Bonnie Miller-McLemore's phrase of the 'living human web',[24] which begins to move pastoral theology away from its traditional focus on the psychology of the individual and has echoes of Arendt's thinking. She uses this to demonstrate the ways in which feminist understandings of pastoral care have moved away from a focus on the one-to-one encounter of counselling and the 'living human document'[25] of clinical pastoral education, to consider the lives of individuals within systems of families, churches and institutions which are characterized by power dynamics that can be, and often are, exploitative if not oppressive and unjust.

The disciplines of counselling and psychotherapy have sometimes been criticized for being too individualistic, and their influence on pastoral care decried as taking away from a focus on community and justice. Within the secular professions, however, there is an increasing awareness of the social and economic forces which impact on clients' lives and shape their self-understanding, and pastoral theologians too are beginning to broaden their perspective. Riet Bons-Storm[26] writes of the ways in which women's stories are often negated or trivialized in the context of pastoral care and counselling, and the women perceived as unstable or abnormal. This, she argues, is because their stories are heard in the context of wider narratives – psychological, sociological and theological – with a masculine or patriarchal bias, which trivializes or victimizes women. Women's 'problems' need to be seen not as their misfortune or weakness, but as symptoms of power imbalances in wider church and society.

Work such as this within the fields of pastoral and practical theology increasingly highlights the systemic nature of discourse which victimizes women and implicitly legitimizes abuse. Here there are issues of power and oppression that need to be publicly challenged and debated, and research into women's spirituality and feminist theology has an increasing role to play in offering a prophetic voice.

---

[23] Zoë Bennett Moore, *Introducing Feminist Perspectives on Pastoral Theology* (Sheffield, 2002).

[24] Bonnie Miller-McLemore, 'The Living Human Web: Pastoral Theology at the Turn of the Century', in Jeanne Stevenson-Moessner (ed.), *Through the Eyes of Women: Insights for Pastoral Care* (Minneapolis, MN, 1996).

[25] This phrase was first used by Anton Boisen in the early part of the twentieth century and has been significant in the development of clinical pastoral education, particularly in the United States, but also in Britain; see for example, Frances Ward, *Lifelong Learning: Theological Education and Supervision* (London, 2005).

[26] Riet Bons-Storm, *The Incredible Woman: Listening to Women's Silences in Pastoral Care and Counseling* (Nashville, TN, 1996).

Celebrating Same-Sex Relationships

Five years ago, my partner and I celebrated our civil partnership with a service of blessing in our local church.[27] Over many years of being lesbian in the Church, I had always imagined that, were I to celebrate a committed relationship, it would be in a small private ceremony, with a few close friends. My partner was adamant that she wanted a church blessing, and our local church had already declared itself to be an 'inclusive congregation'. In the event, what we held was a public ceremony, in many aspects resembling a wedding, but with some subversive touches – rainbow ribbons on the car, two women walking (or in my case dancing!) down the aisle to the music of Melissa Etheridge, and a blessing ceremony using ribbons knotted together by members of the congregation and wrapped round us. It was, in Elizabeth Stuart's phrase, a 'parody', a 'repetition with a critical difference',[28] which both resembled but also subverted a traditional patriarchal ceremony.

In her auto-ethnographic account of her research, Ladelle McWhorter[29] tells her story of celebrating her relationship with her partner. Initially reluctant to enter into something which she saw as a conventional ceremony, she found the process transformative, and named it, in Michel Foucault's terms, as a 'practice of freedom', enabling members of an oppressed group (in this instance, the gay and lesbian community) to claim power and identity. The private joy of their relationship became a public, transformative act.

The introduction of a law permitting civil partnerships indicates and partially constructs a shift in public attitude towards lesbian and gay relationships. Much of this is commercially driven – there are new opportunities for merchandise and new business for party planners. Whilst it is easy to dismiss much of this as an unthinking adoption of heteronormative conventions, that is to miss the point; a public act of commitment is a political – and in the instances of church blessings, a theological – statement and a claim to empowerment.

Issues of gay sexuality have of course figured largely in the public debates of the Church; but much of this discourse has been in the liberal framework of equal human rights. This is necessary and to be welcomed; but I would like to see a greater attempt to articulate theologies of marriage and sexuality which do not simply request the same rights (rites) for gay people, but seek to ask questions

---

[27] See Elena Buch and Karen Staller, 'The Feminist Practice of Ethnography', in Sharlene Nagy Hesse-Biber and Patricia Lina Leavy (eds), *Feminist Research Practice: A Primer* (Thousand Oaks, CA, 2007) for auto-ethnography as a feminist research method using the researcher's 'personal lived experience as the primary source of ethnographic data' (p. 189).

[28] Elizabeth Stuart, *Gay and Lesbian Theologies: Repetitions with Critical Difference* (Aldershot, 2003), p. 108.

[29] Ladelle McWhorter, 'Rites of passing: Foucault, power, and same-sex commitment ceremonies', in Kevin Schilbrack (ed.), *Thinking Through Rituals: Philosophical Perspectives* (New York and London, 2004).

about the relationship of personal commitment to public life and values. Sexual orientation and preference is no longer a private matter, but is taking its place in law and religious ceremony.[30] Early lesbian and radical feminist voices challenged the patriarchal hegemony of marriage, but feminist theology offers the possibility of a stronger re-engagement with a theology of desire, power and mutuality. Directions are emerging in the work of Carter Heyward on mutuality, Lisa Isherwood on embodiment, and Elizabeth Stuart on queer theology.

Running through Heyward's work[31] is a deep insistence on the value and importance of mutuality. It is mutuality, not hierarchical transcendence, that characterizes the divine/human relationship, and so should be reflected in all human relationality. Human loving is an act of justice making, of 'godding', which shares in the process and activity of God/ess in the world. The implications of this understanding for human sexuality is that all our expressions of human loving, including the erotic, must exclude any domination of one by the other. Patriarchal views of marriage as a legal transaction which gives one person rights over another's body or property are a denial of justice and mutuality, and human love and commitment find expression in a mutual passion for justice.

The dualism of public and private, male and female, has been mirrored by a dualism of mind and body, in which rationality and cerebral understanding have been considered superior to emotion, bodily experience and instincts. Part of the enterprise of feminist theology, therefore, has been to reclaim and articulate a theology of embodiment. Isherwood[32] roots this in her understanding of the incarnate Christ – the story of a human Jesus is one of flesh made sacred, sharing bodily pain and desire, and enjoying bodily pleasures. An embodied theology recognizes the human body as a site of the sacred, and human desire and sexuality as carrying the possibility of divine encounter. This transgresses the conventions of body shape and size, and heterosexual relations, to embrace a multiplicity of forms of sexual expression; though retaining an opposition to any form of sexual relations which objectifies, exploits, or abuses the other.

Along with secular theorists such as Judith Butler,[33] Stuart emphasizes the social construction of gender and sexuality, arguing that our sexual identities and understandings of gender are shaped by social forces and competing discourses. Whilst we may perceive them as fixed and absolute, they are relative and fluid. Our

---

[30] At the end of 2012, the UK government announced its proposals for equal marriage in England and Wales that would enable same-sex couples to marry. This follows similar proposals for Scotland announced by the Scottish government earlier in the year.

[31] Carter Heyward, *Our Passion for Justice: Images of Power, Sexuality, and Liberation* (New York, 1984).

[32] Lisa Isherwood, 'The Embodiment of Feminist Liberation Theology: The Spiralling of Incarnation', in *Embodying Feminist Liberation Theologies: A Special Edition of Feminist Theology* 12/2 (January 2004): 140–56.

[33] See, for example, Judith Butler, *Gender Trouble and the Subversion of Identity* (New York, 1990).

identity as baptized Christians subverts all distinctions of gender and sexuality, and renders them queer:

> Christianity has a divine mandate to be 'queer', to perform our socially constructed roles, our gender, our sexuality, our race, our class, and so on, in such a way as to point to their non-ultimacy.[34]

Our theological understandings of relationship, commitment and marriage are part of these constructed identities. Queer theology subverts traditional views to point us toward a fluid, interpretive and intersubjective understanding of human identities and relationships.

For feminist theologians, then, female sexuality is not simply a private matter, but is a voice that needs to be heard in the multi-layered and competing discourses of marriage and family, sexual ethics, and individual and social commitment, speaking of a theology which takes seriously the reality of bodies-in-relation.

Conclusion

Women's spirituality and ritual making often begin in the private domain, and need the safe space of intimate knowledge and friendship to grow and flourish. But in that flourishing, in its creativity and playfulness, it is reaching out to speak with a more public voice, with what Walter Brueggemann calls 'prophetic imagination',[35] and Elisabeth Schüssler Fiorenza 'a hermeneutic of creative actualization'.[36] Research into feminist theology, in making public women's stories and experiences of faith, challenges us to re-examine the dualism of public and private, to transgress the boundaries, and to move from privacy to prophecy.

---

[34] Elizabeth Stuart, 'Exploding Mystery: Feminist Theology and the Sacramental', in *Embodying Feminist Liberation Theologies: A Special Edition of Feminist Theology* 12/2 (January 2004): 34.
[35] Walter Brueggemann, *The Prophetic Imagination*, 2nd edn (Minneapolis, MN, 2001).
[36] Elisabeth Schüssler Fiorenza, *In Memory of Her* (New York, 1983).

PART II
Neglected Ages, Stages and Styles in Women's and Girls' Faith Lives

Chapter 3
Understanding the Work of Women in Religion

Abby Day

Introduction

Researching the faith lives of girls and women has been central to my work since 1999, beginning with a short study of a women's prayer group,[1] followed by long-term fieldwork in England from 2003 until the time of writing in 2011,[2] made possible through three separately-funded studies through the Arts and Humanities Research Council and the Economic and Social Research Council. The longitudinal studies spanned three generations of people ranging in age from 14 to 84, from different social classes and evenly split by gender. My current project, again funded by Economic and Social Research Council, focuses exclusively on Anglican women born in the 1920s and '30s, the cohort I have named 'Generation A'. In this chapter, I draw on some of that theory to illuminate cases from my longitudinal studies; I focus on women of faith, looking beyond a narrow conception of faith as 'belief' alone. My research concludes that exploring the interaction of different dimensions of belief and belonging reveal a richer nature of religiosity. That was why I developed an interpretive model to focus not just on the content of belief but belief's *resources*, *practices*, *salience* and *functions*. To study belief longitudinally, new elements of *place* and *time* were incorporated. This holistic, organic, multi-dimensional framework developed the research beyond standard sociological techniques to an enhanced anthropological approach introducing a performative, dynamic element. This process, which I termed 'performative belief', refers to a neo-Durkheimian construct where belief is a lived, embodied performance brought into being through action. Within a social context are social relationships: performative belief plays out through the relationships in which people have faith and to which they feel they belong. Belief in social relationships is performed through social actions of both belonging and excluding.

---

[1] Abby Day, 'Doing Theodicy: an Empirical Study of a Women's Prayer Group', *Journal of Contemporary Religion* 20/3 (2005): 343–56.

[2] Abby Day, 'Doing Qualitative Longitudinal Religious Research', in Linda Woodhead (ed.), *Innovative Methods in the Study of Religion* (Oxford, forthcoming).

Applying this theory to gender is instructive. Women in Euro-American countries are apparently more religious than men, and older women more religious than younger women. That generalized statement seems to be supported by large-scale quantitative data on Christianity in the UK: about 40 per cent of Church of England monthly attendees are women aged 60 or over, twice the number of men of a similar age.[3] Older women are represented disproportionately: 4 per cent of the general population attends the Anglican Church regularly; about 10 per cent of women over 60 attend and less than 2 per cent of women under 60. Evidence suggests that this is a unique generation that will not be replaced: women under the age of 60 attend church much less often than their mothers and their participation has not been increasing over time.

Such behaviour sometimes leads scholars to conclude that women are more religious than men. That claim is supported by some research, as described above, but leaves a counter-argument unexplored: if, indeed, women are 'more religious' than men, how do we account for widespread evidence that men near-exclusively occupy the most senior strata of religious institutions? Feminist inroads have been made in liberal forms of Judaism and Christianity, but these have been recent, hard-won battles that have caused schisms on an international scale as men have resisted such intrusions. Religious power and authority has been and generally remains a male domain. When, therefore, people suggest that women are more religious than men, they must be restricting their analysis to certain behaviours and kinds of lay religiosity. This lack of a definition of what is construed as religious and what may be explained by gender may speak to a wider unease about gender in the sociology and anthropology of religion.[4] Only quantitative surveys asking such limited and thin questions as, for example, 'do you believe in God?' provide evidence of more female than male religiosity but, as feminist researchers have long argued, such forced and skewed questions do not accurately explain the nature of what people may actually believe and feel to be religious or spiritual. Quantitative studies continue to ask forced religious questions about apparent beliefs in God, heaven, hell and so on without pausing to interrogate what those terms mean on the ground. From that 'evidence', they construct theories of biological, psychological, or sociological explanations often centring on ideas about deprivation, status, guilt, socialization, personality, or even a lack of testosterone.[5]

---

[3] *British Social Attitudes, the 24th Report* (London, 2008).

[4] Linda Woodhead, 'Feminism and the Sociology of Religion: from Gender-blindness to Gendered Difference', in Richard K. Fenn (ed.), *The Blackwell Companion to Sociology of Religion* (Oxford, 2001), pp. 67–84; Day, 'Doing Theodicy', pp. 343–56; Fiona Bowie, *The Anthropology of Religion* (Oxford, 2006); Fenella Cannell (ed.), *The Anthropology of Christianity* (Durham, NC and London, 2007).

[5] Tony Walter and Grace Davie, 'The Religiosity of Women in the Modern West', *British Journal of Sociology* 49/4 (1998): 640–60; A.S. Miller and R. Stark, 'Gender and

Work that challenges those theories attempts to re-introduce power, agency and complexity,[6] with several small-scale studies focusing on gender, if not older women specifically.[7]

This chapter provides two illustrations drawn from my longitudinal research to act as emblematic examples of why I challenge existing theories about gender and religion. I will argue here that through qualitative research it becomes apparent that other explanatory values, such as relatedness, power structures and sociality, may explain gender discrepancies. What may be at stake is the kind of religiosity that is valued and then accorded to men or women. For example, sociologists of religion may minimize the power of women's spiritual labour. In Wuthnow's study of small groups, including church-based groups dominated by women, he concluded that a certain type of wisdom was missing because members did not pay sufficient attention to theological arguments: 'In simplest terms, the sacred comes to be associated with small insights that seem intuitively correct to the small group rather than wisdom accrued over the centuries in hermitages, seminaries, universities, congregations and church councils.'[8]

Wuthnow seems to be implying that women who discuss and pray about everyday problems are not doing serious work whereas men, who inhabit male institutions and spend time in contemplation and discussion of centuries-old theological ideas constructed by other men, *are* doing serious work. His orientation reflects other male-constructed theories and definitions in anthropology and sociology which tend to focus on milieux inhabited by men and thus tend to universalize and marginalize women through ignoring anything specific about women's experience and constructs.

In what follows, I will conclude that faith is hard emotional work and, like most emotional work, it is usually assigned to women. Further, it is work that is mostly spent not in the service of 'religion', but in the service of society through a

---

Religiousness: Can Socialization Explanations Be Saved?', *American Journal of Sociology* 107/6 (2002): 1399–423.

[6] Abby Day, 'Wilfully Disempowered: a Gendered Response to a Fallen World', *European Journal of Women's Studies* 15/3 (2008): 261–76; Elizabeth J. Ozorak, 'The Power, but Not the Glory: How Women Empower Themselves Through Religion', *Journal for the Scientific Study of Religion* 35/1 (1996): 17–29; Louise Mari Roth and Jeffrey C. Kroll, 'Risky Business: Assessing Risk Preference Explanations for Gender Differences in Religiosity', *American Sociological Review*, 72/2 (2007): 205–20; and Donald Paul Sullins, 'Gender and Religion: Deconstructing Universality, Constructing Complexity', *American Journal of Sociology* 112/3 (2006): 838–80.

[7] Helen Cameron, Philip J. Richter and Douglas Davies, *Studying Local Churches: A Handbook* (London, 2005); Nancy Nason-Clark, 'Ordaining Women as Priests: Religious vs. Sexist Explanations for Clerical Attitudes', *Sociology of Religion* 48/3 (1987): 259–73; and Julie Manville, 'The Gendered Organization of an Australian Anglican Parish', *Sociology of Religion* 58/1 (1997): 25–38.

[8] Robert Wuthnow, *Sharing the Journey: Support Groups and America's New Quest for Community* (New York, 1994), p. 358.

gendered allocation of responsibility for moral integrity. Taking as I do that faith often involves emotional work, I would argue following, for example, West and Zimmerman,[9] that processes of social differentiation have assigned faith and other emotional labours to women. That women are responsible for society's moral health or downfall is a familiar assumption, argued Brown.[10] This relates to a gendered Christian discourse that located piety in femininity from about 1800 to 1960. He argued that the age of 'discursive Christianity' collapsed during the 1960s when women stopped subscribing to that discourse and 'the nature of femininity changed fundamentally.'[11] While I think Brown has a powerful argument about the nature of discursive Christianity, I am not convinced that the nature of femininity has changed fundamentally for all women. Women do still look after their husbands and children, even while working outside the home.

Hochschild and Machung's 'second shift' argument illustrates that women in dual-income households still perform the majority of domestic labour, as well as care duties for their immediate and extended families.[12] Women, as fully conscious agents, are aware of the gendered normative roles and practices operating in contemporary UK society in general, not only in conservative wings of Christianity but more widely, where men oppress and exploit women. Frequently during my interviews, I found that women who maintain their places within the domestic, 'feminine' sphere are revered, and women who leave that sphere and subordinate roles risk hostility and blame for the downfall of their children and communities. This apparently 'natural' scheme of gender relations can be supported through what Walby describes as 'discursive patriarchy', being 'a system of social structures and practices in which men dominate, oppress, and exploit women'.[13] Her analysis focuses on how patriarchy can be understood best through exploring structures of production, paid work, the state, male violence, sexuality and cultural institutions, to which I add religion and the family. This is a case of how religion may function to support wider social norms.

Method

My original study[14] featured two characteristics that are somewhat unusual in my field: I did not use religious questions to research religion and I did not

---

[9] Candace West and Don H. Zimmerman, 'Doing Gender', *Gender and Society* 1 (1987): 125–51.

[10] Callum Brown, *The Death of Christian Britain* (London, 2001).

[11] Ibid., p. 195.

[12] Arlie Hochschild and Anne Machung, *The Second Shift: Working Parents and the Revolution at Home* (Berkeley, CA and London, 1989).

[13] Sylvia Walby, *Theorizing Patriarchy* (Oxford, 1990), p. 20.

[14] Abby Day, 'Researching belief without asking religious questions', *Fieldwork in Religion* 4/1 (2009): 89–106.

recruit people on the basis of their interest in religion. During the first phase of the research, my questions, asked in semi-structured interviews, were designed to probe the content of what they believed in: about their moral beliefs, what was important to them, how life began, how it might end, what, if anything, life meant to them, what frightened or delighted them and where those emotions and beliefs came from. It soon became evident that content was only part of the story and that belief's sources, practices, salience and function were just as important.

During the follow-up phase (2009–11), I lived in the same village of many of my participants, and bordered others, and conducted what I have categorized as 54 fieldwork data collection events, of which 22 were formal interviews recorded and transcribed, 32 were visits to people's homes, social events, places of worship, schools, significant sites (market, shops, cafes, taxi ranks) prompted by informants' insights and often accompanied by them. I will turn now to my illustrations.

Working for God's Love

Vera,[15] 84, had been a local village resident since 1945 when she and her husband moved to the village when they married. She came from a hard-working family of manual labourers: her father laboured on road-building and her husband was a quarry-man and then worked in the mill. She had never taken paid work; she told me 'my husband wouldn't allow it.' When I met her, she was living in sheltered housing, where she had moved four years earlier when her husband died. She had suffered a stroke three years before that, and as a result could not use her left arm.

During our conversations it became clear that for Vera, God's grace was the most important evidence of God's existence. It was how she explained her everyday spirituality and her moment of divine protection. She told me that when she had her stroke, the doctor was surprised that she had survived. At first, her main reaction to the stroke was to blame herself for making it happen: she said, 'My first question was why, what had I done that I should be … .' It took a long time and much thought, soul-searching and prayer before she could accept that the stroke did not happen through something she had done, but 'was just one of those things'. On further reflection, and following her doctor's reassurance that she was not going to die, she became convinced that God had protected her: 'I was certainly looked after that night, by something or somebody that was looking after me, either he or she.'

What seemed at first to be a gender-neutral way of conceiving God quickly changed during the interview when Vera added immediately a proviso that 'I think it's a he. I don't think for one minute they would call God a she. I think it's a he, but it's spiritual, you know what I mean. It's not the same as me looking at you here … it's something spiritual, way out there, you know [*she points to the sky*]. Whatever it is, it's marvellous.'

---

[15] All names have been changed.

To understand why Vera stressed so vehemently why God could not be a she may require consideration of her wider social relations. She was raised in an era where women who could afford to did not work. Her father and then her husband were providers who looked after her both financially and materially. She was comforted by that kind of male relationship:

> Yes, I've had a wonderful life, really. As I say, I had a nice childhood, with a very happy childhood, I had. And even my husband, he was good to me. I don't think we had a cross word at all all our lives. I don't mean to say we didn't have our little bits of ups and downs, but I mean we didn't fall out, if you understand me. If we did have a tiff we always managed to make it up before bedtime. We didn't go to sleep on it, you know, anything like that. So, yes, I mean I think I've been very well looked after. Very well. Yes. [*pause*] As they keep telling me, things could have gone a lot worse. But, here we are.

After her stroke, her husband ensured that she did not attempt any difficult activities, such as shopping, alone:

> My husband would be pushing me and ... he was very protective, but he would never let me try to walk. I could stand up to see things in the supermarket, and I used to try to stand, but I always used to get 'sit!' [*she adopts the tone and action of someone commanding a dog*] but I wasn't – he was over-protective, really.

Vera talked in the same way about her doctor, who prescribed her medicines that she took unquestioningly, saying that 'the doctor says I mustn't stop that. It's something to do with the blood, with the circulation.' The portrait I am painting thus far about Vera presents her as someone who accepted her place in a male-oriented universe, and therefore her acceptance of a male God who controlled and protected her fits unproblematically with that worldview. But her faith was not an unquestioning, passive acceptance. It was a specific kind of practice, requiring hard work, emotionally, physically and mentally.

First, there is the matter of retaining faith. It was not easy for her to accept that she had a stroke. Nor was it easy for her to lose her husband, a loss that was only bearable because she thought that they would meet again: 'But, uh, I do believe there's a possibility that we'll all meet again somewhere. And, we'll recognize each other. We must do, really. I try to hold on to that. I won't let that go. I hold onto it as much as I'm able to.'

While that element of her faith – a belief in the life hereafter – was comforting, it did not signal that she accepted unquestioningly a hard doctrinal view of what might be described as credal or propositional belief. As I have discussed elsewhere,[16] the demarcations between so-called propositional or emotional forms

---

[16] Abby Day, *Believing in Belonging: Belief and Social Identity in the Modern World* (Oxford, 2011).

of belief are less rigid than might be argued by others. Rather, her belief was more 'performative', in that it came into being to reinforce an element of her identity that was important to her. This arose in particular when we discussed her small ornament of a brass Buddha:

> Abby: I notice the brass Buddha you have there, on your windowsill.
>
> Vera: Oh yes, I bought that in a charity shop. And, there was somebody once came here and she said to me, you shouldn't have that, that thing on your window sill, she said you should throw it in the dustbin and I said what for? Well, she said it's a sin, like, and I said, why? I don't pray to him, or anything like that. He's just a little ornament. In fact I think I used to use him as a little stop, when I put papers down. [*She shows me how she would use him as a paperweight.*] I used to put it on top so they wouldn't be blown away. And the same as my little swans [*she indicates a pair of small brass swans on the window ledge near the Buddha*]. I bought them in a charity shop. I like brass. Used to have horse brasses on the walls, but I can't clean them now. I took them all off. Those, fortunately, they don't tarnish. You can just wash them in soap and water.

Vera's pragmatism about what she enjoyed and what she carefully looked after in practice overcame what her visitor saw as idolatry. Did this mean, out of context, that Vera was non-religious? I suggest it simply meant that a religious interpretation of her charity-shop Buddha paperweight was not salient for her, which in no way detracted from the salience and passion with which she often spoke of her devotion to God. In contrast, another charity-shop item carried with it great weight of religious significance. It was when she showed me a cardboard copy of a prayer that she began the story about her stroke. We had been discussing prayer, and whether the way she prayed had changed over the years:

> Vera: No, no. I just pray the same that I've always done. Thank him for everything, I mean. [*She reaches to the shelf beside her and brings out a large and slightly faded card with text on it and hands it to me. I read the title: 'A Prayer of Gratitude'.*] That was something I bought in a little shop when I was out on one of my holidays. I thought it was rather nice.
>
> Abby: Yes, that's nice.
>
> Vera: I mean, you do forget to say thank you sometimes, like. I mean, something good happens to you, like you should always say thank you for it. Although I must admit, when I had my stroke, I couldn't see the, couldn't say.

Charity-shop Buddha and charity-shop holiday prayer-card: both had different religious significance but were valued in their own ways.

In Vera's experience, the sociality of her lived religious experience was sometimes as salient as her faith in God. She talked about being a child, and attending church with her friends:

> I had all my friends and where they went I went. So I just sort of automatically went to the Church of England school. Another thing – we got prizes at the end of the year. You know what children are ... you get a nice book and a prize for attending Sunday school – and that was very nice. And then we went on church little trips, with the church like, you know. I just went along with my friends.

That form of sociality continued throughout her life, although now many of her friends had died and some who still lived in the village like her, found it too arduous to attend church regularly. She could, however, attend the village hairdresser regularly because she had a carer who would take her. She enjoyed those visits because 'when I go to the hairdresser's very often there's one or other at the same time, getting their hair done, like, and we'll meet then and talk.' The function of friendship and sense of community she enjoyed at church was partly retained through her visits to the hairdresser but not by the parish priest's visits to her. She told me she was grateful that the priest came regularly to give her communion, but her telling lacked the warmth and emotional vibrancy that touched her story about the hairdresser: 'They bring me communion. So I still keep with that.' I note her use of the plural pronoun 'they', which is a corporate 'they', as in 'they of the church'. It is an impersonal, institution-based relationship. I contrast that now with my interviews with Jane, conducted over a period of six years.

Working for the Moral Community

When I first interviewed Jane, then a 61-year-old married teacher and mother of adult children, and asked what she believed in, she said: 'I believe in God, one God, which I define as a spiritual being or a spiritual presence, no gender, all loving, all powerful, all mighty, creator.'

She told me she attended church regularly, prayed, and felt she carried out God's work in her role as a teacher. It had not always been easy: like Vera, Jane often found faith was hard work. Although, she said, she thought she had 'always believed', there were times when it was a struggle: 'You know, teenage times, mid-twenties, I think belief is a struggle. I don't think it's easy.' But even when she was older, in times of crisis or personal suffering, or confronting difficult world events, her faith was shaken. One significant event was the end of her first marriage and divorce which, she said, 'without wanting to sound pompous' was like a crucifixion, with the aftermath like a resurrection: 'There was a whole lot of grief to go through and suffering, and sometimes I felt God was there and sometimes I felt he wasn't, and it took me a long time [*pause*]. But I felt like I'd come out better at the end of it, a much stronger person.'

It was her hard work, faith and church community that helped her, she said. God gave her a reason for being: 'I couldn't contemplate life without him, and I couldn't contemplate life without there being something at the end of it.' Jane said she believed that the church was the source of moral teaching and that people who did not attend church had 'no sense of community for a start'.

Communities were, for most of my informants, places where they lived and belonged, and where they recognized those who did not belong. I found little resonance with Wilson's assertion that 'the secularized salvation of modern times surrenders the community: the survivor becomes the self.'[17] Although the word 'community' may have meant something quite specific to Wilson, what it seemed to mean to most of my informants was a place to which they had not surrendered but to which they belonged and in which they felt safe. When I met Jane again after a five-year gap, we returned to the idea of community. She felt that it still played an important role in her life, although with church attendance decreasing, it may have been less obvious elsewhere. As with my observations above with Vera, the concept of community entailed hard work. Jane described her sense of community:

> A sense of community – I think on a practical level it means that people help one another. People who attend that church help one another and are aware of one another's needs and one another's sufferings. And also, you get the sense of celebration when good things happen. It's a sharing, I think, and I think that's an important part, really.

Changes in society that have occurred had, for Jane, affected changes in community and stemmed from the changing nature of girl/womanhood. Girls, she suggested, had become more confident, leaving boys without a clearly defined role, and the implication was that more assertive women made for looser sexual morals that led directly to teenage pregnancies. Jane was, however, hard-pressed to articulate the nature of the change. Her examples of change seemed trivial – men were less chivalrous and opened doors less, and therefore women had lost that aspect of femininity. Just as in our first interview, she stressed the role women have in raising moral, well-adjusted children. When we discussed where she had learned about her sense of morality and community, she was quick to answer that the source of these beliefs was her mother: 'I think my mother. My mother and my faith. My mother was a very selfless person, had tremendous faith. She was a good wife and a good mother and I think that's possibly where I learned it, if you do learn these things.'

Her linking of mother, faith, and 'good' was nearly seamless. The gender role of morality and responsibility for children's upbringing was clear for her, just as it was clear that things have changed. When I interviewed her several years later, she

---

[17] Bryan Wilson, 'Salvation, Secularization, and De-moralization' in Fenn, *The Blackwell Companion*, pp. 39–51

had retired and lacked the excited energy she had when we first met at the school where she worked. More sombre, and pessimistic now, she bemoaned the lack of discipline at home. This recalled for me how Vera had also talked about lack of discipline. Vera said that young people today lack self-discipline and expect to earn money for doing little. This was mainly because they did not have enough discipline at home and in the schools, she said. When I asked her what she thought the reason was for what she perceived as young people's bad behaviour, she said:

> I can't imagine really, other than the way they're educated at home, how the parents sort of bring them up. 'Cos I think some parents are what I'd call lax with their children, they tend to let them do, I once heard someone say, oh, let them get it out of their system, let them do it, get it out of their system like. But I think a little bit of, um, discipline, I think. That's what they're lacking today. Discipline.

Given that women are the ones usually charged with raising children, I suggest here that Vera's criticism of young people was also a criticism of their mothers. Women were frequently blamed in many of my interviews for acting in ways that differed from the roles they held in society in a previous generation. They are still seen as the primary source of socialization and when they abandon that role, many people argue, this results in a general breakdown in the family unit, leading to an increase in bad behaviour amongst young people.

Conclusion

The case examples above point to the often-neglected nature of women's faith work and how this acts to support their personal lives and the lives of their families and communities. Women who perform faith work on behalf of themselves, their husbands, their families and their communities can be seen as not more or less religious than men, but only performing religious work differently. The idea that women are more religious than men is, I suggest, contestable and only appears so through presenting limited quantitative evidence that measures limited aspects of religiosity. Through appreciating the multi-dimensional nature of belief, women's religiosity is seen as not simply passively held but performed through a multi-dimensional construct of belief's content, resources, practices, salience and function, all of which are situated specifically in places and times.

It appears that performing faith work on behalf of others has a long tradition crossing the generations: what has changed today is not so much the nature of faith, but the unwillingness of younger women, Generations X and Y, to perform invisible, unpaid faith work. We may need to examine the way women are reconfiguring their roles in society rather than only within their religions to understand more about why that is so.

A methodological implication is to pay close attention to the lived narratives people employ, and to a multi-dimensional analytical framework that allows us to consider more than just the content of people's beliefs, but the way those beliefs are sourced and practised, and how their salience and function may change over time and place.

Chapter 4
Feminist Faith Lives? Exploring Perceptions of Feminism Among Two Anglican Cohorts[1]

Sarah-Jane Page

Introduction

Feminism is a broad term, but can be conceptualized to mean addressing gender inequality in society. As Jones articulates, feminism has traditionally endorsed two aims: 'First, feminists sought to identify the various forms of oppression that structured women's lives, and second, they imagined and sought to create an alternative future without oppression.'[2] But feminists have undertaken this project in multifarious ways.

Christianity and feminism are often considered incompatible,[3] but this does not necessarily reflect the historical relationship between the two. Broadly speaking, early feminist concerns were often underpinned by a Christian religious ethic;[4] justice-seeking Christianity was often perceived to be fully compatible with the goals of feminism. By the emergence of a second-wave feminist movement in the 1960s onwards, a greater incompatibility emerged. As Redfern and Aune note, the second wave was more secular in nature, and religion was perceived in negative terms.[5] Klassen links this to the way in which de Beauvoir, a key influence within early second-wave thought, positioned religion as a chief oppressor of women.[6] As Trzebiatowska and Llewellyn note, a disciplinary disconnection occurred between religion and mainstream feminism; although feminist work was conducted in theology and religious studies departments, this was not necessarily integrated

---

[1] I would like to thank the editors as well as Professor Andrew Kam-Tuck Yip for offering valuable feedback on this chapter.

[2] Serena Jones, *Feminist Theory and Christian Theology* (Minneapolis, MN, 2000), p. 3.

[3] Mary Daly, *Beyond God the Father* (London, 1986); Daphne M. Hampson, *Theology and Feminism* (Oxford, 1990).

[4] Darlene M. Juschka, 'A General Introduction to Feminism in the Study of Religion', in *idem* (ed.) *Feminism in the Study of Religion* (London, 2001), p. 6.

[5] Catherine Redfern and Kristin Aune, *Reclaiming the F Word* (London, 2010), pp. 153–4.

[6] Chris Klassen, 'Confronting the Gap', *Thirdspace* 3:1 (2003).

or woven together with the mainstream feminist movement.[7] Key texts that did emerge which undertook a feminist critique of religious institutions (for example, Daly and Trible)[8] were utilized by the broader feminist movement to dismiss religion as a worthy category of critical investigation, with a lack of nuance regarding how women were situated *vis-à-vis* religion – rather, religion was seen as simply bad for women.[9]

More recently, the new context for discussing feminism has been in terms of whether we are witnessing a postfeminist era. Faludi has outlined that feminist ideas have been subject to a backlash rhetoric, where feminism is ridiculed, challenged and considered against women's interests.[10] Some have charted more complex developments, arguing that new discourses mesh together both anti- and pro-feminist perspectives.[11] As Scharff articulates, feminism is 'viewed positively (valuable but no longer necessary) and negatively (extreme and ideological) ... The two sets of narratives about feminism resonate with, and reflect, a postfeminist sensibility where feminism is both taken into account and, simultaneously, repudiated.'[12] The realm of popular culture has been a crucial space for examining this phenomenon, where young women are told they now have unlimited opportunities. Educational and career success is highlighted, along with the ability to consume. Choice is the buzzword.[13] At the same time, this is underpinned by new expectations and intensifications surrounding femininity, with television programmes, magazines and other ephemera encouraging women to be slim, beautiful and sexy. Indeed, a key angle of this trend has been the increased sexualization of women's bodies, with consumerism being the platform through which such a femininity is promised to be achieved. 'Choice' thus becomes narrowly defined, restrictively enabled through consumer products, with a feminist politic being muted in the process. As McRobbie argues: 'The young woman is offered a notional form of equality, concretised in education and employment, and through participation in consumer culture and civil society, in place of what a reinvented feminist politics might

---

[7] Marta Trzebiatowska and Dawn Llewellyn, 'The Changing Feminist Face of Christianity', *British Sociological Association's Sociology of Religion Study Group Annual Conference: The Changing Face of Christianity* (Edinburgh, 2010); Tina Beattie, 'Religious Identity and the Ethics of Representation', in Ursula King and Tina Beattie (eds), *Gender, Religion and Diversity* (London: 2004), pp. 65–78.

[8] Daly, *Beyond God the Father;* Mary Daly, *The Church and the Second Sex* (Boston, MA, 1985); Phyllis Trible, *Texts of Terror: Literary-feminist Readings of Biblical Narratives* (Philadelphia, PA, 1984).

[9] Redfern and Aune, *Reclaiming*, pp. 157–8.

[10] Susan Faludi, *Backlash: The Undeclared War Against American Women*, 15th anniversary edn (New York, 2006).

[11] Rosalind Gill and Christina Scharff, 'Introduction', in Rosalind Gill and Christina Scharff (eds), *New Femininities* (Basingstoke, 2011), p. 4.

[12] Christina Scharff, *Repudiating Feminism* (Farnham, 2012), p. 1.

[13] Angela McRobbie, 'Preface', in Gill and Scharff, *New Femininities*, p. xi.

have to offer.'[14] Ideas of gender equality abound, but feminism itself comes to be problematic territory, because it would destabilize the merely surface equality that is being offered through new consumerist forms. Feminism therefore must be vilified in order to be contained.

Some formulations of a postfeminist sensibility have included religion, with religion being grounded as a site of gender oppression. Scharff's illuminating study of young German and British women's perceptions of feminism highlights that an overwhelming number use the notion of the religious woman (more specifically, the Muslim woman) as the 'oppressed other', who is subject to patriarchal cultures and processes.[15] This construction allows seemingly choice-laden privileged young women to situate themselves as part of a liberated, western nexus. Muslim women are thus used as a convenient oppositional rhetoric to support western claims of gender freedom. Aune, examining postfeminsim from the perspective of conservative Christianity, has argued that postfeminist sensibilities can also be located actually within religious spaces, highlighting the complex ways in which religious groups intertwine religious and secular discourses.[16]

The relationship between Anglicanism and gender is a long and complex one, where traditional outlooks have been endorsed alongside more progressive stances, and where ideologies about gender have not necessarily corresponded with the realities of women's lives.[17] In the latter half of the twentieth century, women's ordination to priesthood provoked much debate, with a variety of positions taken. Discussing the ensuing debate, Furlong commented that:

> In speech after speech at General Synod an extraordinary misogyny emerges. Women are seen as about to 'dismember' the Church, to 'destroy' relations with the Orthodox. The Bishop of London described the ordination of women as being potentially 'an ineradicable virus in the bloodstream' of the universal Church.[18]

However, since the first ordinations of women priests in 1994, the gender landscape has changed enormously.[19] Women themselves are now more firmly established as part of the church hierarchy, although, at the time of writing, they are still not authorized to become bishops. Rapid changes have occurred in attitudes to women, with dioceses overwhelmingly supportive of women becoming bishops. Despite an increased emphasis on women's inclusion at the level of faith leadership, at a

---

[14] Angela McRobbie, *The Aftermath of Feminism* (London, 2009), p. 2.
[15] Scharff, *Repudiating Feminism*, pp. 45–67.
[16] Kristin Aune, 'Marriage in a British Evangelical Congregation', *The Sociological Review*, 54/4 (2006): 638–57.
[17] Sean Gill, *Women and the Church of England* (London, 1994).
[18] Monica Furlong, 'Introduction', in Monica Furlong (ed.), *Mirror to the Church* (London, 1988), pp. 7–8.
[19] Gill, *Women*; Ian Jones, *Women and Priesthood in the Church of England Ten Years On* (London, 2004).

deeper level, gender inequalities remain, especially in relation to the gendering of certain sacerdotal roles, difficulties in obtaining senior church posts, the need for women clergy to negotiate a broader masculinist culture, as well as the specific issues clergy mothers face, whose motherhood responsibilities are often constructed as being in conflict with their ministry responsibilities.[20] Therefore, although a notion of gender equality is being promoted, this is not twinned with a more in-depth critique of the ways in which the constructions of identities such as femininity and masculinity, as well as roles such as priesthood and motherhood, structure women's inclusion. It should also be remembered that inequality is still embedded in the very legislation authorizing women's priesthood, with resolutions allowing parishes to opt out of having a woman priest being in place. Despite only a minority of parishes taking up this clause, it is still notable that religious institutions have greater scope in authorizing unequal codes, due to exemption from some elements of the equality legislation, and opponents remain very vocal in their opposition to women's faith leadership.[21]

Studying the Faith Lives of Women

This chapter draws on data from two separate projects, where detail was gathered on the relationships between Anglican women and feminism. The first project, conducted between 2006 and 2007, sought to examine the experiences of Anglican clergy who had dependent children.[22] Starting with the question, 'Tell me how you came to be a priest', in-depth narratives were generated, charting the experiences patterning this journey, with insight being generated on participants' relationships to feminism. Overall, 17 clergy were interviewed – 15 priests and two deacons. Women were aged between 31 and 54; some were part of the first cohort of priests to be ordained in 1994, others were very new to ordained ministry, having been made deacons, and imminently to be priested.

The second project had quite a different focus. Entitled *Religion, Youth and Sexuality: A Multi-faith Exploration*,[23] this study was comprised of three methods

---

[20] Barbara Bagilhole, 'Prospects for Change?', *Gender, Work and Organization*, 10/3 (2003): 361–77; Sarah-Jane Page, 'Negotiating Sacred Roles', *Feminist Review*, 97/1 (2011): 92–109; Sarah-Jane Page, 'Femmes, Mères et Prêtres dans l'Eglise d'Angleterre', *Travail, Genre et Sociétés*, 27 (2012): 55–71; Helen Thorne, *Journey to Priesthood* (Bristol, 2000).

[21] Page, *Femmes*.

[22] The project entitled *Masculinities and Femininities in the Church of England* was conducted by Dr Sarah-Jane Page and funded by the ESRC (Award no: PTA031200400290). The research would not have been possible without the support of both those who helped in recruitment and the participants themselves.

[23] The project entitled *Religion, Youth and Sexuality: A Multi-faith Exploration*, was funded by the Arts and Humanities Research Council/Economic and Social Research

(questionnaires, interviews and video diaries) which focused on 18 to 25-year-olds (men and women) from six different religions, living in the UK. Undertaken between 2009 and 2011, the project commenced with a questionnaire, to which 57 Anglican women responded. Six Anglican women who participated in the questionnaire were interviewed, and were asked about their understandings of gender equality and feminism.

For both projects, the exploration of faith lives was integral. For the clergy, this was often about the way in which their faith informed their decision to become a priest, as well as how faith was utilized in order to negotiate ensuing challenges. Meanwhile, for the young women, they were negotiating the relevance of Christianity for their own identity, articulating the ways in which significant issues such as sexuality and gender were integrated with their faith. But the projects were also quite different, with various aims, methods and time frames. Therefore, the aim of this chapter is not to compare the cohorts directly (especially as one group was comprised of lay women, and another group of ordained women), but rather to offer up the two examples as case studies in exploring the relationship of different age cohorts to, and how different life experiences impacted on, their negotiations of feminism. This data illuminates the diverse and rich accounts obtained from a small number of Anglican women, but does not claim to be representative, or demonstrate all perspectives towards feminism. The interview samples were generated for a broader purpose than examining feminist attitudes per se (clergy motherhood and sexuality respectively) and both samples are predominantly made up of white middle-class women, which fits the broader profile for UK-based Anglicanism, but does not capture its full diversity.[24] Pseudonyms have been used throughout. Each case study will now be considered in turn, starting with women clergy.

Clergy Women, Feminism and Faith

The clergy women interviewed were a diverse group, comprising different theological traditions within the Anglican Church and occupying a variety of church posts. Some were directly involved in the campaign for women's ordination throughout the 1980s and early 1990s. In terms of these women's formative experiences, many had encountered some form of feminism at college and university, and in religious contexts, this could be impacted upon by wider issues about women's inclusion in ordained ministry:

Council Religion and Society Programme (Award no. AH/G014051/1). The research team consisted of Professor Andrew Kam-Tuck Yip (Principal Investigator), Dr Michael Keenan (Co-investigator) and D. Sarah-Jane Page (Research Fellow). The research team is grateful for the funding, as well as the invaluable contribution of the respondents, individuals and groups who helped with the recruitment of the sample and the members of the advisory committee.

[24]   Thorne, *Journey*; Clare Walsh, *Gender and Discourse* (Harlow, 2001).

> I can remember as a teenager totally misunderstanding what feminism was all about. Finding out more about it as a young woman and at theological college looking at feminist interpretation of scripture, of the Bible, and that I was really interested in it. (Amanda, aged 41)

> When we were training there was a lot of feminist stuff going on. Because obviously it was when the vote was going through and all of that. (Isobel, aged 37)

From the 1970s onwards, a key issue being debated in the churches was whether women could be faith leaders. The Church of England's Synod[25] voted in 1975 in favour of the motion that there were no theological objections to women's priesthood, but the process to remove the legal barriers preventing their ordination was not endorsed. Synod voted again on the issue in 1978 but the motion was again defeated.[26] Galvanized by this situation, the campaign group, the Movement for the Ordination of Women (MOW) was formed.[27] However, MOW was perceived as endorsing 'strident' feminism. Scharff argues that feminist ideas are dampened by negative stereotypes and labels being attached, something she calls 'the mythic construction of "the feminist"'.[28] In labelling MOW's stance as strident, opponents sought to diminish its power. As Webster has noted, 'it was strange to find myself and my rather serene, thoughtful MOW friends pigeon-holed in this way.'[29] Such attempts at castigating feminism in negative terms can be seen as part of a feminist backlash, which was pervasive at this historical moment.[30]

Throughout the 1980s, debate on the issue of women's ordination remained strong, with some, such as Laura, a 43-year-old priest, recalling, 'I belonged to the *Movement for the Ordination for Women*; I spoke to groups all over the place ... about the arguments for and against the priesting of women, all those campaigning things – t shirts and I sat in Parliament when the vote went through.'

The MOW campaign was about raising awareness, through publications as well as direct protests at ordination services.[31] In many instances, the tactics used by campaigners for women's ordination were similar to those adopted by the broader feminist movement a decade earlier, with Kate, a 54-year-old priest outlining, 'I was one of the women who stood outside ordinations and held up placards.'

These experiences also propelled some who had been relatively neutral about the issue of women's inclusion to become ardent supporters of women's faith equality, as Harriet, a 51-year-old priest, discusses in relation to inclusive language:

---

[25] Synod is the legislative body of the Church.
[26] Margaret Webster, *A New Strength, A New Song* (London, 1994), pp. 39–46.
[27] Ibid., pp. 47–50.
[28] Scharff, *Repudiating Feminism*, p. 2.
[29] Webster, *New Strength*, p. 53.
[30] Faludi, *Backlash*.
[31] Gill, *Women*, p. 254.

> I used to underline the hymns in the hymn books in the chapel ... and would put another word in instead ... And I think I went not being totally convinced of women's ordination as priests because you know, I was going to be a deaconess, which wasn't a priest. But I was soon converted by the men who were anti-women, pretty soon – I mean that was pretty swift.

The 1980s were formative times for those training to be deaconesses and deacons,[32] with opposition directly encountered. Feminist activism within the Church, spearheaded by groups such as MOW, helped such women to make sense of, articulate and voice their experiences, and theological colleges and universities were fertile grounds for encountering feminism. Some identified with feminism (or at least a gender-equalist approach) as a result of their experiences of exclusion, even if the feminist label was not used. Some became active in relation to gender issues for the first time because of the gender oppression encountered, but this was experienced in a context of great mutual support, as Rachel (age not disclosed) recalled:

> It was like being in a wilderness because there was a real injustice about what was going on and there was a real sort of deprivation and yet that deprived wilderness place was a very rich place of community and learning and the kind of immensely strong relationships that were formed among the women.

After the 1992 vote, however, and when the ordinations to priesthood commenced for women, the landscape shifted. Laura discussed the taming of activism:

> There used to be a group in the late '80s which I belonged to – there was some great thinking going on there. And it disbanded in the end. And it became quite wacky before it disbanded ... it was interesting, it was good interface with people communicating, but in a way, it had run its course.

By the time Laura was priested, association with such groups had waned. Other research has indicated how priests distanced themselves from the feminist label in the post-ordination climate, highlighted in Thorne's research where 75 per cent of her sample of women priests viewed feminism with antipathy.[33] Some have attributed this to the way feminism had been portrayed in the ordination debate. MOW had been castigated as very radical, and some had viewed any

---

[32] The Deaconess Order was started in 1861 and was only open to women, who were excluded from the Orders of Deacon, Priest and Bishop. By 1987, the diaconate was opened to women, and the Deaconess Order was subsequently closed.

[33] Thorne, *Journey*, p. 113; Clare Walsh, 'Speaking in Different Tongues?', *Sheffield Hallam Working Papers on the Web* 1 (2000).

feminist impetus as damaging to the very ordination campaign itself, particularly if women's ordination was seen as piggy-backing on a secular feminist agenda.[34]

In addition, parishioners had already showed concern about having priests who were perceived to be too 'stridently' feminist, hence a need to be careful in how gender-egalitarian ideas were presented.[35] Some of the clergy discussed how they introduced gender-equality issues delicately in their preaching:

> [Feminism is] something I use with great discretion ... I want to do it sufficiently gently so that people aren't confronted and hurt and upset by it. (Eleanor, aged 43)

> If I said I was going to preach a sermon about feminist theology, I'm sure people would have sort of thrown tomatoes at me but actually I did and they liked it.

> *You didn't use the 'f' word?*

> Yes, that's right. And why do you need to? If you're talking about the concepts and you're helping people to think about different images of God, different pictures of church, why do you need to label it? (Laura)

Feminism in this context was a dirty word. Whilst gender equality and justice could be endorsed and theologically linked, the 'f word' could not be utilized.[36] Meanwhile, those who were not part of the campaign for women's ordination sometimes drew a clear line of demarcation between their own gender-equal principles and those perceived as being endorsed by the campaigning generation:

> This militant thing allows people to say 'they're just being feminists. They're fighting for the cause.' I think it's very destructive but the ones that are more militant, their focus is on how soon women can be bishops, which I think it's right that women should be bishops at some point [but not as a result of militancy]. (Lois, aged 31)

> I often feel that feminists are actually being very masculine in the way they go about things. And I've tended to distance myself from the feminist kind of movement really ... I do think it's really important that women are able to work out what it means to be a woman rather than to have to almost become like a man to survive in a man's world, which the church has been for all these years. And you know, it's obviously becoming much less so now ... I'd say I was supportive of feminists but certainly I don't, I wouldn't call myself a feminist. Because I don't like the way I see them going about things. (Isobel)

---

[34] Sue Dowell and Jane Williams, *Bread, Wine and Women* (London, 1994); Gill, *Women*.

[35] Jones, *Women*, p. 23.

[36] Redfern and Aune, *Reclaiming*.

These younger priests saw feminism as a dangerous thing that could impede women's inclusion. Although these priests were not against gender equality per se, any concept of equality was decoupled from the feminist label. Negative ideas circulated about achieving equality through feminist means, with the associated links to militancy, extremism and masculine personas.[37] Some of the older generation of priests were well aware of such sentiment, with Harriet articulating that 'I know [the women before 1994 are] considered 'before the war' ... we're sort of seen as being that much more campaigning and so on. Whereas women now just think it's all fine and get on with it. Until they get a bit later and find that it isn't quite as they thought.' Indeed, evident in Isobel's narrative was the idea that things have moved on – the Church is no longer a male bastion and there is little need for radical feminist intervention.

However, the lack of explicit feminist engagement and discussion meant that younger participants could feel ill-equipped to deal with gender injustice when it arose, and some priests did not necessarily feel they had the resources to challenge sexism. For example, Dawn, a 38-year-old priest, experienced great negativity from a colleague in college when she attended a WATCH support seminar (the group that superseded MOW after the 1992 vote, standing for Women And The Church) discussing women's equality in the Church:

> I was stunned by the backlash, I mean we were called witches ... one guy even said 'You're like a bunch of witches, they should call it *WITCH* not *WATCH*' ... it was like an unmasking of institutional sexism at its most difficult and ugly form ... but I've got to say ... some of our friends couldn't just hold it, couldn't listen.

Dawn had no outlet to discuss her experiences. Ironically, the space opened up for the exploration of injustices and discriminatory practice was closed down due to the policing of other students. The term 'witch' has traditionally denoted danger and fear of women, and is linguistically powerful in securing negative connotations.[38] On using her own personal resources (that is, her friendship network in the Church), Dawn again felt any discussion of negative experience was blocked.

The clergywomen interviewed had a range of experiences with many who were part of the campaign for ordination fondly remembering the camaraderie and support networks it generated. However, on becoming part of the institution, the participants' contact with explicit feminist activism had waned and although gender-equal perspectives were gently introduced within preaching contexts, the 'f word' was considered beyond the pale. Meanwhile, younger cohorts interviewed

---

[37] Pamela Church Gibson, 'Introduction: Popular Culture', in Stacy Gillis, Gillian Howie and Rebecca Munford (eds), *Third Wave Feminism* (New York, 2004), pp. 137–8; Barbara Findlen, 'Introduction' in Barbara Findlen (ed.), *Listen Up* (Seattle, WA, 1995), pp. xi–xvi; Scharff, *Repudiating Feminism*, p. 1.

[38] Rosemary Radford Ruether, 'Women's Body and Blood', in Alison Joseph (ed.), *Through the Devil's Gateway* (London, 1990), pp. 18–19.

either eschewed the feminist label altogether, or struggled to generate the necessary support systems when gender injustice was encountered.

Young Anglican Women's Negotiation of Feminism in Postfeminist Times

For the young Anglican women aged between 18 and 25, their formative experiences were somewhat different. Raised in an era which Baumgardner and Richards have characterized as having 'feminism in the water',[39] gender equality was taken as a given, as 20-year-old Claire notes: 'We haven't been brought up as feminist by any means but we have been brought up as equalists. My brother can't even intellectually understand how, why women are treated differently ... So I guess I'm kind of similar.'

This group of Anglican women were young children when the vote for women's ordination to priesthood went through and many have come of age at a time when opportunities for women appear endless. A belief in equality was evident when women were talking specifically about their own faith traditions. In our questionnaire, of the 54 Anglican women who responded, 83.3 per cent strongly disagreed or disagreed with the statement, 'Religious authority figures should be male.' Meanwhile, in interviews, women pinpointed the endeavours of women priests they knew as offering positive role models, not only in terms of faith equality per se, but also how that transpired in terms of domestic roles, as 22-year-old Heather indicates:

> In terms of women being priests and religious authority roles, when I got married it was a woman priest who married us and she is in our local church. I think it is great. Her husband stays at home and looks after the kids ... I am not a feminist but it should be equal rights for all people.

Feminism is not endorsed, but gender equality certainly is, captured in the common phrase, 'I'm not a feminist, but ...'.[40] At the same time, the participants recognize that gender inequality does exist, for example, 23-year-old Helen, who discusses the relationship between Christianity and gender:

> That is another bugbear ... where the woman has to do what the man says ... I wouldn't say I'm a massive feminist but I don't appreciate it no [*laugh*], again it's that message of equality and unfortunately at times it seems to contradict itself if you take only the Bible. But no I think equality in all forms is certainly what I believe and yes, I would have a problem with anything that contradicted that.

---

[39] Jennifer Baumgardner and Amy Richards, *Manifesta* (New York, 2000), p. 17.
[40] Sylvia Walby, *The Future of Feminism* (Cambridge, 2011), p. 3.

Helen was utilizing the language of gender egalitarianism to challenge more conservative interpretations of biblical passages. These young women were therefore agentic in utilizing the 'feminism in the water' around them to dismiss any conservative religious counter-narrative encountered, but without using the feminist label. Similar to Scharff's research on young women, inequality is certainly challenged, but it is not done so through using explicitly feminist discourses. Rather, a more general 'common-sense' egalitarianism is alluded to.[41]

Meanwhile, some young women did openly endorse feminism as a positive label, such as 22-year-old Jenny:

> I think I am quite feminist although I think a lot of friends would blanch at the fact that I call myself a feminist. For them feminist is always radical. It is very much Mary Daly, I do like Mary Daly. But from them it is very much Germaine Greer is the face of radical feminist. It is very much men hatred, which it isn't about at all. I think it is actually incredulous when women say they are not feminist. When you say do you like the fact you can vote, yes, then you are a feminist.

Jenny had dismissed the popular rhetoric surrounding feminism[42] and aligned feminism firmly with a positive embrace of gender equality. Some, such as 24-year-old Emily, utilized reinterpreted texts as a means of strengthening faith as well as interpreting faith in a relevant and contemporary light:

> There's this book called *The Red Tent*. It's wonderful. That's all about [the biblical character] Dinah … [the author] just expands this wonderful world of women. And the red tent is the tent where they go and sit to have their period every month … I love Mary Magdalene; I think she's wonderful because she's kind of this oddball really. And she's been branded this harlot or obviously in *The Da Vinci Code* where they say she was his [Jesus'] wife. I just love that.

In both Jenny's and Emily's narratives, secular and the religious resources interweaved. Making sense of faith and gender equality was not something separated off, but integrated with populist novels and the broader context, enacted beyond the borders of 'church'. It was premised on individualized investigation and interpretation.

The young Anglican women interviewed who overwhelmingly endorsed gender equality used a diverse range of resources to support their view, such as holding up women's priesthood as a marker of equality, and seeing such women as role models, as well as utilizing secular and religious literature. But feminist identities were individualized in nature, and the 'f word' was not usually adopted.

---

[41] Scharff, *Repudiating Feminism*, p. 10.
[42] Gibson, *Introduction*, pp. 137–8; Findlen, *Introduction*, pp. xi–xvi.

As Hughes asserts, young women believe in equality even when they do not believe in feminism.[43]

Conclusion

Gender equality was positively affirmed across both groups of participants, although endorsing such equality did not necessarily mean that feminism itself was used as a term to describe this perspective. In line with Porter's research on Christian women, 'general support for women's equality is not connected to an embrace of feminism.'[44] Feminism is a contested term, connected with radicalism, man-hating and women's superiority.[45] Negative attitudes towards feminism were to be located both amongst clergy and younger lay women. As Scharff asserts, feminism 'is frequently allocated to the past and depicted as no longer relevant – to both older and younger women'.[46]

Gender-equal attitudes were automatically taken up by the younger cohort of Christians, as a form of 'common sense'.[47] Meanwhile, clergy had often encountered feminist discourses later in their lives, for instance, at theological college/university. Clergy were more likely to have experienced gender-unequal situations. Both cohorts had developed individualized negotiation with feminism. Some priests actively introduced feminist thinking in their preaching; some of the younger women were engaging in their own hermeneutical critique of biblical texts and reinterpretation of key figures, but the feminist label was rarely used to describe this endeavour.

Discussions of postfeminism have articulated why it might be the case that feminism comes to be vilified in contemporary culture. Feminism is seen as no longer relevant in a gender-equal world where women's educational and occupational success is foregrounded. To bring feminism fully into being would highlight the endemic gender inequality underpinning women's lives, both within the Church and outside of it. The inclusion of feminism would undermine the façade of equality that is presented to women.[48] In wider society, religion is usually positioned as a bearer of traditionalism that disempowers and reduces choice for women. This is a strategy in emphasizing the surface-deep gender egalitarianism on offer for young, western (usually white and middle-class) women.[49] This

---

[43] Katie Hughes, "'I've Been Pondering whether You Can Be a Part-feminist'", *Women's Studies International Forum* 28 (2005): 37–49.

[44] Fran Porter, *It Will Not Be Taken Away From Her: A feminist engagement with women's Christian experience* (London, 2004), p. 20.

[45] Walby, *Future*, p. 3; Scharff, *Repudiating Feminism*, p. 2.

[46] Scharff, *Repudiating Feminism*, p. 9.

[47] Ibid., p. 10.

[48] McRobbie, *Aftermath*, pp. 1–7.

[49] Scharff, *Repudiating Feminism*, pp. 1–5.

supports the view that gender equality has been achieved, and is premised on secular normatives – indeed, religion is expunged from this framework and is constituted as the space in which inequality continues to reside.[50] This helps to conceal the injustices experienced by women in secular culture, particularly in relation to the narrow range of femininities on offer.[51]

Meanwhile, the women interviewed, living within the contours of Anglicanism, are negotiating these perceptions and configuring gender equality within their faith tradition. Indeed, young women especially subscribe strongly to a view of gender equality (yet repudiate feminism in the process) and fashion ways of emphasizing this as an egalitarian terrain, through reference to women's inclusion in faith leadership. Meanwhile women clergy themselves are the ones facing the contradictions of inclusion and exclusion first hand. On the one hand, their inclusion is encouraged and held up as the marker of a progressive church, but on the other hand, great structural barriers remain, especially for mothers who are negotiating the twin demands and expectations of both priesthood and motherhood.[52] The diminution of feminism reduces the likelihood of critical spaces and debates emerging, with participants who encountered opposition constrained in managing this. Therefore, the Church is not an unambiguously patriarchal space against which secular equality agendas can be measured, but like other societal domains, gender injustices are still embedded. It appears that a postfeminist sensibility can be located amongst women in the Church; gender equality is supported but not necessarily through endorsing feminism and those priests explicitly supporting feminism are careful in its deployment, due to anticipated negative reactions. As women's inclusion in the episcopate becomes ever-more likely,[53] further claims to gender equality are likely to be made, but this should not be at the expense of examining deeper-level inequalities that go beyond mere inclusion.

---

[50] Ibid., pp. 45–67.

[51] Michelle M. Lazar, 'The Right to be Beautiful', in Gill and Scharff, *New Femininities*, pp. 44–7; Scharff, *Repudiating Feminism*.

[52] Page, *Femmes*, pp. 55–71.

[53] At the time of writing, the draft Measure for the consecration of women bishops was defeated, after narrowly missing out on the two-thirds majority required from the House of Laity. The vote has, however, provoked much debate about how to speed up the process to legislate for women bishops in the near future.

Chapter 5

Being in Communion: Patterns of Inclusion and Exclusion in Young Lay Women's Experiences of Eucharist in the Church of England[1]

Kim Wasey

Introduction

The Eucharist is the most universally acknowledged and frequently practised sacrament in the Church of England. There has been considerable feminist theological work on women's experiences and understandings of church, and on ways of seeking development and transformation in the institutional churches and beyond them.[2] There is also some qualitative research specifically into women's Eucharistic practices outside the Church, including Sheila Dierks' *WomenEucharist*.[3] In the Church of England context, concerns about women's priesthood have dominated.[4] More recently, focus has shifted from women's exclusion from the Eucharistic ministry of the priesthood, to the experiences and theology emerging from those women who are now able to exercise ordained ministry at the altar.[5]

Other recent publications have begun to consider how a feminist reclamation of the sacraments can embrace the need for a theology which takes account of female embodiment. Susan Ross proposes the model of family as a context for forming

---

[1] Material in this chapter is drawn from Kim Wasey, 'Being in Communion: A Qualitative Study of Young Lay Women's Experience of the Eucharist' (unpublished ThD thesis, University of Birmingham, 2012).

[2] For example, Rosemary R. Ruether, *Women-Church: Theology and Practice of Feminist Liturgical Communities* (London, 1985); Marjorie Procter-Smith, *In Her Own Rite: Constructing Feminist Liturgical Tradition* (Nashville, TN, 1990); Letty M. Russell, *Church in the Round: Feminist Interpretation of the Church* (Louisville, KY, 1993).

[3] Shiela Dierks, *WomenEucharist* (Boulder, CO, 1997).

[4] Liz Barr and Andrew Barr, *Jobs for the Boys? Women who became Priests* (London, 2001); Christina Rees, *Voices of this Calling: Women Priests – the First Ten Years* (Norwich, 2002).

[5] Ali Green, *A Theology of Women's Priesthood* (London, 2009).

sacramentality which is firmly embodied,[6] and Natalie Watson develops a feminist sacramental ecclesiology founded on the principle of celebrating embodiment, which is particularly concerned to engage with the wholeness of creation, justice and transformation.[7]

In contrast to the dominant focus on women's priestly ministry, this chapter focuses on the experiences of young lay women in relation to the Eucharist. If the patterns of predominantly female and older congregations continue, such women will be crucial to the future of the Church and should rightly have their part in shaping the developing life of the Church as a Eucharistic community, along with ordained women. I examine women's experiences of interacting with the liturgy, teaching, physical context and practice of Eucharistic liturgies in the Church of England. Some of the women embrace traditional understandings and practices of communion as vital and meaningful to their own lives; others subvert these teachings and practices, subtly or overtly, to claim new and liberating meanings for themselves and their communities.

My research data comes from semi-structured interviews with ten women of diverse backgrounds, cultural heritage and social contexts, ranging in age from 19 to 34 years.[8] Several had experience of living and worshipping in different countries. All had experience of communion in the Church of England but their current church membership ranged from Catholic-Anglican to Free Church and alternative worship (Fresh Expressions) communities. All were educated to at least undergraduate level, though this was coincidence rather than design.

Through the voices of the women I interviewed, I explore how women's experience of exclusion is bound up in their gendered experience. Examining women's desire for personal inclusion through finding a sense of belonging, I survey the ways this is facilitated through Eucharistic practice and teaching, set against the negative impact of experiences which thwart this desire and the implicit threat and fearfulness this creates. In doing so, I highlight the ambiguity of boundaries which serve as markers of positive inclusion, as well as painful exclusion and disempowerment. I then consider the women's desire to deconstruct these boundaries, creating a vision of inclusive and egalitarian Eucharistic community which embraces freedom for choice and dissent and where loci of power and authority are challenged by the quest for personal autonomy and relationship in community. This leads to the conclusion that a shift is needed, beyond the identified need for a more generally embodied sacramental theology, to locate women's selves and bodies explicitly at the heart of Eucharist theology.

---

[6] Susan Ross, *Extravagant Affections: A Feminist Sacramental Theology* (New York, 2001), pp. 97ff.

[7] Natalie K. Watson, *Introducing Feminist Ecclesiology* (Sheffield, 2002), pp. 88–100.

[8] The names used are a mixture of real names and pseudonyms of the participants' own choosing, according to the women's individual wishes.

Encountering the Boundaries

The experience of being excluded or included involves the concept of boundaries between those who are inside and outside. The women I interviewed identified both explicit and implicit boundaries, marked in a whole range of ways including specific rites, church rules and teaching, dress, physical space and language. It is important from the outset to highlight the ambiguity of women's relationship with these boundaries. Many of those aspects which were experienced as exclusive also had the power to mark inclusion and belonging, something which was deeply important to the women I talked with.

Initiation Rites

The event which most frequently marked a transition from being an 'outsider' at communion to becoming an 'insider' was confirmation, or baptism as a comparable rite of adult initiation. Confirmation provided both a gateway *and* a barrier to communion, and awareness of this formed at an early age, as was the case in Grace's experience:

> The church that I went to when we were growing up would only let you be confirmed at fourteen ... by the time I was eleven I was really quite miffed that we couldn't be confirmed ... so when I first got confirmed it was partly 'yeah, real Christian', and 'yeah, we can actually do communion properly'.

Claire also recounted her wait to reach the age of confirmation and full access to communion:

> I had to be confirmed at my church before I could start taking communion, but ... because I was very inquisitive about these things before I was confirmed [*laughter*], my mum used to give me, well, a half or a quarter of her little bit of bread ... my mum didn't really agree with, you know, that you had to wait that long until you would be able to take communion ... I used to think it was really silly that I couldn't get, that I could only have a blessing.

Confirmation none the less remained a significant point in her journey to feeling fully included and later in the interview, Claire returned to reflect on the impact of confirmation for her own sense of belonging: 'I remember when I was confirmed and started getting the communion that I did feel very included in the Church then and I think the Church really tried to make me feel more included.'

For Khadijat, it was baptism rather than confirmation which gave her the sense of being *allowed* to receive Holy Communion, although in fact she had been receiving it for some time previously: 'Recently when I got baptized, my first, like, official communion, I felt like it was the time, like, I was actually allowed to go for communion.'

In this way, her baptism was an inclusive act which enabled Khadijat to experience feeling fully incorporated and accepted into the Eucharistic fellowship for the first time. The Church-instituted rite provided the context in which participation in communion became explicitly permitted, and the boundary which prevented access to communion was crossed or removed.

Although the women's views about confirmation varied significantly, there was an overarching theme of permission and 'being allowed', which demonstrated how strongly authority over admission to communion resides outside the control and agency of women themselves. The example of confirmation highlights the ambiguity surrounding the women's experiences of boundaries in the Church. Confirmation provided both the point of exclusion, frustration and alienation, but also the means of obtaining a concrete experience of feeling 'taken in' and fully included within the Church.

Receiving Communion

Alice described early experiences of kneeling before the altar as feeling 'kind of otherworldly'. A transcendent or 'otherworldly' quality of worship is something which many churches would hope to convey. Commonly, however, the women described the sense of otherworldliness as negative and contributing to feelings of discomfort and alienation. As Alice described,

> I remember as a child going up to the, sort of, altar bit where you take communion ... being told this is the blood of Christ and everything, and just thinking 'wow this is very strange', you know, very weird ... a sort of response ... almost like a taboo thing that I need to, kind of, overcome to have access.

There is a latent sense of fear in Alice's descriptions of communion and when I asked her about feeling happier to go forward and receive a blessing she responded, 'I don't feel, you know, I don't feel as threatened by it in a strange sort of sense. And I do like that, you know, receiving a blessing. I like the ritual, I like it, you know.'

Her repetition of the word 'threat', along with the use of descriptions such as 'freaked out', 'very strange', 'very weird', 'a taboo thing', paint a picture of discomfort and unease. The sense of fear was also evident in Claire's interview as she recounted a particularly negative experience of communion at a school mass in her Roman Catholic secondary school:

> I got the wafer stuck straight in my mouth and it absolutely scared me to death ... I was worried about transubstantiation as it was ... and I'd been kind of told, it was drilled into us 'you're not a Catholic and it's the Catholics who take the Eucharist and you don't' ... it still stays with me now, horrible, *horrible* experience, and I was so worried that something awful, like, you know, God would be very cross with me because I'd taken the communion, and it was a complete accident.

The horror of this experience was so great that despite the efforts of her mother and another lay minister she still was not reassured.

What became clear through the interview analysis was that the Church was communicating threat to the women, whether intentionally or not, both implicitly in its practices, and more explicitly in its teachings and prohibitions. The awareness of the alienation and control experienced as young gendered individuals was palpable in the language and stories the women shared throughout the interview material. The Church in its celebration of communion must therefore recognize the need for women to renew and re-create self understanding, to practise faith and religious ritual in a way which nurtures our ability to conceptualize ourselves and God, which is so vital to a healthy relationship with ourselves and with ultimate divine being. As Rosemary Radford Ruether propounds, women 'desperately need primary communities that nurture their journey into wholeness, rather than constantly negating and thwarting it'.[9]

Being Refused Communion

The women recounted many experiences of communion being refused, both to them personally and in experiences of close family members being refused communion, when the sense of outrage was articulated even more powerfully. In the majority of cases, the women's reaction to these experiences was to argue for more radical inclusion. There was a deep and instinctive sense that, regardless of the teaching of the Church, this exclusion was wrong, unjust and damaging.

Ann had experienced refusal twice, once where she was refused communion outright and a second time where she had eventually been given communion, but not straight away:

> One was at my home church when a visiting minister was giving communion. The other church I visited once and I never went back. They didn't recognize me. I am short and people often think I look younger than I am, and they didn't give me communion, and it made me feel really upset inside. I felt powerfully upset, possibly, probably angry.

Like Ann, Laura had been deeply affected by the impact of exclusion from communion, though in her case it was her father who had been excluded in the Roman Catholic Church as he had been previously married and divorced:

> He was about to die before having an operation ... my mother called a priest and they gave him communion after many, many years because my father was divorced and so he was completely marginalized from the Church. And I, all the time I've had communion, and it makes me cry even remembering.

---

[9] Ruether, *Women-Church*, p. 5.

For Laura the effect of engaging with the deep emotional impact of exclusion in this way had been to shape more firmly her own theological position of inclusion. She described what she liked about communion, and the juxtaposition of the two perspectives (Church and personal) is revealing of how her theology has developed through her experiences and reflection. She talked of 'a food that is available for everybody. Something there that is endless and that it's really open to everybody who wants to receive it ... this gift which is open to everybody ... what I feel about communion is that it's something that should be open to all, to everybody.'

Claire tried to make sense for herself of the complex situation of participating in communion on a pilgrimage she joined, where both Anglicans and Roman Catholics were present:

> It's a Catholic pilgrimage so they have the Catholic mass, so I don't take part obviously in that part of the Eucharist, but they also have an Anglican priest who says some, so it's, kind of, separate communion. They don't call it that. They call it something else that sounds more inclusive than separate [*laughter*] ... But for me, I really do feel that the table should be open to all people. And it really stands out when we stand there going to separate priests ... I spoke to another friend of mine and she's Catholic and she said 'well I don't know whether I'm allowed to take Anglican Eucharist because the Catholic Church says you're only supposed to take it from a Catholic Church.' So it's difficult to know isn't it, what's right and what's wrong and when a doctorate says something?

Again Claire expresses awareness that there is an authority which lies elsewhere, and outside her control, in what she describes as 'a doctorate'. Although her experiences leave her with some degree of confusion, and a feeling that the power to determine 'what's right and what's wrong' lies elsewhere and beyond her, Claire is still able to assert her own belief, clear in her personal conclusion that 'the table should be open to all people.'

Being refused communion was just one of a number of aspects of communion which revealed how the women experienced power dynamics within the Church. Reflecting on her experiences in various countries and cultures, Khadijat considered how distinctions within the Church were symbolized in dress and ritual. She valued this symbolism highly, but I observed that it also had an ambiguous effect upon her own self-perception. Khadijat viewed those with Church role and authority as being 'holy enough'. She spoke of lay assistants distributing communion, saying 'I wouldn't mind doing it but somehow I feel as if I don't have the authority to do it, you know, like I'm not holy enough or something.'

The perception that she was *not* 'holy enough' lessened her own sense of worth and equality and she echoed Alice who described 'almost not feeling worthy enough' to receive communion. Alice also saw the wearing of robes as a powerful symbol of distinction and authority and she described how breaking down distinctions within the church was very important in enabling her to feel at ease: 'They also have ... is it lay people? – who aren't dressed in sort of robes and everything and they'll be giving out the ... So there's no kind of clear authority ... It's, kind of, making it less strange, you know.'

A theme emerged in my analysis of the interviews around feeling unworthy or unclean in a way which left women feeling they were outside the boundaries of purity and holiness which brought full inclusion. These feelings of unworthiness and uncleanliness were often latent in the women's voices and they highlight what women inherit in their self-understanding and what they absorb and internalize about gender, value and self-worth from the history and culture of the Church.

Laura had a keen awareness of the division between the laity and priests and was sensitized to the separation present in celebrating communion. With her 'anthropologist eyes', she was critical of the physical setting and structuring of the ritual, questioning both the role of the priest and the way in which the 'protagonists' are 'somewhere else':

> I don't feel that the mass itself is a nice, is an attractive rite. So yes, and I feel that actually a lot of people don't feel attracted in the mass because it's not, because it's too hierarchical and it is not cheerful enough, and the organization of space is, you know, yeah ...
>
> [*Interviewer*] *Tell me about the space?*
>
> Yeah, it feels like you are a more ... d'you know what it feels like, you are in front of a kind of performance but that, and the audience participates a lot in that performance, but finally the main act is elsewhere, is in front of them.

This problem has been considered in Steven Shakespeare's critique of non-inclusive aspects of the Eucharist:

> As a spectator sport, the Eucharist falls prey to the besetting sins of the age: first, to turn religion into a ready-made object or teaching which we have to contemplate from afar or understanding intellectually in order to be a part of; and second, making communion into an essentially individualistic act between me and my God. To put it strongly, the Church was not shaped by Jesus' kingdom banquet. It administered it in the name of its own authority to control the life of the believer.[10]

Ultimately, this led Laura to a place where she imagined ways everyone could participate together in remembering the Last Supper:

> Sometimes I wonder if we could, like, try to experience the moment that Jesus Christ had with his disciples, eh, in a more similar way ... like sitting all together

---

[10] Steven Shakespeare and Hugh Rayment-Pickard, *The Inclusive God: Reclaiming Theology for an Inclusive Church* (Norwich, 2006), p. 95.

maybe, you know, sitting on the floor and just receiving some bread and so to make it more, you know, to make it more like, just like sharing some food together and in the name of Christ.

She was the most radical of the interviewees in directly confronting the dilemma of the alienation caused by the hierarchical separation of power between priests and laity in the Eucharist and seeking solutions.

Women Taking Control: The Ability to Dissent and Freedom to Choose

Alice was unique amongst the interviewees in describing herself as never having received communion (in the form of bread and wine): 'I still go and get the blessing, which often is quite strange I think because people assume, you know, that I'm happy to sort of be a full part of it and I don't feel like I am.'

She had made an individual and proactive choice to exclude herself from the act of communion and was very articulate in talking about her decisions and feelings about attending communion services: 'It's important to me to be making my own choice about going. I still feel uncomfortable if I go with my parents because it was a very forced thing.'

She picked this theme up again later in the interview, reflecting on what had made communion feel uncomfortable for her and echoing her earlier words: 'For me it's very much a thing of being forced, and again that might be something to do with it, you know, being forced to take something, you know, and perhaps that's a part of the reason why I don't, I don't want it, you know.'

Her decision to self-exclude was a means of taking control of a situation where she felt that things were strange, almost 'weird' and often 'forced' and therefore her control and autonomy were under threat. By excluding herself of her own volition, she removed the ability of these perceptions and feelings about communion to be in control, and to exclude her through their power.

Alice's response to the communion ritual and her decision to participate on her own terms offers an interesting reflection on Marjorie Procter-Smith's argument that 'Univocal prayer creates a coercive space in which consent is assumed and *yes* is the only possible response ... our practices of prayer and ritual presume the agreement of the participants, and assume that the participants are capable of consent.'[11] Rather than articulating her position as being excluded *by* the ritual of the church, Alice is confident in her 'self-exclusion'. This is a very clear and assertive response to the 'coercive space' in which she has found herself. Whilst it is true that consent is assumed in the ritual practice of communion, Alice's practice states a clear, self-chosen 'no'.

---

[11] Marjorie Procter-Smith, *'Praying With Our Eyes Open': Engendering Feminist Liturgical Prayer* (Nashville, TN, 1995), pp. 41–2.

Unlike Alice, many of the other women I interviewed chose to remain living within the tension of participating fully in communion and at the same time wrestling with experiences of exclusion and alienation, but they shared with Alice an emphasis on the importance of choice and personal autonomy. Claire felt there should be space for individuals to come to their own decisions: 'I think everyone comes to these things differently don't they? And I personally probably don't think it's right to force things on people.'

Grace too, wanted to maintain her own autonomy against a 'coercive space'. She talked with confidence about being able to hold her own perspectives, challenge established positions and for this to be accepted within her church community regardless of her age and, implicitly, her gender:

> I'd actually rather disagree with, like, the Church's teachings as a whole rather than not know what they are ... you're actually on an equal level with everybody else ... I've never gone to a house group where I've felt, like, 'oh but you're a student and you're only twenty and oh you can't really give me advice', you know.

Laura was self-aware about how she chose to dissent from doctrine she had received from the Church. Not only did she speak of her 'own re-interpretation of what I've learned from church and from catechism', but very early in her interview she wrestled with her desire to find a channel for her own voice and those like her to be heard and to be effective within the Church:

> There are aspects of the church I go to I don't like ... but at the same time I feel that I don't do anything to change, so as a member of the church I just take but I'm not contributing too. I don't know whether there's really the space to do that but sometimes I feel uncomfortable with this ... I don't know how I could express, sometimes I, maybe you could organize like a kind of movement in which we could just speak out ... I always pray, like, to God to give me some point the chance to do something or to show me the way how to express myself.

The diversity of the women's responses offers insight into two different moments of women's reaction to the power of the Church in deciding the limits of inclusion: resistance and dissent. The examples of being refused communion give a particularly clear demonstration of these two moments of reaction.

Resistance can be seen in the women's emotional responses to experiences which felt instinctively wrong. It is the first movement away from acceptance of the status quo. Most of the women who had reframed their belief and practice of communion, described having been through times of distress and anger. This was particularly true for Ann who described being 'powerfully angry' when refused communion. It can be seen more widely in feelings of resistance, including Claire's sense that exclusion was 'silly' and Laura's distress at her father's excommunication.

Ultimately the experiences of exclusion and alienation led many of the women to a point where they chose to dissent and take ownership of their own understandings. Laura's reaction to the control of the Church over the individual's access to communion was to reject the underlying principle of the Church's position, to reconstruct her own understanding of what was right and develop her personal practice accordingly. She used imagination to reframe her views of what communion means and how this could be enacted in the Eucharistic community. Alice sought out contexts which normalized communion into a world which she recognized and identified with and maintained her early decision not to conform to the expectations of the Church in her own practice. Claire also exemplifies articulate opposition to coercive space, nurtured by her mother's reworking of the rules to enable Claire to share in communion as a child, and Grace echoes the importance of autonomy in her wish for knowledge in order to choose agreement or dissent for herself.

These different moments of response can be seen in many of the other areas of women's experiences of the Church and it was possible to discern a sense of journey and trajectory through these stages. Those who had adopted a position of dissent and self-determination in their thought and practice had deliberately and consciously moved away from a place of acceptance, usually through experiences of resistance and anger, and at times still drawing upon these experiences, to form their own dissenting view.

Conclusion

The women I interviewed demonstrated a deep desire for personal inclusion and belonging. Most reacted strongly to boundaries and experiences which excluded themselves or others, as well as aspects of communion which left them feeling alienated or fearful. The symbolism of vestments and robes, the use of liturgical space, limiting access to special or holy areas of the church, all marked out distinctions for the women between 'them' and 'us', those who were powerful, enacting the ritual and in control, and those who were passive recipients of this.

What became clear to me in analysing the interviews was that the women were *feeling* excluded from the Eucharist at a much more fundamental level than simply in the tangible and individual instances they described. The sense of exclusion and alienation penetrated beyond external experiences and was grounded in an internalized sense of women being 'other', while power, authority and holiness were perceived as located elsewhere, that is, outside or beyond women. Consonant with this lack of self-assurance in the Church was the women's powerful desire to belong and feel accepted and fully included within communion.

The negative aspects of the life of the Church which have been identified in the ongoing work of feminist theologians and practitioners are borne out specifically in relation to Eucharistic practice and theology as experienced by young lay women in the Church who took part in this research. The powerlessness and sense of unworthiness experienced by so many women arises from the multi-layered experiences of fearfulness, alienation and exclusion.

Ultimately the belief, meaning and yearnings which the women bring to their personal engagement with communion are beyond the control of the Church and the interviews revealed a strong desire within women to stand against marginalization and inequality and assume control and personal agency for themselves in the face of ecclesiastical power and authority, in order to create a context of equality for all participants in the celebration of communion. It is vital, therefore, to create an understanding of Eucharist which enables women to feel that sense of authority and identification within themselves, both corporately as a gender, and flowing on from this, individually.

Tina Beattie sees the role of women priests as pivotal in bridging the gap between 'them' and 'us', bringing the priest's female body into the interplay between people and God in the Eucharist.[12] Despite the progressive step of ordaining women to the priesthood in the Church of England since 1994, I did not find any evidence in my research interviews that the experience of women's priestly and Eucharistic ministry amongst the lay women I spoke to was impacting significantly on their understanding or internalized experience of exclusion and alienation. I was genuinely surprised at the paucity of reference to the impact or significance of receiving women's ministry. This led me to conclude that, for some women at least, it is unrealistic to expect the role of the woman priest to mediate the full inclusion and integration of women into the life of the Eucharist, or mitigate the negative impact of the Eucharistic milieu they experience in the Church.

Whilst the woman priest may stand as transformative symbol, challenging the established separation and exclusion of women, this transformation must be more thoroughgoing and integrated. It must permeate every aspect of the Eucharistic life of the Church in order to redress the negative and destructive impact of Eucharistic theology and practice upon lay women. There is therefore an urgent need for the creation of a theology of the Eucharist which places the female body at the centre and recognizes the fullness of all women's bodies, nature and identity as being in the likeness of Christ in a Eucharistic context.

The effect of addressing this fundamental bias against women's bodies directly in the theology and Christology of the Eucharist could, I believe, have far-reaching consequences. It could meaningfully address the many concomitant dualisms which operate in the Eucharistic celebration as identified by the women I interviewed – dualisms of 'them and us', of the holiness of the priest and robed participants versus the unworthiness of the people 'watching', of the fear of the bread and wine which are 'taboo', and the powerlessness and vulnerability expressed in the threat of 'being forced' by those who have power.

---

[12] Tina Beattie, 'Vision and Vulnerability: The Significance of Sacramentality and the Woman Priest for Feminist Theology', in Natalie K. Watson and Stephen Burns (eds), *Exchanges of Grace: Essays in Honour of Ann Loades* (London, 2008), p. 247.

A Eucharistic theology which locates power and meaning in the female body rather than in the person and role of a female priest or even bishop, owning its creative power, inherent wisdom and autonomy, has the potential to offer women a theology which is liberational and emancipatory.

Chapter 6
God Talk/Girl Talk: A Study of Girls' Lives and Faith in Early Adolescence, with Reflections on Those of their Biblical Fore-sisters[1]

Anne Phillips

Introduction

I had worked for many years on theologies of childhood and women's religious and spiritual experience in feminist perspective, when it hit me: where are the girls? My daughter was growing through her teen years, and there was a gap where Bible and theology might have helped her interpret her identity and faith as a girl growing within a Christian context.

Most theologies of childhood are written by men and thus reflect a male standpoint. Biblical examples regularly cited as evidence for a theological perspective on childhood are male – Samuel, David, Jesus. Feminist theology is ambivalent about girls, marked as it often is by an adultism in which girls are either overlooked, or trail along in women's wake on the assumption that what is true of them also applies to girls.

This was a lacuna that cried out to be filled. So I embarked on an empirical study of this overlooked group at an age, between 11 and 13, broadly coinciding with the onset of puberty and arguably the most formative stage of their development. Existing research into girls/boys[2] is largely gender neutral, and usually clearly age-defined – 'children' up to 11, and 'young people' from 14 upwards; thus the difficult years of transition in between are neatly avoided. Following the modernist trend to categorize and label societal groups and thus objectify and dehumanize them, this group has even been labelled 'tweenagers'.[3] From my research data, there were two strands I wanted to interweave: first, analysis of findings from my interviews with girls growing up within a church context; and secondly, reflection

---

[1] Material in this chapter is adapted from Anne Phillips, *The Faith of Girls: Children's Spirituality and Transition to Adulthood* (Farnham, 2011).

[2] I adopt this term instead of 'children' to highlight the fact that 'childhood' is peopled by both genders; this is significant in the research process.

[3] Peter Brierley, *Reaching and Keeping Tweenagers* (London, 2002).

on pre-pubertal biblical girls in order to suggest a theological base on which girls – and women – might build their spirituality and faith. In this chapter, I will summarize the process and the results of my research with girls who were part of church communities, and then trace the trajectory of my biblical and theological reflection, which is ongoing.

Learning from Girls

Qualitative research with girls/boys has evolved methodologies informed by sociological research which views them as subjects, agents in their own development, at a stage in their lives which is 'socially, culturally and temporally specific',[4] and commands respect as a distinct social world. I chose an ethnographic methodology which is consistent with feminist research; this sets aside traditional views that the researcher retains a critical distance to maximize objectivity, but recognizes instead that the quality of data is strengthened if relationships are developed with subjects, consistent with the desire for connection, while maintaining awareness of the potential influence of the researcher's standpoint on the outcome.

My research data were gathered through interviews with 17 girls from Free Churches in a variety of geographical location and social and demographic context, in a process messily constructed to fit in with the demands of full-time teaching and ministerial responsibilities, and family commitments. The semi-structured interviews were largely in small groups (maximum of four), to help the girls gain confidence from one another, but with sufficiently varied methods that all had an equal opportunity to share their thinking, however quiet they were. I was able to spend time with most groups on several occasions, and share in the activities of which our conversations formed an integral part either within a weeknight meeting or during and after Sunday morning worship. It was important to try to redress the power imbalance between us by meeting in their space, either on church premises or in a home where my guest status gave the girls a measure of authority, which in Nesbitt's experience 'encourages children's confidence in speaking'.[5]

At all times, ethical considerations with such young subjects were to the fore. My access was through the minister as gatekeeper; they, their leadership teams and the girls' parents were given an introductory sheet containing my CV, assurance of my adherence to best practice and official clearance[6] with regard to child protection, and an outline of my research with the invitation to discuss

---

[4] Ruth Emond, 'Ethnographic research methods with children and young people', in Sheila Greene and Diane Hogan (eds), *Researching Children's Experience: Approaches and Methods* (London, 2005), p. 124.

[5] Eleanor Nesbitt, 'Researching 8 to 13-year-olds' perspectives and their experience of religion', in Ann Lewis and Geoff Lindsay (eds), *Researching Children's Perspectives* (Buckingham and Philadelphia, PA, 2000), p. 143.

[6] Through an Enhanced Criminal Records Disclosure.

any aspect of it with me. I planned the physical space for each interview with an eye to comfort, but also balancing transparency and openness with security and confidentiality; where practical, doors were left ajar, but in all cases, the girls were seated where they could leave the room unhindered should they so wish. In some cases adults entered the room, but rather than disturbing the process it enhanced the relaxed atmosphere, and served to build group identity and cohesion in which I was included; on one occasion, the girls were given further power of choice when towards the end of our allotted time, they were offered an alternative activity which they refused, opting to continue the conversation.

I devised a common process which combined open questions with activities, allowing both group and individual voices to be heard through speech and writing, with scope for 'chatter',[7] quiet for thought, and flexibility for tangents to be followed but with sufficiently light steering to prevent one voice dominating. The starting-point for each interview was crucial, both to establish their trust in me and to foreground as their frame of reference their identity and experience as girls. The first question: 'What do you enjoy about being a girl?' was light-hearted and elicited some responses which captured the tone, but as the conversation became more serious, many girls still limited their self-definition to 'not boy'. This could suggest a lack of encouragement or opportunity to explore their gendered identity perhaps in the interests of equality, but once given permission to do so, many offered uninhibited reflections on their experience, and later their faith. The most informative data emerged from an exercise in 'telling it slant',[8] drawing on methods employed successfully in earlier research on girls'/boys' spirituality by Tamminen,[9] using photographs to invite both cognitive and affective responses in terms of 'what do you think?' and 'what do you feel'? The images were not obviously 'religious' but potentially suggestive of deeper meanings; they were selected carefully from within their cultural context, from girls' and other magazines, and from among images freely available in stores girls would frequent.

Having recorded and transcribed the interviews, immersing myself in the data, I began my analysis, following textbook protocols to develop grounded theory which emerges out of the data instead of being imposed upon it, seeking categories through sequential coding.[10] I used both inductive and deductive strategies, and engaged in something akin to the 'free-flowing dialogue' Slee describes to draw out themes and categories, and followed hunches to wander in fields of 'interpretative

---

[7] Rebecca Nye, 'Psychological perspectives on children's spirituality' (unpublished PhD thesis, University of Nottingham, 1998), p. 229.

[8] A phrase originating with poet Emily Dickinson: making connections not dependent on cognition alone.

[9] Kalevi Tamminen, *Religious Development in Childhood and Youth* (Helsinki, 1991).

[10] Anselm Strauss and Juliet Corbin, *Basics of Qualitative Research: Techniques and Procedures for Developing Grounded Theory*, 2nd edn (Thousand Oaks, CA, 1998), p. 12.

creativity'[11] about what was going on for the girls at this time of transition. Since it is a common assumption that 'children are ... incapable of articulating their own spiritual and religious longings', and 'many would question whether children have the requisite cognitive capacity to formulate conceptual understandings of existential realities',[12] I saw my task as one of advocacy,[13] redressing girls' invisibility in ecclesial settings.

Girl Talk

Published resources on girls in academic fields were hard to unearth; the richest seam I found was in sociology and in cultural studies where the social construction of girls was discussed in some depth.[14] Much of what I read was substantiated in my interviews, although no sociological resources took account of the place of spirituality, let alone religion, in girls' experience. Mercer comments aptly that 'when researchers, fearful or unaware of the multiplicity of religion's presence in women's lives, neglect it in young women's experience, they ignore a vital but complex feature of these girls' lives.'[15] Studies of girls'/boys' spirituality, such as that of Hay and Nye, demonstrate the prevalence of spiritual experience; this is indicative of the gravity of the omission in psychological and sociological studies of all girls/boys, particularly in the light of their emphasis on well-being and fulfilment. Reciprocally, however, many churches show little if any engagement with the complex social and political contexts within which girls are attempting to structure their faith lives; the physically maturing female body and adolescent heterosexual relationships are commonly sites of disturbance and fear, yet are rendered invisible or repressed by church workers.

In analysing my data, these resources helped me to identify the struggle many girls have between Christian teaching which pays little attention to embodiment, and their growing awareness of their changing bodies, which some desire to beautify – for their own sake, and not only in response to advertising. I found that the relentless growth away from the freedom of childhood into a more restricted womanhood (menstruation, sexualization, assumptions of future maternity, which can become deterministic), are to them a source of grief: pubertal transition is for

---

[11] Nicola Slee, *Women's Faith Development: Patterns and Processes* (Aldershot, 2004), p. 57.

[12] Eileen W. Lindner, 'Children as Theologians', in Peter B. Pufall and Richard P. Unsworth (eds), *Rethinking Childhood*, (New Brunswick, CT, 2004), p. 60.

[13] See David Jensen, *Graced Vulnerability, A Theology of Childhood* (Cleveland, OH, 2005), p. xiii.

[14] For example, Catherine Driscoll, *Girls: Feminine Adolescence in Popular Culture and Cultural Theory* (New York, 2002).

[15] Joyce Ann Mercer, *Girl Talk, God Talk: Why Faith Matters to Teenage Girls – and their Parents* (San Francisco, CA, 2008), p. xxii.

most their first experience of bereavement, and its impact can be intensified by the imposition by adults of negative attitudes regarding healthy relationships. As Lucy[16] woefully commented: 'you think of boys differently; cos you don't think of it as friends any more and I think that's actually a shame ... if you're seen with boys it's considered straightaway that it's girlfriend/boyfriend and it's not!'

Other changes, caused by moving to new schools or by geographical mobility of families, serve to intensify this so that, even when not obvious, many girls interpreted in terms of loss images which to me represented intimate relationship. To several girls, two pictures spoke eloquently of brokenness: one was of an adult hand holding that of a small child, the other showed adult and child feet sole to sole. Julie saw in the first an example of the 'cycle of life', that someone had died and was being 'replaced', and Bryony felt 'like it's me reaching out to God for help'. The other reminded Bethan and Martha, independently, of the separation between mother and child which is a consequence of growing up. Such grief is acknowledged by Carol Gilligan in her psychological studies: aside from her work on women's moral voice in defining her ethic of care, she and her colleagues did extensive research with girls in schools, where they uncovered this feature of adolescent girls' experience.[17]

Psychology and philosophy also contributed to data analysis. In the writings of Erik Erikson, usually dismissed by feminists for his assertion of a woman's destiny being determined by her anatomy, I found an unexpected awareness of women's psyche and role. Sensitized to 'life on boundaries'[18] by his own life experience, he identified the liminal nature of puberty, and grief as in some sense intrinsic to it. Furthermore, he affirmed women's preference for negotiation and relationship rather than confrontation and conflict, which could, he thought, be the salvation of humankind in an era bent on mutual destruction through technological warfare promoted by men.[19]

The work of clinical psychologist Robert Kegan formed another strand in the framework I adopted for the analysis of my research findings. In a similar way to Erikson, and contrary to malestream developmental theories which correlate maturity with independence and autonomy, Kegan recognizes the need to balance individuality with the interdependence found in healthy relationships. Besides naming the stages or balances in the self's evolution, he also attends to the factors

---

[16] Pseudonyms are used throughout.

[17] Carol Gilligan, 'Women's Psychological Development: Implications of Psychotherapy', in Carol Gilligan, Annie G. Rogers and Deborah H. Tolman (eds), *Women, Girls and Psychotherapy: Reframing Resistance* (New York, London and Sydney, 1991), p. 26.

[18] L. Friedman, *Identity's Architect: A Biography of Erik H. Erikson* (New York, 1999), p. 344.

[19] Erik Erikson, 'Womanhood and Inner Space', in *Identity: Youth and Crisis* (New York, 1968), pp. 278, 284, 293–4.

that trigger transition – for girls, the shifting identities in which they test out new ways of being and relating as they move into adolescence.[20]

As with sociology, so in psychology, spirituality does not feature, although both Erikson and Kegan do admit to a spiritual dimension inherent in human experience. Academically credible qualitative research on girls'/boys' spirituality[21] and faith[22] at this transitional age is sparse, but the studies by Tamminen, and by Smith and Denton, show that in pre- and early teen years, girls are more positive than boys in their attitudes and beliefs and have a deeper sense of relationship with God; they thus give more place to faith practices in daily life. Research by Heller provides a more nuanced understanding; consistent with Brown's findings,[23] he uncovered girls' ability to stretch boundaries in their faithing,[24] while being fearful of articulating views divergent from their leaders or parents for fear that deviance will be demeaned as immaturity, and relationships will be broken.[25] This supports the findings of Gilligan and others, that girls are socialized into compliance, and lose their own voice at the onset of puberty. It was only as confidence in my trustworthiness and confidentiality grew that, in my interviews, girls began to push at the boundaries of faith and spiritual experience.

Carol Lakey Hess applied both Gilligan's and Kegan's work to a church context, and identified the pressure on girls of the self-sacrificial imagery which forms a significant part of their teaching – dying to self – which breeds and feeds a loss of self-worth.[26] Hess recognizes that the Church can be restrictive, even abusive to girls; this resonates with philosopher Luce Irigaray, when she says that 'holiness is often presented to women as being a relation to the other gender through self-abnegation.'[27]

---

[20] Robert Kegan, *The Evolving Self: Problem and Process in Human Development* (Cambridge, MA, 1982).

[21] David Hay, with Rebecca Nye, *The Spirit of the Child*, revised edn (London and Philadelphia, PA, 2006).

[22] Heller, *The Children's God* (Chicago, IL and London, 1986); Tamminen, *Religious Development*; Christian Smith, with Melinda Lundquist Denton, *Soul Searching: The Religious and Spiritual Lives of American Teenagers* (New York, 2005).

[23] Lyn Mikel Brown, *Raising their Voices: The Politics of Girls' Anger* (Cambridge, MA, 1998), p.107.

[24] I follow Fowler in using 'faith' as an active verb: James Fowler, *Stages of Faith: The Psychology of Human Development and the Quest for Meaning* (San Francisco, CA, 1981), p. 16.

[25] Heller, *The Children's God*, p. 74.

[26] Carol Lakey Hess, *Caretakers of our Common House: Women's Development in Communities of Faith* (Nashville, TN, 1997), Chapter 1.

[27] Luce Irigaray (ed.), *Luce Irigaray: Key Writings* (London and New York, 2004), p. 154.

God Talk

Girls on the cusp of adolescence are on a threshold, not just physically, but emotionally, intellectually and spiritually; they are capable of articulating in a profound way aspects of their experience, and their intellectual and faith processes.

These formed the next stage of my investigation as I studied their spiritual lives through what they had to say about the things of God and their strategies of faithing. The maturity of their construction of theological argument was only constrained by their limited life experience and vocabulary: when I analysed their arguments, I was able to correlate them with the writings of major contemporary theologians: the 'problem of evil', and the Trinity are two examples. Lucy offered a balanced view of the 'bad things' touching on all the great theological themes within theodicy; although at first sight her thoughts appear incoherent and immature, careful attention revealed justice and mercy wrestling each other, with mercy winning out as the quality that sustains relationship. Amber's language suggested a rounded Trinitarian awareness, describing alternately the transcendence and immanence of the Father and the Son and the 'mist-like' working presence of the Spirit.

My findings support feminist critique of structural faith development theory[28] which exposes its weaknesses in its application to women and girls,[29] and corroborate studies which find that women's spirituality is founded on relationship, both with God and in the faith community: relationality and caring underlay all that the girls said. In my analysis, I addressed their God-talk first in order to counter the assumption noted above about the limitations of their conceptual understandings. In their faithing, relationship with God was desired above all, but some were fully aware of the contextuality of belief and the ambiguity of their position as faithing people still subject to the teaching and doctrinal formulations of adults. Karen voiced the tension:

> 'it's like having two things,
> one that you've been taught to believe
> and one that you do.'

Lucy, two years younger, makes a similar point less succinctly:

> a lot of the stuff that we've been taught when we were younger
> was like ...
> stories so you start to think:
> 'well these stories have got to be perfect you know
> and if anyone says anything that these stories are wrong,
> then they're wrong',

---

[28] See Fowler, *Stages of Faith*.
[29] Slee, *Women's Faith Development*, pp. 28–32.

but ... we realized that there were millions of different ways of,
every single person has a different way of describing God.

Unprompted, Ruth initiated her own dialogue between religion and science:

'I've had this feeling before about creation.
I wonder if the Bible and the scientists' theory and all the different theories,
I think they all seem to make sense in different ways to me
but God is still in there somewhere.'

God was still, however, looked to for security and protection as both transcendent ('It's amazing that he made the world, made things and made us and knows everything', said Suzanne), and immanent (like 'your best friend sat next to you', said Ruth); as many of them, like Lucy, struggled with living in a flawed creation, an ethic of care, divine and human, was central. God empathized with their experience through the incarnation. Jesus was the 'parable of God'[30] to Martha who described Jesus as 'a symbol of how it was, like, before your eyes'. But he was also the companion on the way whom Mary was 'hanging out with' and who will 'support you and things'. It was with discussion of the Holy Spirit that the relational dimension was paramount. Although Ruth said 'I've never really been told much about the Holy Spirit', she and others recounted real experiences, some with physical manifestations, others as a presence 'just there around you'. A few girls drew on doctrinal clichés while others clearly reflected the influence of adults whether from home or church; yet most began to think outside the box, using original language and imagery to explore their thoughts, a capacity Büttner has also observed with even younger girls/boys who, facing new challenges, 'experiment with new ideas based on their knowledge'.[31] The interviews gave the girls a valuable opportunity to think and talk freely and creatively, not having to 'say what we're supposed to', as Karen put it.

Styles of Faithing

Their God-talk was, however, based on and filtered through their own relationship with God, characterized by varying degrees of closeness, so next I identified 'styles of faithing', which again have close internal connection. Recognizing, as some girls did, their own vulnerability, God was safe to trust themselves to in difficult times. 'Safe faithing' has close links with 'empathic faithing'; not only

---

[30] Sallie McFague, *Metaphorical Theology: Models of God in Religious Language* (Philadelphia, PA, 1982), p. 165.

[31] Gerhard Büttner, 'Where do children get their theology from?', in Annemie Dillen and Didier Pollefeyt (eds), *Children's Voices: Children's Perspectives in Ethics, Theology and Religious Education* (Leuven, 2010), p. 372.

do they look to adults, especially mothers, for understanding because as Bethan said, they've also 'been in the situation of developing and things', but they can also relate to God because in Mary's words he 'walked on the earth like we do', so much so that for Michelle, 'he knows what you're going through.'

There is a darker side, however. At the interface of church and school, the girls lost their confidence and felt threatened, so to live a Christian life beyond the security of the Church context was a 'daunting' style of faithing, requiring courage. A peer group and mentoring by older girls and women were vital to the growth of their self-confidence as faithing people. Girls from churches which self-identified as evangelical felt under pressure to witness to their faith in word and deed, increasing their sense of vulnerability among their peers.

'Relational faithing' involved caring for others, which individual girls exhibited by acting as peacemaker, giving to the poor, and caring for family and friends in practical ways and through prayer support.

Faith had its sensual side, too, and I identified a category of 'girlie faithing' not as a derogatory term but, according to their definition, originating in the part that fantasy or illusion played in helping them to enter into genuine relationality with that which cannot be seen or touched, but which is still real to the senses. Much of this corroborates and extends the 'generative themes' which Slee developed in her patterns of women's faith development.[32]

Finally, I identified 'biblical faithing'. Although outright knowledge of biblical narratives was often sketchy, in deeper theological reflection, some were able to mine its resources to construct faith dialogue by which they showed how deeply embedded some passages were. Some girls were alert to the Bible's androcentrism ('it's more of a story for boys'), but those who questioned its relevance to girls based its redemption on contextualization ('if Jesus was around ... now, then I don't think it would be just all boys'), and the authority they gained from their own relational experience of God as girls.

The Church's Role

On the basis of this evidence, how best can the Church fulfil its obligation, and girls' expectations, to care for them and assist their nurture toward womanhood? The rich imagery of the womb suggested itself as a metaphor as I unpeeled the layers in my data. It features in much contemporary feminist writing as well as in the psychological writings of Kegan and the biblical scholarship of Phyllis Trible. I approached it rather differently, however, identifying the girls' chief needs as space to grow through play with their theology and their faith, and protection from the sexualization and cynicism that surrounds them.

I ventured, then, to explore the womb's physiology, and found that these needs are met in foetal gestation by the two separate uterine membranes, the chorion

---

[32] Slee, *Women's Faith Development*, p. 59 and Chapters 5–7.

and the amnion: the outer chorion protects from the knocks of accident, and the amniotic sac holds the waters in which the baby enjoys free play. Playspace is a key to thriving in liminal space, as Watts, Nye and Savage recognize when they describe play's supportive function through the losses of transition; play makes it easier, they say, to respond positively to cognitive conflict as schemata begin to crumble.[33] Kegan, directing our attention to the cultures in which girls are growing, describes as an 'amniotic environment' the space which holds without constraining the reorganizing of who the person is in the next step of growth.[34] Likewise Trible, with whom the wombing image is closely associated theologically, attests to its function to protect and nourish while not possessing and controlling.[35] The analogous relationship thus set up between the physical maturing of a girl's uterus and her psychological and spiritual growth offers a rich metaphor for the safe space a girl needs to flourish spiritually, one which offers nurture and holding as she actively engages in the gestation and birthing of herself as woman. These images enabled me to focus on key facets of the optimum 'holding environment', a concept Kegan uses to denote holding on, letting go, and third but often forgotten, remaining in place as a secure home to which the wanderer may return.[36] If the girls' progress through puberty is seen as wombing, the outcome is birth; the Church's role then finds its descriptor in another metaphor, that of midwife. In extending care for both the one giving birth and the one birthed, the midwife comes alongside as trusted companion offering assistance and support as girls negotiate this liminal space, transforming 'the authoritarian discourse of the past into an internally persuasive discourse ... that breaks open the traditional formulations about God'.[37] To Hess, the Church's task is the empowerment of girls in 'creative defiance' to 'wrestle together to prevail against those things that deprive women of their well-being',[38] a safe place in which girls can be coached and mentored, learning to resist compliance but be critically inquiring, and challenge interpretation of texts and discriminatory practices which dehumanize, inhibit, or deny their flourishing.

---

[33] Fraser Watts, Rebecca Nye and Sara Savage, *Psychology for Christian Ministry* (London, 2002), p. 125.

[34] Kegan, *The Evolving Self*, p. 162.

[35] Phyllis Trible, *God and the Rhetoric of Sexuality* (Philadelphia, PA, 1978), pp. 33–4.

[36] Kegan, *The Evolving Self*, pp. 121–32.

[37] L. Juliana M. Claassens, 'Rupturing God-Language: The Metaphor of God as Midwife in Psalm 22', in Linda Day and Carolyn Pressler (eds), *Engaging the Bible in a Gendered World: An Introduction to Feminist Biblical Interpretation in Honor of Katharine Doob Sakenfeld* (Louisville, KY, 2006), pp. 170–72.

[38] Hess, *Caretakers of our Common House*, p. 181.

Theological Reflection

I can now begin to weave together this analysis of my living texts with a reflection on pre-pubertal biblical girls. Hitherto, girls have been offered no strong peer foundations in either scripture or theology; nowhere can they find resources offering girlhood as an icon through which we see God or God might be revealing Godself to us. So what connections could I find between my data and the Bible?

My path began with Trible's pursuit of the journey of the womb (*rechem*) metaphor 'from a physical organ of the female body to a psychic mode of being ... from the wombs of women to the compassion of God'.[39]

Thence to Lo-Ruhamah, the one named girl in the whole of the Bible whom we can claim with certainty is not of marriageable age. The middle child of Hosea and Gomer, she was so named to identify her bodily with her father's prophetic announcement of God's refusal any longer to have compassion for the people. What an abuse to name your daughter, the fruit of your womb, 'the one for whom I have no compassion'! Clearly, Gomer defies the signification, and has motherly compassion by breastfeeding her for the normal two to three years; maybe by this means Hosea realizes the bond between mother and child which no divine word can break, and teaches a lesson about God from motherhood.

Other girls are agents in God's story: some are heroic like Moses' sister and Naaman's wife's slave girl, others abused like the slave girl Paul healed.[40] I will isolate two, however, whose brief appearances suggest a direction for a theology of girlhood. Jairus' daughter's story is known for being part of a 'women subplot' which highlights how women's bodies, suffering and healing are models for the body, suffering and resurrection of Jesus; if her rising is also to womanhood, its interlacing with the healing of the haemorrhaging woman symbolizes that the flow of blood which marks (or mars) womanhood is not impure but the way women are intended 'to live in the well-being of God's reigning presence'.[41] Her Old Testament counterpart appears briefly in the prophecy of Ezekiel. The whore Israel has become was left for dead at birth. YHWH rescued her while still in her amniotic fluid and uterine blood, had compassion and called her in her blood to live and flourish. There are difficulties for women with the way the prophecy develops (and much ink has been spilt over chapters 16 and 23) but along with the other texts, it supports a theology in which girls symbolize natality. Here I draw on the work of Irigaray again, and the writing of Grace Jantzen whom she inspired. Girl narratives or references in scripture promote life. They bespeak natality in contrast to the 'obsession with death and other worlds' of the western 'masculinist

---

[39] Hebrew for 'compassion' is *rachamim* or *rachum*: Trible, *God and the Rhetoric of Sexuality*, p. 33–4.

[40] Exodus 2:1–10; 2 Kings 5:2–3; Acts 16:16–19.

[41] F.J. Moloney, *The Gospel of Mark, A Commentary* (Peabody, MA, 2002), p. 111.

imaginary'.[42] As they grow towards their bodily birth (or rebirth) as women, they bring with them, unless conditioned or constructed out of them, the desire and gift for creativity 'from the beginning contained in a web of relationship and in a shared world'.[43] Here is Jantzen's imaginary of natality which she frees from the limitations of its associations with motherhood; it can then serve to free girls from cultural as well as physiological predetermination of their identity and destiny and allow them to flourish as daughters of God. Thus, understanding girlhood theologically is to affirm who girls are in and for themselves, not for who or what they will become. Nurturing them on this journey is a shared task for us all.

---

[42] Grace Jantzen, *Becoming Divine: Towards a Feminist Philosophy of Religion* (Manchester, 1998), p. 129.

[43] Ibid., p. 149.

PART III
Female Faith in Diverse Ecclesial and Geographical Contexts

Chapter 7
The 'In-the-Middle' God: Women, Community Conflict and Power in Northern Ireland[1]

Fran Porter

Introduction

Civil conflict with its social, cultural, political, religious and economic aspects has been part of the pervasive backcloth against which women in Northern Ireland conduct their lives.[2] The violence and awfulness of this civil unrest, known as 'the troubles',[3] with its thirty plus years of accumulated memory and experience, is imprinted on all aspects of life in Northern Ireland. This is true not only for those whose painful encounters with the more brutal manifestations of the conflict have left deep marks on their lives. It also applies to those who, by virtue of their social and geographical location, appear to have been left relatively untouched by the more obvious elements of community divisions. As a Methodist woman encapsulated: 'The troubles have done more than just the killings, it's the whole culture.'

With the paramilitary ceasefires and political accommodation of the 1990s peace process, culminating in the 1998 Belfast Agreement, Northern Ireland is now post-troubles but it is not post-conflict. It still struggles with sectarian[4] division, and this

---

[1] Material in this chapter was adapted from Fran Porter, *It Will Not Be Taken Away From Her: A feminist engagement with women's Christian experience* (London, 2004), Chapter 6.

[2] An accessible and comprehensive account of the conflict in Northern Ireland from the inception of the Northern Ireland state in 1921 to the 1998 Belfast Agreement and its immediate aftermath is David McKittrick and David McVea, *Making Sense of the Troubles* (London, 2001).

[3] The term 'the troubles' refers to the conflict in Northern Ireland that began in 1969 and is generally understood to have ended with the signing of the 1998 Belfast Agreement. The euphemism probably originates from its use as an expression of condolence at times of bereavement: 'I'm sorry for your troubles.'

[4] Part of the definition of sectarianism as defined by Joseph Liechty and Cecelia Clegg, *Moving Beyond Sectarianism* (Dublin, 2001), p. 102, is that it is a 'system of attitudes,

is played out in the political arena. It took ten years for the Belfast Agreement to be fully implemented, during which time the Northern Ireland Assembly, the legislative body integral to that Agreement, was suspended four times due to political stalemate. Sectarian violence and public disturbance has not disappeared and in recent years, paramilitary activity that had never completely ceased has increased in visibility and effectiveness. Northern Ireland remains a divided and conflicted society. Reasons for hope about building a better and shared future live alongside signs of vulnerability to the fragile peace. Northern Ireland is still a society engaged in a peace process, struggling to deal with the many legacies of the past.

It was while we were in the middle of the 1990s peace process that I was researching about Christian women's lives. I interviewed 55 Protestant and Catholic women aged between 21 and 73 who were based throughout Northern Ireland and from a range of theological outlooks as well as denominational affiliations.[5] My research was a feminist engagement with women's Christian faith experience that focused on women's understanding of God, their self-understanding, their relationship to church institutions, and their life experiences. The troubles, how women's lives had been affected, and their various responses to it, emerged as a common and prominent feature in our conversations.

Responding to the Troubles

The women interviewed had a range of experiences and attitudes in respect of the troubles, indicating the pervasiveness of the conflict. There were those who, either personally or through their family or close friends, had been involved in bomb explosions, shooting incidents and arson attacks; experienced verbal assault and physical injury; known employment discrimination; received intimidation or death threats; and witnessed death and bereavement.

Some women were actively endeavouring to address sectarianism. 'I wouldn't be in the job I'm doing now if it hadn't been for the troubles', said a community sector worker. 'I've always had a thing about trying to ... as an individual responsibility, do something rather than hide ... [What] bothers me in sectarianism [is] the hate and so I would want to do something about it rather than be passive.' Others, however, felt like they coexisted with the situation. 'I feel affected because of [where I lived]', a Presbyterian woman in her forties explained,

---

actions, beliefs and structures – at personal, communal, and institutional levels – which always involves religion and typically involves a negative mixing of religion and politics'.

[5] In order to include a diversity of women, I identified groups/communities of women which between them accommodated the four characteristics of denomination, age, theological outlook and geographical location. I contacted 13 groups (ten of which reached province wide), circulated over 800 letters, and received 76 responses (almost a ten per cent response rate), 55 of whom I interviewed (between May 1996 and October 1997).

... but in many ways I've kept my head down, it's been a matter of tolerating it and getting on, that attitude, you know, keeping it in the background and just getting on with life. I've detached myself from it all at the same time living through it. A number of my neighbours were murdered, I've been in shooting incidences and murder incidences so it has impacted quite a bit and yet in another way it hasn't.

For some, there was a sense of feeling physically or emotionally removed from the community conflict. 'I can be objective about it', commented a Catholic woman in her seventies. 'I would tune into the world service and the BBC and listen in to all the things that are happening around the world, you know, and they would be just as equally oppressive and upsetting as what is happening here.' A Presbyterian woman over fifty stated: 'Fortunately the troubles have not had much impact on our lives in that ... we haven't had any close family relations killed or injured or anything like that. We know people who were bereaved, but it hasn't touched on us really.'

The idea that the troubles 'hasn't touched us really' refers to not being direct victims of violence or injustice, the more overt hallmarks of the conflict. However, the reality of living in a divided society is reflected in the way that issues of national or religious identities and loyalties dominate social relations. Speaking of her time as a nursing student, a Protestant woman commented how she and her roommates automatically introduced themselves to each other in terms of their names, hometown and religion. A Catholic woman expressed how pervasive is such identification: 'It is intrinsic in all of us – no matter whether you intellectually want to or not – if you've grown up in Northern Ireland it is second nature to you to suss out someone's religion ... It's not necessarily for any ulterior motive. It's just ... indigenous to growing up here.'

Such categorization is accompanied by expectations of behaviour that support and sustain particular identities. 'I was expected to be very republican, nationalist,' said a Catholic woman referring to the views of other Catholic people, 'and I wasn't prepared to go into that mould.' She spoke of her experience in a cross-community prayer group when a Catholic member said to her, 'Oh, I thought you were Protestant.' This 'was a very subtle way of saying you do Protestant things, you know. And that was because I wouldn't fall into the stereotype, you know, of what was expected of Catholics in the Catholic group.' A Methodist woman protested about experiencing a similar dynamic. 'I hate people put into boxes', she stated emphatically, 'I don't want to be put into a box, I want to be myself ... I don't want people thinking "she's a Protestant, so she must vote this way or be this way or think this way".'

These dynamics that reflect the systemic sectarianism[6] in operation have an imprisoning effect that stifles proactive engagement. For an Anglican woman:

---

[6] The systemic nature of sectarianism means that 'a sectarian system can be maintained by people who, individually, do not have a sectarian bone in their bodies' (Liechty and Clegg, *Moving Beyond Sectarianism*, p. 9).

Most of the time, I have to be honest, it just goes on ... it's just a bit of the background. But every time I go away and come back it's just so suffocating. I just feel so oppressed and I feel why can't it just stop ... I go through periods of intense praying about it and asking for peace and what can I do, and then other times it just goes on.

Disempowerment or Agency

This last woman's fluctuating relationship to the situation, from intensity to 'it just goes on', reflects a sense of powerlessness among some women in the way they relate to the situation of community conflict. This powerlessness is a sense of women feeling unable to change or alter their situation on either a personal or social level. Sometimes this is expressed in terms of frustration, confusion, pain, or helplessness, of feeling 'like there was no hope'. Sometimes it is about a sense of disempowerment through lack of political or cultural identity, of not being able to own being Protestant, Catholic, Irish, Northern Irish, or British, because to be those things was to be expected to behave, talk, or vote in certain ways. In a society where national or religious identity is the first thing that people want to know about someone and that people are judged by because of what it implies, women talked of a disempowering detachment. One woman spoke of how she had 'closed off from [the troubles] a long time ago' and hence, 'wouldn't dream of being involved in politics'.

This feeling of powerlessness contrasts with the notion of empowerment, which has been described as

> ... the process by which individuals, families, groups, and communities increase their personal, interpersonal, socioeconomic, and political strength and influence in order to improve their well-being. Empowerment is not granted from an external source but emerges from within as persons and communities acknowledge and appreciate their gifts and their responsibilities.[7]

Clearly, this is different from an understanding of power as something a person or group of people exercise over others. Rather, empowerment is experienced by individuals or groups as they assume responsibility for themselves. While this does not mean that they can completely control their social environment, it does mean that they become active agents in their situation, seeking to address it in whatever form is appropriate for constructive purposes.

An example of this comes from a Catholic woman who spoke of how she had joined the Alliance Party – a cross-community party formed in the early years of the troubles, which advocated an alternative to the two stark choices of unionism or

---

[7] Marie J. Giblin, 'Empowerment', in Letty M. Russell and J. Shannon Clarkson (eds), *Dictionary of Feminist Theologies* (London, 1996), pp. 83–4.

nationalism. Joining was very hard for this woman to do, but was a response to the powerlessness she felt at the time in the face of discrimination and sectarianism. As she said: 'With all this going on, what could you do? You were powerless and [the Alliance Party] came along and that was an opening for working with Protestants and Catholics together.'

One woman attributed her alienation from political involvement to a sense of powerlessness which was forged not only as a result of growing up as part of a minority community, but also to her experience as a woman:

> Research would indicate that women feel more powerless because they see that things are more personal ... Research [into] promotion [shows] women invariably thought that they had been promoted because they had been in the right place at the right time whereas men ... [it was more] that you were the best person for the job. And I think that translates itself into women's perception on whether it is possible for them to influence societal events.

There are a number of interrelated reasons for women's feelings of powerlessness or empowerment in respect of community conflict. Individual personal biographies, of course, affect women's attitudes and actions. A woman whose husband's life had been threatened had lived for many years with the fear that 'at the back of my mind I was aware that I could become a widow.' She had conducted her life taking this into account, ensuring work for herself that energized her and which she loved. Yet she did not shirk from doing what she felt was right in regard to community issues, 'we ... can justify our actions, you know, nothing we have done we would regret.' Against this background, she also was reticent about expressing herself:

> I sort of keep things under my belt and you don't see ... the whole of me, that's just me ... There's a certain reserve within me that will not speak out about my innermost feelings. So when it comes to the troubles, I'll not speak out about my innermost feelings and certainly not to those who would oppose me.

Political Priorities

When a society is immersed in the middle of a volatile sectarian situation, the question of women's empowerment frequently is seen as a non-priority. What life is like for women, what their concerns may be, their own personal development or public involvement, are very much secondary concerns to what is viewed as the so-called 'real' issue, namely resolving the constitutional matter as to which political jurisdiction Northern Ireland belongs: the United Kingdom or the Republic of Ireland.[8] To counteract this marginalization of women, the Northern

---

[8] The 1998 Belfast Agreement provided a democratic framework to resolve this matter. Any change in Northern Ireland's constitutional status is now dependent upon a

Ireland Women's Coalition (NIWC), a non-sectarian, broad-based coalition of women of all political hues and religions, made up of academics, trade union activists, and voluntary sector and community workers, emerged. It was formed just six weeks prior to the May 1996 elections for the Northern Ireland Forum for Political Dialogue, to ensure that women's voices would be included in the political process. Winning two seats on the Forum enabled the NIWC to participate in the multi-party talks that began in June 1996 and which culminated in the 1998 Belfast Agreement. While addressing all the issues inherent in the peace process, it was the presence of the NIWC that ensured that women's rights were stipulated in that Agreement.[9]

In practice, seeing women's status and participation as secondary to other concerns not only postpones, belittles, or refuses to acknowledge women's reality. It also suggests that issues of gender are irrelevant to the national question. In doing this, it overlooks the interlocking nature of oppressions that may be at work in a society, including patriarchal agendas evident in sectarianism. A woman who had been terrifyingly intimidated by paramilitaries had been told that this intimidation was directly linked to the content of her work with women in community education. She was working with women from the other side of the community division to her own and they

> ... were beginning to do a lot more studying around ... this whole thing that they can't say no within a marriage – sex and things like that. And the fact that they aren't just here to have children and there's other alternatives and other ways of looking at things and thinking about things. And marriage being a partnership rather than a dominant partner. And that whole query about self-assertiveness within women ... I found that quite funny because I knew it was very strong in [my] faith, you know, the dominant male thing, but that was my first real experience of it being very, very strong within [their] faith.

As a result, 'the men weren't just having it all their own way, you know. And some of them weren't particularly liking this.'

This is not only a story about sectarian oppression. It is also the story of men intimidating one woman in order to maintain dominance over other women. Yet it is not two distinct stories, but a tale of two injustices woven together into an oppressive whole. Women's empowerment is not a separate or neutral matter in a conflicted society.

---

majority vote of the people of Northern Ireland and not solely a decision for the British or Irish governments.

[9] Kate Fearon, *Women's Work: The Story of the Northern Ireland Women's Coalition* (Belfast, 1999), pp. 106–7. The NIWC formally ended in 2006.

Faith and Empowerment

'I suppose really when it comes down to it we've had to trust the Lord a lot, lot more in this situation than what we would have to do in many's another situation.' These words of a Presbyterian woman are an expression of trust in God in a context of conflict in which personal vulnerability is exposed. A Catholic woman spoke of 'a tremendous level of dependence on God because you had to sort of say, well I'm going to have to go out and just get on with this ... recognize the fear is there and try to work with it.'

It is not that trusting God for these women is simply an acknowledgement of their own powerlessness and, hence, a sense of their own empowerment would make their faith redundant. Dependence upon God is assumed in the understanding of God as loving creator from whom humanity receives the possibility of existence and well-being. Situations that expose human vulnerabilities bring this aspect of the relationship to God into sharper focus. Faith is a complex interweaving of life experience, personal commitment, belief and practice, and involvement with a community of believers. The trauma of life in a violent, divided society (as with other life experiences and situations) subjects faith to critical questioning. Speaking of the sectarian murder of her friends, an Anglican woman explained, 'I sort of thought, well God why didn't you stop them, but again I sort of feel that God allows us to do our own thing. I find that a bit hard to accept at times ... I think why doesn't he interfere and get involved? So ... the troubles have made me question an awful lot.'

A Catholic woman reflected on her personal experience of the trauma of her family being caught up in a bomb explosion: 'I don't believe that God would want anybody to be taken in a bomb, but I think God can change a bad situation and bring good out of it. That's different to saying it's God's will ... I don't think half of the things that are said to be God's will are God's will.'

Trusting in God for each of the above four women is a matter of personal faith and integrity. It does not preclude active involvement in facing the community division in Northern Ireland. Each of these women is engaged in addressing sectarianism in their respective situations. However, for other women, trust in God, when combined with a lack of personal or communal agency, finds expression in a dependence on God's actions to the exclusion of their own. 'A lot of people say, where is God in the midst of all this? And I think you can't help asking that sometimes,' said a woman in her sixties. 'My faith tells me that he is there and he's in control, but it's just very difficult to understand sometimes why it's all been let happen.' A Methodist woman echoes a similar thought, 'The troubles don't bother me because I have the theory that God is working through them. I don't mean that I'm not sad when there's a tragedy. I feel very much for people ... who suffer. But I've accepted that God is working.'

In contrast, for a Presbyterian woman, Christian faith implicated her in her social surroundings:

> I suppose living here if the troubles haven't had an effect on our Christian faith – I suppose I should talk about myself – if the troubles hadn't had an effect on *my* Christian faith, I would feel it would say something about my faith, you know. Because we can't live in and around violence and hatred ... without taking account of it ... we can't just say well that's just ten percent of the population and that's nothing to do with us.

An Anglican woman put it succinctly, '[If] the gospel isn't relating to Northern Ireland then what are we at here?' A Catholic woman explained that for her this meant

> ... that I was going to try do something. So I became known ... as the liberal one that would go to all the Protestant services. And that I would try and cross the divide and all that ... try and break down the barriers and let each other see that the horns the other person has aren't real horns at all, you know, it's just because of what we're carrying from our background and it's so silly carrying all this ... I just had a calling to have a deep relationship with God and this all just came out of it, you know. And once you start having a relationship you have to start opening out to everybody.

Part of what makes the difference between those women whose trust in God goes with their own passivity and those whose trust in God compels them to get involved is their view of God. Engagement with the difficulties of life in a conflicted society reveals an understanding of God as caught up in the trauma of human reality rather than detached from it:

> I've had so much, because of working in [a hospital in Belfast] in the early seventies, terrible pain ... I can remember going on duty as a very junior student nurse to work in theatre or recovery ward ... and there had been some atrocity during the night and you'd have all these bags sitting at theatre door and these were all the limbs of people that had been blown up during the night. And ... going in and seeing all these people ... innocent victims ... people just going about doing their own thing and just caught up in things. And I ... felt an overwhelming sort of grief ... and felt that it was all so ... just wasted and feeling ... how much more must God feel that, you know, because we'd been given so much and yet we do this to each other.

It is one of the continuing creative tensions in Christian faith how to hold together the understanding of God as wholly other, as divine not human, the creator not the creature, as holy, with the belief that God has become known to humanity and experienced human reality, through the person of Jesus. This is the transcendent God and the incarnate Christ. Much of Christian theology has tended to emphasize God's transcendence, and has done so by defining it not simply as other than or different from but as opposite to human existence. This dualistic worldview that separates spirit and matter has kept God apart from the ordinary, earthly, everyday matters of life. This has had detrimental consequences for women in particular who, in dualistic thought, have been associated with that which is physical, natural, material and, hence, have been seen as corrupting influences and kept away from that which is seen as holy. In so far as dualism perpetuates an understanding of God and all that is associated with the divine as needing to be kept separate and above material realities, it provides no model or incentive for Christians to engage in the risky and difficult work of resolving community conflict.

The 'In-the-Middle' God

In contrast to the idea of God as removed and above human concerns, one woman, out of her own experience of conflict, understands God to be in the most difficult of places, that is, in the middle of conflict. Early on in her interview when asked how she would describe God, this was her response:

> God is able to be in the middle of situations of total opposites and not be crushed by them. The difference between God and us is that when we get stuck in the middle we get pulled apart and, for me, you have to choose sides because it's too painful to be on two sides at once. Whereas God can stay in the middle and survive. I suppose for me God is love but what it means is ... for me it became clearest when somebody I knew was very, very badly [injured in the troubles] ... and I was working with people who belonged to the organization who did that ... Or another [example] would be where you're working with ... two people in love who are trying to go in different directions, and ... there came a point where I realized that to stay sane I could only work on one side, I would choose one side. I think I chose generally ... the side without power. But that was in order to stay [sane] because to stay there in the middle was such a crucifying experience that there was no way you could live there, it was too painful. For me that was the difference that God can actually be there in the middle and fully feel and everything else, the different sides, and still stay there. To me that was the difference ... between God and us.

To listen to more of this last woman's story is to understand that actually she is staying 'in the middle' in a number of courageous ways as part of her daily life. The picture she and others provide is of God immersed in the pain of human conflict rather than removed from it. An Anglican woman spoke of the bigotry she had been subject to because she was married to a Catholic. Experiencing the vulnerability of her own situation, she reflected:

> I suppose the fact that Jesus was vulnerable, you know, I think it has made me understand more how much he did ... what the cost was ... I mean, nobody was more abused than he was, and he didn't have to do it. And I think experiencing

[vulnerability] a bit ourselves, I think I feel the pain of the divisions here very, very strongly and, again, I think that must be what God feels like.

Both of these women are developing the idea of incarnation, of 'God with us', in the context of the many manifestations of community conflict. An incarnational theology provides these women with a model of God being with them in their difficulties and in their endeavours to work in situations of conflict. Hence, empowerment is not a smooth continuum of increasing ease of being. It does not preclude suffering or anguish.

For Christian women, a theology that endorses the value of human existence and understands God as immanent as well as transcendent to the realities of Northern Ireland's particularity is part of a faith that energizes them to deal with conflict. Their involvement may be on any number of levels. Not all engagement is dramatic. Several women referred to their contributions in the diminutive. A Methodist woman living in a particularly volatile area, talking of her desire to cross the boundaries to Catholic people in that region, said, 'I feel a tremendous responsibility to pray about … the troubles. And … I would love to have a role in being a bridge and there is no big bridge open to me at the moment or obvious [one] – there are lots of little ones and I jump at every opportunity and have done since 1969.'

To do something rather than nothing was expressed by a Catholic woman in her sixties:

> God was asking me to do this, there was some drive in me asking me to do this. I wouldn't have been aware of it say in the beginning, but when I'm looking back on it I can see that God was choosing somebody to try and, you know, do their wee bit, not much but I mean that wee bit was given you to do.

While this woman describes her engagement as a 'wee bit', it was actually both courageous and at the time prophetic.[10]

An incarnational theology that views God as involved in all human affairs can provide people of faith with an impetus to be involved regardless of personal experience of violence or injustice. One woman spoke of coming from an environment where she had never experienced overt discrimination or sectarian violence and going to an interface area.[11] There she became

---

[10] I use the term 'prophetic' here in the sense of speaking and acting in ways that reveal the realities of a situation that others refuse or are unable to acknowledge.

[11] An interface area is a boundary between Nationalist and Unionist areas, especially where two highly segregated areas are closely situated. They are regularly sites of high tension and sometimes violence. In Belfast, many of these interfaces have physical barriers know as 'peacelines'.

... involved in the life of the people and saw things and heard things that really were very foreign to me, but I took on board and again I tried to make sense of for the people. And that was very often kind of going against my own middle-class background ... and my own image of church and my own concept of right and wrong ... I think that was one of the graces of God really that I held myself open to new things and tried not to be judgmental.

For some Christian women in Northern Ireland, from a variety of life experiences, their incentive or encouragement or reason that they should, at times, try and be in the middle between different and even hostile groups, is found in the understanding that that is where God is. This theology overturns a dualistic understanding of the relationship of God to human reality and provides women with a sense of personal agency, enabling them to actively involve themselves in whatever way they can in a divided society. The identity of 'God-with-us' and 'in-the-middle' of conflicting situations is both commitment and companionship and, hence, part of women's empowerment.

Chapter 8
Fat Chicks, Blue Books and Green Valleys: Identity, Women and Religion in Wales

Manon Ceridwen James

Introduction

In this chapter, I describe research into the extent and nature of the dominant religious tradition's influence on the identity of Welsh women. I am particularly interested in the role religion plays in forming positive, negative and ambivalent personal and social identities.

My interest arose through being aware of my own struggle with self-confidence and agency in the different spheres of work, community and family life. I could identify with Bennett Moore who wrote about her fight 'for self-confidence as a woman in the face of the kind of role, status and character for women projected by my father and my early Christian teaching, which made men the gateway to the real world'.[1] Through my work as a priest and theological college tutor, I found that this experience was widely shared, and agree with Bennett Moore that this is an urgent pastoral issue for the Church to address.

I considered self-esteem and agency as useful psychological concepts, but in the end decided to focus on identity as an all-encompassing term looking at how someone thinks and feels about themselves (personal identity) and the social groupings to which they belong (social identity). The research investigates how religion influences the social identity of Welsh women, and in turn the effect this has on their individual identity.

Identity

Beliefs about identity seem to lie at the heart of postmodern debates about the self. I have been influenced by thinkers such as Butler,[2] who views identity as something that is performed and socially constructed. In other words, we don't have an 'essential' core self, and neither do our social identifiers (such as being female or Welsh) mean that we have particular characteristics (such as being emotional, or being able to

---

[1] Zoë Bennett Moore, *Introducing Feminist Perspectives on Pastoral Theology* (London, 2002), p. 134.

[2] Judith Butler, *Gender Trouble*, 10th anniversary edn (New York, 1999).

sing). However, we do not generally get out of the bed in the morning and decide to assume a new personality and character; we act as if we have a continuous and stable identity, although we also act differently in different situations and our identities do change and develop. Therefore I hold both views of the self – that it is continuous as well as performed and contextual – in tension.

In terms of theological debates, again there seems to be a difference between, on one side, queer and feminist theologians such as Althaus-Reid[3] who recognize a performative and non-essentialized view, and, on the other, systematic theologians (even those influenced by postmodern thinking) such as Grenz,[4] who speak about identity as if there is an essential, unified self.

I have also been influenced by the argument that identity is formed or recognized when we realize our difference from an 'Other'.[5] This can be a negative and disempowering experience when one group is considered normative, as explored by postcolonial and critical theorists.[6] A Welsh woman's identity, it can be argued, is created in contrast to a powerful and normative Englishness and maleness.

According to the literature, Christianity (particularly nonconformist traditions) has had a significant effect on the Welsh mindset,[7] particularly women's.[8] It has been suggested that this influence has been detrimental, even oppressive. Beddoe claims that nonconformity has been historically 'the agency of the social control of women'[9] in promoting a chaste and repressed ideal of womanhood.

However, negative emotions about the self are hardly unique to women, or to people living in Wales. 'Impostorship' seems to be a common experience in education generally, whereby both students and teachers describe feelings of alienation, of not having a 'right' to be either educated or educators, an overwhelming emotion that cuts across racial, gender and class lines.[10] My

---

[3] Marcella Althaus-Reid, *Indecent Theology* (London, 2003).

[4] Stanley J. Grenz, 'The Social God and the Relational Self: Toward a Theology of the Imago Dei in a Post Modern Culture', in Richard Lints, Michael S. Horton and Mark R. Talbot (eds), *Personal Identity in Theological Perspective* (Grand Rapids, MI, 2006), pp. 70–92.

[5] Stuart Hall, 'Who needs Identity?', in Paul du Gay, Jessica Evans, and Peter Redman (eds), *Identity: a Reader* (London, 2002), pp. 15–29.

[6] For example, Edward Said, *Orientalism* (London, 2003), pp. 27, 332.

[7] See, for example, Merfyn R. Jones, 'Beyond Identity? The Reconstruction of the Welsh', *Journal of British Studies* 31/4 (1992): 338; Mervyn Phillips, *Wales: Nation and Region* (Llandysul, 1997), p. 3; Paul Chambers and Andrew Thompson, 'Coming to Terms with the Past: Religion and Identity in Wales', *Social Compass* 52/3 (2005): 337.

[8] Jane Aaron and Teresa Rees, 'Introduction', in Jane Aaron, Teresa Rees, Sandra Betts and Moira Vincentelli (eds), *Our Sisters' Land: The Changing Identities of Women in Wales* (Cardiff, 1994), p. 11; Deirdre Beddoe, *Out of the Shadows: a History of Women in Twentieth Century Wales* (Cardiff, 2000), p. 179.

[9] Beddoe, *Out of the Shadows*, p. 177.

[10] Stephen Brookfield, *The Skilful Teacher* (San Francisco, CA, 2006), pp. 76–83.

research explores how Welsh women negotiate their identities within a particular and challenging historical, sociological and religious context.

Blue Books and Green Valleys: Welsh Women in Historical Context

My research into the historical context suggests that these dominant and negative influences on women are recent, socially constructed and run counter to older traditions. Brown, Baker and Day comment that the pious respectable image of Welsh womanhood was 'invented during the nineteenth century'.[11] This is borne out in my own reading, particularly Welsh women's poetry. This tradition, stemming from as early as the fifteenth century, records the coexistence of erotic and devotional themes often in the same poems, which Gramich and Brennan call the 'bi-textuality' of the Welsh tradition.[12] The best example of this is one of the earliest poets, Gwerful Mechain, who wrote 'An Ode to the Vagina', and several similar poems. It could be argued that she was the first exponent of an Indecent Theology:

> *Trwsglwyn merch, drud annerch dro,/ Berth addwyn, Duw'n borth iddo.*
> [A girl's thick glade, it is full of love / Lovely bush, blessed be it by God above].[13]

This interconnection of sex and religion contradicts the nonconformist ideal of repressed respectability, and the celebratory religious view of sexuality could be attributed to the more positive medieval attitudes towards sex untouched by Victorian inhibition. However, writers such as Aaron also argue that an educational report, colloquially called the 'Blue Books', had a significant effect on Welsh women. Instead of only charting the poor educational provision in nineteenth-century Wales, the report also took the opportunity to highlight the apparent sexual immorality of Welsh women, based on interviews with Anglican clergy who used the inquiry to sow seeds of doubt regarding the respectability of the emerging popular nonconformist churches. This was 'proof' that Wales needed to be 'civilized', or rather Anglicized – that is, instilled with the values and language of the English middle class.[14] For example, the Vicar of Nefyn was highly critical of his female parishioners' morality, compared to that of English women, and

---

[11] Brian Brown, Sally Baker and Graham Day, 'Lives Beyond Suspicion: Gender and the Construction of Respectability in Mid-Twentieth Century Rural North Wales', *Sociologia Ruralis* 51/ 4 (2011): 371.
[12] Katie Gramich and Catherine Brennan, *Welsh Women's Poetry 1460–2001: An Anthology* (Dinas Powys, 2003), p. viii.
[13] Gwerful Mechain, 'To the vagina', in Gramich and Brennan, *Welsh Women's Poetry*, pp. 4–5.
[14] Aaron, *Sisters' Land*, pp. 185–6.

commented that 'in England farmers' daughters are respectable; in Wales they are in the constant habit of being courted in bed.'[15]

Therefore women in nineteenth-century Wales faced a dilemma in working out their identity. The easiest route was to adopt a genteel English definition of respectability. Alternatively, they could have accepted the report's descriptions of Welsh women as wild, uncontrollable and sexually immoral. A third option, considered more desirable for women who were proud of their nationality, was to create the new version of propriety that later emerged within nonconformity, that of sexual repression. As Aaron argues, none of the available options gave women a 'voice of their own' and their identity became subjugated to the greater good of saving the reputation of the new Free Churches.[16]

An iconic image of this control is seen in Richard Llewellyn's *How Green was My Valley*, where an unmarried woman is cast out of chapel for being pregnant, to the shouts of an elder that her body is the 'trap of the devil'.[17] Aaron argues that the dominant and virtuous male deacon 'hounding out' a sexually permissive woman is 'a characteristically Welsh image'.[18]

Stereotypes have a profound influence on us, even if they have little basis in actual experience. They can be a means of empowerment or disempowerment, stigmatization, as well as political threat.[19] They become influential in that we compare ourselves and others to them; they become part of our stories, jokes and our common discourse – our 'reality'. My research is concerned to find out how powerful these tropes still are, and whether these oppressive religious narratives still affect women today.

The Fieldwork

In order to investigate women's individual and social identity I decided to conduct semi-structured interviews with a strongly biographical element. Narrative researchers argue that this approach is particularly appropriate for investigating individual and social identity.[20] Biography forms an important part of identity,[21] and even if we question the idea of an unchanging, essentialized self, it is still

---

[15] Reports of the Commissioners of Inquiry into the State of Education in Wales 1847, The National Library of Wales <http://www.llgc.org.uk/index.php?id=thebluebooks> accessed 17 April 2009.

[16] Aaron, *Sisters' Land*, p. 188.

[17] Richard Llewellyn, *How Green Was My Valley* (London, 2001), pp. 104–5.

[18] Aaron, *Sisters' Land*, p. 184.

[19] Susan R Pitchford, 'Image Making Movements: Welsh Nationalism and Stereotype Transformation', *Sociological Perspectives* 44/1 (2001): 45–65.

[20] Catherine Kohler Riessman, *Narrative Analysis* (Newbury Park, CA, 1993), p. 5.

[21] Anthony Giddens, *Modernity and Self-Identity: Self and Society in the Late Modern Age* (Cambridge, 1991), p. 55.

possible and productive to speak of a 'narrative identity' as something that is relatively stable and coherent.[22] Moreover, narratives are not just individual and personal: stories also construct cultural identities by producing stereotypes and discourses that create boundaries and connect groups of people together.[23]

I asked women first of all to tell me their life story, and how, if at all, religion had influenced it. I then followed up with questions about being Welsh and female, and their perceptions of stereotypes of Welsh women, and the role of religion in creating them. Following Slee,[24] I believe that my own reflectiveness and attention to issues of power is vital, especially given that this is 'insider research'. I have attempted to be as transparent as possible about my commitments, assumptions and beliefs and also to reflect on and be critical of my practice as I interview. Far from being a detached observer, I have taken the decision early on to engage fully with the conversations as a way both to elicit data and be better able to analyse the data in context.[25] This is why reflectiveness and transparency on my part is vital, along with a concern to empower the research participants and to hear their voices.

Findings

In many participants, there seems to be a link between nonconformity and Welsh identity, and conversely a sense of alienation for those who are not 'chapel'. Bethan[26] described the bullying she experienced at school for being a Catholic: other children would gesture at her, pretending their hands were guns, mouthing that she was a member of the IRA. She is now attending the Presbyterian chapel with her children, as this is more of a 'traditional Welsh' thing to do. Jessie, in a very lively interview, was very harsh about what she considered to be the moral and political power of the Welsh-speaking ruling class, whom she called the 'Plaid Cymru Methodists', who nevertheless held a Thatcherite Tory 'I'm alright Jack' approach to life. Stefania, identifying as dual heritage Italian and Welsh, described her feelings of alienation springing from religion, when she moved to Italy as a teenager:

---

[22] Jane Elliott, *Using Narrative in Social Research: Qualitative and Quantitative Approaches* (London, 2005), p. 1.

[23] Donileen Loseke, 'The Study of Identity as Cultural, Institutional, Organizational, and Personal Narratives: Theoretical and Empirical Integrations', *The Sociological Quarterly*, 48 (2007): 661, and Riessman, *Narrative Analysis*, p. 5.

[24] Nicola Slee, *Women's Faith Development: Patterns and Processes* (Aldershot, 2004).

[25] As argued by Elliott G. Mishler, *Research Interviewing: Context and Narrative* (Cambridge, MA, 1986).

[26] All the names are pseudonyms and participants have given permission to quote from the interviews.

> I was just a nanny so I didn't fit in that way so the only person who would talk to me was another Italian and I just felt even though I'm in a Protestant church … I don't know any of the songs, I couldn't do the Lord's Prayer in English, because I was used to doing it in Welsh and I just went away feeling quite empty.

There is a link between some participants' experience of faith and religion and its effect on their agency and self-esteem, though there is also evidence of ambivalence. Elinor described how the condemnatory Christianity she experienced as a young person led her to feel worthless and to practise self harming. After a few years of marriage, she realized she wanted a divorce, but felt huge pressure not to do so because of the influence of 'chapel culture'. Ironically, it was her newfound Christian faith in middle age which led her to leave her unhappy marriage.

Welsh women also experience misogyny within church life. Stacey referred to sexist comments made by her previous church leader, joking that he wanted his female members to be pretty, in order to attract newcomers:

> He was on about this mini bus which goes around town picking up all the women to go to a nightclub and it says on the mini bus 'no fat ugly chicks allowed'. And he said from the pulpit, 'I want this church to be like the minibus … I don't want any fat ugly chicks in this church.'

Whilst this is an instance of humour used at women's expense, I also detected in her interview particularly, and in others, that humour seemed to play the part of a dissenting discourse,[27] offering a strategy to deal with oppressive practices or pressures.

The pastoral care that women have received seems to have been crucial in enabling them to grow in confidence and self-belief. Encouragement from her minister father enabled Marged to explore different Christian churches and groups and this broad experience helped her openly to challenge the inherent sexism of her denomination, where women have to 'stay behind' to organize the refreshments and have very little role in the public life of the Church, despite official equality. Mari describes how her minister (at the time) preached a sermon supporting her as a young single mother raising a mixed-race child. She attributes the fact that the minister insisted on a public rather than a private baptism as a contributory factor leading to her growing into the strong faith that she has today. A private baptism, she believes, would have turned her against the Church and God for ever. Finally, Anwen explored with me the struggle of wanting to live honestly and openly as a gay woman in a rural community, and although it would be difficult to do so at the moment given the inherent conservatism of her area, she has had unstinting support from some (Christian) family members as well as her local minister. However, homosexuality is a long way from being accepted as something that

---

[27] Hayden Teo and Donella Caspersz, 'Dissenting Discourse: Exploring Alternatives to the Whistleblowing/Silence Dichotomy', *Journal of Business Ethics* 104 (2011): 237–49.

affects Welsh people; it is generally considered to be alien and 'English'. Anwen, in speaking about the discussions about civil partnerships in her Free Church denomination, said:

> The impression you get from the denominational newspaper is that we are talking about an 'us and them'. It's OK for these gay people, probably English people, living in a city, it's OK for them to have their civil partnerships but they need to leave us alone, and not come to our chapels. Why would they want to come? [*laughs*]. So, yes, it was a good time, a time to speak more about it, but the best thing was being able to come out to my local minister who is *so* supportive.

It would seem, then, that religion, particularly nonconformist Christianity, is still thought of as a contributor to a Welsh identity, and according to the data so far, that this is an ambivalent contribution both to social and individual identity, and to women's lives both politically and personally.

Conclusion

In this chapter, I have described some interim findings within a longer project researching the extent, nature and influence of religion on women's identity in Wales. I have found that historically there has been a significant variety in the expectations placed on women by religion, especially in terms of sexual morality, as well as general teaching about behaviour.

Attempts by nonconformist leaders to transform the image of Welsh women, following on from the criticisms of their immorality in the 'Blue Books' report, seem to have been highly effective. My participants reported that the social pressures to behave respectably are still immense – what one referred to as 'what would Mrs Jones down the road say?' The hypocrisy involved in maintaining a respectable persona was referred to by several participants – something which non-Christians within my sample were highly critical of and found deeply unattractive. However, there are resources within Welsh women's writings (such as the poetry of Gwerful Mechain) for a more integrated spirituality which is not afraid of bodily expression and challenges Victorian sexual repression.

There is also evidence that some women in Wales are growing in confidence to utilize what is life-giving within the Christian tradition, whilst discarding what restricts and diminishes growth and flourishing. The role of humour is also important for them, and is one of the strategies they use to challenge and live with oppressive practices. Good quality and supportive one-to-one pastoral care has also been seen to be vital for individual emotional and spiritual well-being. This needs to be replicated and reinforced within the churches at an institutional level if women are to fulfil their potential in their private and public lives.

Chapter 9
Searching for Sisters: The Influence of Biblical Role Models on Young Women from Mainstream and Charismatic Evangelical Traditions

Ruth Perrin

Introduction

Much has been written of the relational character of women's faith. In her research, Nicola Slee identifies a strong sense of relationality in women's faith development.[1] Other research suggests that both the sharing of story and the part played by fore-sisters are significant in nurturing women's faith journeys.[2] Elizabeth Schüssler Fiorenza's 'hermeneutic of remembrance' also illustrates this.[3] Studies in sociology and psychology support these findings; many women testify to inspirational role models who might intuitively understand them, particularly those who feel marginalized such as women in male-dominated professions.[4] Developmental models further suggest this need for community and identification is particularly significant for young adults.[5] At this exciting and complicated time,

---

[1] Nicola Slee, *Women's Faith Development: Patterns and Processes* (Aldershot, 2004), p. 24.

[2] Leonora Tubbs Tisdale, 'Women's Ways of Communicating', in Jane Dempsey Douglass and James F. Kay (eds), *Women, Gender and Christian Community* (Louisville, KY, 1997), pp. 104–14; Elizabeth Schüssler Fiorenza, *Bread not Stone* (Edinburgh, 1984), p. 19.

[3] Elizabeth Schüssler Fiorenza (ed.), *Searching the Scriptures* (New York, 1993), vol. 1, p. 339.

[4] Cecilia L. Ridgeway and Lynn Smith-Lovin, 'The Gender System and Interaction', *Annual Review of Sociology* 25 (1999): 210; Penelope Lockwood, 'Someone like Me can be Successful', *Psychology of Women Quarterly* 30/1 (September 2006): 43.

[5] Sharon Parks, *The Critical Years: The Young Adult Search for a Faith to Live By* (San Francisco, CA, 1986), pp. 87–9.

young women will often look for examples of those who have walked a similar path before them as they explore their identity, potential and faith.[6]

Despite the patriarchal and individualistic tendencies it has embraced, the Judaeo-Christian tradition is rooted in relationality and role modelling. Examples include the Gospel writers' narratives of Jesus both teaching and living this way of life,[7] and the 'body of Christ' metaphor expounded most clearly in 1 Corinthians 12 exhorting believers to interrelatedness, mutual encouragement and care.

Method

After a decade of ministry with young evangelical adults, I undertook a project to explore young women's attitudes towards role models in their faith, how they used the Bible in this quest and how far their churches facilitated their learning.[8]

The British evangelical tradition is diverse in many ways, not least in its attitude towards women's leadership. Since the 1980s a growing 'reformed' tradition, described as 'complementarian', has argued that men and women have complementary roles which exclude women from leadership.[9] Alternatively, many charismatic and mainstream (or open) evangelicals define themselves as 'egalitarian', allowing (although not always actively encouraging) women's leadership.[10] This project focused on these egalitarian groupings, although many evangelicals are trans-denominational, attending a wide range of churches, conferences and para-church groups and thus are likely to have been influenced by a spectrum of traditions.[11]

---

[6] Roberta Downing differentiates between mentors who are personally known and role models who inspire at a distance; thus biblical characters can be effective role models: Roberta A. Downing and Faye J. Crosby, 'The Perceived Importance of Developmental Relationships on Women Undergraduates' Pursuit of Science', *Psychology of Women Quarterly* 29 (2005): 420.

[7] For example, Luke 8:1–3 and John 15:12–15.

[8] Ruth H. Perrin, 'How Might the Evangelical Church use Neglected, Female, Biblical Role Models as a method of Discipleship and Empowerment amongst Young Women?' (unpublished MA dissertation, University of Durham, 2007).

[9] John Piper and Wayne Grudem (eds), *Rediscovering Biblical Manhood and Womanhood: A Response to Evangelical Feminism* (Wheaton, IL, 1991); Andreas J. Kostenberger with David Jones, *God, Marriage and Family: Rebuilding the Biblical Foundation*, 2nd edn (Wheaton, Ill, 2010).

[10] Ronald W. Pierce and Rebecca M. Groothuis (eds), *Discovering Biblical Equality: Complementarity without Hierarchy* (Downers Grove, IL, 2004); Loren Cunningham and David Joel Hamilton with Janice Rogers, *Why not women? A Biblical Study of Women in Missions, Ministry, and Leadership* (Seattle, WA, 2000); Rebecca M. Groothuis, *Good News for Women: A Biblical Picture of Gender Equality* (Grand Rapids, MI, 1997).

[11] David Bebbington, 'Evangelical trends, 1959–2009', *Anvil* 26/2 (2009): 93–101.

The research employed mixed methods. First, I used questionnaires to gather quantitative data, using a Likert-scale format as well as open-ended questions from 50 women aged 18–30 in order to form a broad picture of their opinions. They came from a variety of mainstream and charismatic evangelical churches in the north of England and were primarily white British women with tertiary education, recruited through advertisements in their congregations. This was followed by six qualitative focus groups of between seven and ten women, holding semi-structured discussions on specific biblical narratives containing female characters.

Findings

Role Model Preferences

Even acknowledging the demographic limitations of this project, the questionnaires showed striking unanimity. Nine out of ten participants agreed that the Bible is important for faith development and that biblical figures can be effective role models for today.[12] All of them believed that role models played an important part in faith development, and six out of ten believed that these needed to be the same gender as the subject.

When asked to identify role models in their own faith journey, six out of ten individuals named were women, most significantly female peers and older women in their church communities. Beyond fathers and church leaders,[13] young women did not generally look to men as role models but learnt from other women, many stating that they actively sought older women for faith-nurturing relationships.

However, when asked to identify biblical role models other than Jesus, they reversed these preferences. Thirty-three biblical characters were cited, but only eleven were female. Of those only Esther, Ruth and Mary of Bethany received more than five nominations. Moses, David and Peter were common choices, but nearly half cited Paul. Despite the fact that motivation for their choices was not fully explored, this is a striking reversal of their earlier stated preference. It raises the question of why they predominantly selected male biblical characters, and why so decisively Paul?

---

[12] A role model was defined as an individual you aspire to be like in some way.
[13] In 2010, 82 per cent of leaders in evangelical churches were men. Evangelical Alliance, *Ministers and Church Leaders* (4 May 2012) <http://eauk.org/church/research-and-statistics/ministers-and-church-leaders.cfm> accessed 26 January 2013.

Bible Readers or Bible Admirers?

Despite their conviction about the significance of the Bible, these women appeared to fit the description of 'devoted Bible admirers but not daily Bible readers'.[14] Seven out of ten described their biblical knowledge as coming from being taught rather than personal reading, and a quarter could name fewer than twelve female characters. Noteworthy numbers made negative comments about their biblical knowledge. Hannah[15] stated: 'These passages in Luke are kind of the passages I would glance over. I'd usually not really bother to actually notice that there are women. It's been really good to look at them properly because I don't do that myself, I'm too lazy.'

This was typical of the self-criticism many voiced. They believed in the value of the Bible, its usefulness in life and faith, but many did not engage with it consistently at a personal level. What the (usually male) pastor told them was the sum of what they knew, hence, when selecting role models, they chose individuals they knew most about, reflecting the pastor's choice, which were generally dominant male biblical characters, most often Paul. Of course, there are things to be learnt by women from the faith of such men, but often they do not embody the points of close identification proposed by Bandura in his social learning theory, or the relevance young women might be seeking in role models.[16]

Empathy and Identification

A number of the participants explicitly expressed being drawn to female characters. Discussing 1 Samuel 25 in a focus group, Harriet stated:

> I think Abigail stands out to me from that passage, and obviously I can relate to her more cos she's a woman but – I don't know – the way she deals with situations and the way that she's introduced to the story at the start ... automatically makes me think: 'Oh, here's an interesting woman, what can I learn from her – how has she dealt with situations?' Whenever there are women in the Bible, and there are obviously a lot fewer, I always seem to be automatically drawn to them a lot or I see how they react in different situations.

---

[14] Donald S. Whitney, 'Teaching Scripture Intake', in Kenneth O. Gangel and James C. Wilhoit (eds), *The Christian Educator's Handbook on Spiritual Formation* (Grand Rapids, MI, 1994), p. 164.

[15] All names have been changed.

[16] Bandura argues that an individual with points of commonality is more likely to influence behaviour modification than someone distinctly 'other', thus the more points of identification, the stronger their influence as a role model: Albert Bandura, *Social Learning Theory* (Englewood Cliffs, NJ, 1977), p. 134.

There was a strong sense from the discussions that the women were attracted to and identified with positive female characters, interpreting the narrative with a hermeneutic of empathy, defending the women's actions, as well as exploring what they could learn. They expressed this as obvious. Rather than class, race, or experience, in these cases gender was an instinctive point of identification, both inspiring admiration and providing permission for emulation. Discussing Abigail, Katherine was struck by

> ... the mediator thing, that's a very important role of women and I think it's a role that you play usually in your family first of all and then, I guess it depends what job you do ... but in families there's often a lot of angst and I think a woman can often break that ... so the men would find it hard, but it's easier for a woman to be humble ... but to be wise in the words that you say and the way that you act.

Katherine's desire to resolve conflict with wise dignity had been encouraged by Abigail's behaviour. She had not accepted these attributes blindly; the group discussed at length whether Abigail was manipulative and opportunistic, or shrewd, courageous and diplomatic, concluding a positive interpretation. They accepted the text as literal, but considered historical and cultural settings as well as wider biblical material. Their conclusion was that Abigail was someone to emulate in her initiative and social rule breaking. Suzie was struck by

> ... the whole thing about challenging men actually ... I work with a lot of vicars and actually there are times when ... I don't really like challenging people actually. I know I've been in meetings where someone's said stuff and I've thought what *are* you on about? You know, like – and then times it's like, not wise to challenge that or, you know, does something need to be said? That's quite challenging – to do it the right way. [original emphasis]

Abigail's actions clearly inspired them with confidence. Not only were qualities like courage and initiative biblically endorsed, but they perceived an expectation that women would demonstrate them. Though many would be hesitant to describe themselves as feminists, they were engaging with issues of female empowerment within an evangelical framework and expanding their sense of self from these biblical examples.[17]

---

[17] Groothuis explores the challenges facing evangelical women in embracing the label 'feminist'. Rebecca M. Groothuis, *Women Caught in the Conflict; The Culture War between Traditionalism and Feminism* (Grand Rapids, MI, 1994).

Negative or Negligible?

As well as frustration at their own biblical knowledge, some of the women also expressed frustration with the Bible and particularly the lack of inspiration they received in church. Although there was no suggestion of rejecting the text, there was recognition of the scarcity of positive female characters. Many did recognize that considerable numbers of women were relatively minor in the text, but rather than reject the Bible as irrevocably patriarchal, they wanted to explore it in more detail, believing it must contain useful information. The majority expressed a desire to hear more teaching in their churches about female biblical characters and how to make the most of limited textual information. Over half also made unsolicited comments about the negative portrayal of female characters in sermons, or their being of little interest beyond specialist women's conferences.

During the focus groups, participants appeared encouraged to find women to look up to as positive role models. Typical statements included these:

> I'm inspired by Joanna because she was in quite a high position and she gave all that up, all the prestige to follow Jesus. That challenged me. (Hannah)

> I think I'm the same. Obviously it is probably the fact that she's a woman – which partly makes it easier to empathize – but also I want women in the Bible to be, like, good ... because there's not that many of them, so, like – there were some really good women in the Bible! (Ellie)

Almost all had often heard male biblical characters taught as role models but hardly any had received regular teaching on female ones. Beth commented: 'I think I probably would have said before, that there are quite a lot of women in the Bible, but thinking about it now I think I know them from Sunday school stories.' Once she had reached adulthood Beth had heard little more about women's faith. The adult evangelical world was, for her, one dominated by narratives of male relationships with God. Others commented:

> I think I desperately try to grasp onto anything [about women] because ... there is so little help, you just try really hard to get points out, you try to – maybe learn from things they do wrong. (Katherine)

> Yeah – cos I was really shocked when you got us to do that list of how many women in the Bible. There were loads actually, but you don't really hear them preached on I guess. (Sarah)

The desire to know their biblical fore-sisters was evident, but they struggled to find the kinds of role models they needed. It was evident to them that the teaching they were receiving was neglecting the positive role of women's faith, several postulating that their church assumed men could not learn from female characters. Emma summed up this frustration:

> I really think we need more teaching on women in the Bible in church and that's what I really want. I want to understand it. I mean we get stuff out of guys in the Bible, because it's all we hear – we *have* to, but it's ridiculous to think 'let's leave women out because men don't get stuff out of it', how could men *not* get stuff out of it? Yeah – it's just being lazy! [original emphasis]

Passionate or Passive?

These women took biblical teaching seriously, expecting it to influence their faith and lifestyle, and were willing to submit to the authority they understood to be demonstrated in the text, but they were also aware that they did not know the whole picture. They were conscious of differing interpretations and although they perceived themselves as equal to men, they were unsure which readings were legitimate for them to adopt. Given that most had attended more than one denomination, there was a clear sense of uncertainty about which theological perspectives to embrace. Developmentally, this is typical of young adults who are on a journey to own their beliefs, trying to decide which voices to accept and which to reject.[18] However, despite their education and often professional success, these women appeared to be somewhat passive about, even oblivious to, the absence of their fore-sisters.[19] They were 'making do' with what they were offered rather than addressing the issue or proactively engaging with the Bible. When prompted and given a voice, they were clearly hungry for empowering female biblical role models and wanted help to examine their stories in more depth. Fiona stated:

> I guess we look at, like, Christian women, and I think so many girls are really struggling to know how to be a woman of God. What does that mean? Yeah, you think there are women who are tagging along behind the disciples and doing the cooking and if that's all you know about them then that's all you've got to look at. That's not really a lot of help. It's really important to look at them and what do they *really* do and what does God *really* say?' [original emphasis]

---

[18] Liebert, building on the work of James Fowler, explores the transition of women's faith from 'Conformist to external rules' to 'Conscientious with self-evaluated standards': Elizabeth Liebert, 'Seasons and Stages,' in Jeanne Stevenson-Moessner (ed.), *In Her Own Time: Women and Developmental Issues in Pastoral Care* (Minneapolis, MN, 2000), p. 28.

[19] Glick and colleagues suggest that many women will tolerate discrimination if it appears protective or benevolent towards them: Peter Glick et al., 'Beyond Prejudice as Simple Antipathy: Hostile and Benevolent Sexism across Cultures', *Journal of Personality and Social Psychology* 79/5 (2000): 763–85.

Fiona believed the Bible contains 'what God says'. She acknowledged multiple readings but believed that there is a definitive 'real' answer in the narrative which is affirming of women. However, although she was curious about other interpretations, she had little confidence that she could interpret the plethora of theological readings herself.

Standing Together

Having explored the place of narratives of women in their faith journeys, I found that not only did participants express preference for female role models and inspiring biblical fore-sisters, they also expressed enthusiasm for the research process itself. Many commented that taking part had made them reflect on their habits and ideas, and despite the familiarity of small group Bible studies, this process of intentional examination and discussion was an unfamiliar but positive experience. Indeed, there had been a high level of openness, encouragement and a great deal of laughter confirming other research into female learning environments.[20] Katie commented:

> A really big thing for me is not actually what we've been studying but the fact that we've got together to do it. And that really helps ... I think there's just something really strong about coming together with other girls. Men will try and empathize, but they can't empathize ... so I think there's just something – I've really enjoyed coming together with other girls, I thrive on female company – I think studying the Bible that way really helps.

A Concluding Challenge

In the women's discussion, there was little hostility towards the Bible or the Church, indeed there was considerable commitment towards both. There was however, frustration and a desire for greater inclusiveness and an interest in exploring wider biblical readings to inform their identity and faith. Many would unknowingly fit the description of biblical feminism, holding a conservative moral stance and a pro-women position,[21] embracing the empowering message of the Christian Gospel and seeking to reinterpret or rehabilitate oppressive biblical texts.[22] Part of that journey is discovering those who model these values and illustrate what an empowered faith can look like. Evangelical churches merely paying lip service to

---

[20] Tisdale, 'Women's Ways', pp. 104–14; Ana M. Martinez Aleman, 'Understanding and Investigating Female Friendship's Educative Value', *Journal of Higher Education* 68/2 (1997): 142–4.

[21] Elaine Storkey, *What's Right with Feminism?* (London, 1985), p. 137.

[22] See Phyllis Trible, 'Biblical Tradition and Interpretation', in A. Loades (ed.), *Feminist Theology: A Reader* (London, 1990), p. 25.

the notion of egalitarianism will not help these young women. Such churches must address proactively the issue of biblical teaching and the models they are providing and be intentional about mentoring and developing the faith and abilities of young women, as well as encouraging the whole Church to rediscover and be inspired by their biblical fore-sisters, who received God's affirmation for their faith and courage.[23]

---

[23] Ruth Perrin, *Inspiring Women: Discovering Biblical Role Models* (Cambridge, 2009).

Chapter 10
The Use of Patriarchal Language in the Church of God of Prophecy: A Case Study

Deseta Davis

Introduction

As a female member of the Church of God of Prophecy (CoGoP) for some forty years, I have listened to numerous sermons of varying lengths and on many subjects. I have been taught and accepted that the word 'man' means human beings of both genders and the word 'brethren' means the whole Church. I also believed and embraced the teaching that God (and the Godhead) could only be understood in the male vernacular. However, I have become increasingly aware that a great many of the choruses and hymns sung in CoGoP are very androcentric. As I have listened to preachers, I have felt a growing sense of unease and concern that from the pulpit, women do not appear to be valued in the same way as men. The language used throughout services, but especially in sermons, seemingly views women – if they are included at all – as less than men both in biblical times and today's society. Moreover, there are very few female preachers and these women also seem to preach in similar manner to the men, showing little consciousness of gender within their sermons.

With these experiences in mind, I decided to research the content of sermons preached within one local branch of CoGoP, with a focus on gender assumptions and awareness. The aim was to discover whether the language used was inclusive of women, with a view to exploring whether the Church helps to liberate and empower women or oppress them. In this chapter, I will sketch out something of the background context of my tradition before going on to summarize the methods and findings of my research, ending with reflections on the significance of the research.

The Church of God of Prophecy is a Pentecostal church which has been established internationally since 1903, with its main headquarters in Tennessee, in the US. Although very different in other countries, the Church in Britain, established since 1952, is a Black Led/Majority church. Women within CoGoP can become ordained ministers, lead churches and undertake all manner of ordinances such as baptisms and communion. They have also become pastors and are preachers in their own right, which has been the accepted practice of the church for many years. However, in the UK, only 30 per cent of the pastors are women.[1]

---

[1] Church of God of Prophecy, *Business Acts Directory 2008–2009* (Birmingham, 2008), pp. 22–47.

Sermons within Black Majority Churches are at the core of worship.[2] Within CoGoP, services are organized around the sermon. The theme or topic of the sermon is first given, then the service is planned accordingly. Everything is geared towards the sermon which is regarded as the zenith of the service.[3] Although much shorter in length than in the past, sermons typically average 30–45 minutes. The congregation does not sit passively whilst the sermon is preached, but actively participates in a 'call and response' style.

The language used in preaching and worship within CoGoP is largely androcentric in nature. The use of the King James Version of the Bible has helped to keep preachers tied to an old style of speaking that is very patriarchal. The worship songs and hymns, including modern ones, also mainly use exclusively male language, which results in the whole worship service being male focused.

Gendered Language in Church

Marjorie Procter-Smith maintains that language is more than mere words; it embodies living, feelings and experience.[4] Genesis proclaims that God spoke and the world came into being (Genesis 1:3ff). Barbara Temple argues that language is not only heard in the head, it is also felt in the heart and this is the level where the struggle goes on and faith can be either built up or destroyed.[5] Preaching is a tool used to encourage change and transformation and so the language used needs to be chosen carefully if it is not to have the opposite effect.

Language can either include or exclude people, depending on how it is used. In the hand of the powerful, language can be used to oppress, liberate, or empower. It can also be used to justify dominance, making it seem normal and legitimate to devalue, dehumanize and ignore those who are dominated.[6] Gender-exclusive language can therefore enable women to become passive, accept their imposed status and believe without question.

A survey undertaken in the US by Baptist Pastor Jann Aldredge Clanton suggests that the exclusive use of masculine God-language contributes to the lack

---

[2] Cheryl Townsend Gilkes, 'Some Mother's Son and Some Father's Daughter: Gender and Biblical Language in Afro-Christian Worship Tradition,' in Clarissa W. Atkinson, Constance H. Buchanan and Margaret R. Miles (eds), *Shaping New Vision: Gender and Values in American Culture* (Ann Arbor, MI, 1987), p. 87.

[3] E.K. Bailey and Warren W. Wiersbe, *Preaching in Black and White: What we can learn from each other* (Grand Rapids. MI, 2003), p. 50.

[4] Marjorie Procter-Smith, *In Her Own Rite: Constructing Feminist Liturgical Tradition* (Nashville, TN, 1990), p. 60.

[5] Barbara Temple, *Exclusive Language: A Hindrance to Evangelism Among Women* (Nottingham, 1988), p. 10.

[6] Brian Wren, *What Language Shall I Borrow? God-Talk in Worship: A Male Response to Feminist Theology* (London, 1989), p. 81.

of self-worth in women. The women in her study, whose God was masculine, tended to demonstrate feelings of inferiority, expressing guilt and seeing others as stronger and more worthy than themselves. These exclusive masculine images of God were seen as damaging to men as well as women: 'women found reinforcement for passivity whereas men found support for pride and control.'[7] Barbara Temple fittingly concludes that the sole use of male language 'consciously or subconsciously makes the assumption that men are more representative of the human race than women and thus puts women in a subordinate role rather than that of people of equal worth and value'.[8] When women listen to sermons, they need to be able to recognize themselves and their experiences. This helps them to identify with God, makes them feel of worth and empowers them for the good of themselves and that of the community.

The Research Design

My research was informed by feminist and womanist theological principles, which I brought into dialogue with the selected sermons and used as a framework for analysis and critiquing the sermons.

Feminists have actively fought for women's equality and rights, and have formed the feminist movement for the advancement and emancipation of women.[9] Feminism draws on women's experience and praxis, which are used in critiquing the structures of patriarchy.[10] Lisa Isherwood and Dorothea McEwan believe that women are not interested in reforming bad structures, but in 'transforming structures', which enable them to become equal partners with men.[11] The use of language has played a major role in feminism in helping women to claim their position in a patriarchal world. However, it is deemed by some Black women that feminism does not cater for their experiences and as a response to this perceived lack, womanism was born. Womanist theology draws extensively on Black women's experience, culture and religion, especially as found in the narratives of their lives. Womanist understanding of oppression includes class, race and gender

---

[7] Jann Aldredge Clanton, *In Whose Image? God and Gender* (London, 1991), pp. 75, 81.

[8] Temple, *Exclusive Language*, p. 13.

[9] Pamela Dickey Young, 'Experience', in Lisa Isherwood and Dorothea McEwan (eds), *An A–Z of Feminist Theology* (Sheffield, 1996), p. 61.

[10] Linda Hogan, *From Women's Experience to Feminist Theology* (Sheffield, 1995), p. 17.

[11] Lisa Isherwood and Dorothea McEwan, *Introducing Feminist Theology* (Sheffield, 1993), p. 62.

of all marginalized persons, both women and men, who have been victims of patriarchal dominance.[12]

Using these principles, I analysed and compared 18 sermons preached by seven members of the leadership team of a local branch of CoGoP. This sample included two sermons by women. The sermons lasted between 30 and 45 minutes each, except one sermon which was of ten minutes duration. These sermons were delivered over a six-month period.

In order to analyse the sermons, each preacher was asked to send their written script from their sermon. These scripts were systematically analysed post preaching. Transcripts were made from recordings of some sermons where there were difficulties getting hold of the scripts. The following questions were used for the purposes of analysing the sermons: Who is included in the sermons? What are the women doing? Do they speak with authority? Are they shown in a positive or negative light? What are the dominant images of God used? Are they offered authoritatively? Are they challenged or questioned in any way? Were they majority male or female images?[13]

Main Findings

The analysis found that women on a whole were invisible in the sermons. Out of 18 sermons, women were the main focus in only two, both preached by a man. Women were totally excluded in eight sermons, including one of the sermons preached by a female preacher. This was also borne out by the research of Cheryl Saunders who analysed sermons from African-American women and men of differing denominations. She found that out of 36 sermons analysed, only two of the men's and three of the women's sermons were based on texts that made specific reference to women.[14] By contrast, every sermon mentioned at least one man, including the sermons where women were the main characters.

The only mention of a woman in one sermon was that 'God unrobed himself of his glory and became a babe nursing on a woman's breast'. This sermon did not acknowledge any other part the woman may have played, not even as the person who gave birth to the child, although the bodiliness of the image may be a positive factor. In contrast to the positive female body image of this one example, a sermon which included the woman with the issue of blood saw her as unclean and defiled.

---

[12] Clarice J. Martin, 'Womanist Interpretations of the New Testament: The Quest for Holistic and Inclusive Translation and Interpretation' in James H. Cone and Gayraud S. Wilmore (eds), *Black Theology: A Documentary History, Volume 2: 1980–1992* (New York, 1993), p. 234.

[13] Some of these questions are from Nicola Slee, *Faith and Feminism: An Introduction to Christian Feminist Theology* (London, 2003), p. 29.

[14] Cheryl J Saunders, 'The Woman as Preacher', in David Day, Jeff Astley and Leslie Francis (eds), *A Reader on Preaching: Making Connections* (Aldershot, 2005), p. 213.

This sermon on the whole attempted to be inclusive, stating that everyone could be healed from things like abuse, but the implication was that only women were cursed with disease. This sermon also gave the impression that only women look in a mirror and hate what they see: 'We laugh in the mirror and we put on the nice hats and the nice dresses ... but when we look we hate what we see, we feel so condemned before the mirror.' The fact that women wear dresses and hats (common in many Black Majority Churches) reinforces the negative female stereotype.

One sermon appeared to show a woman in a more positive light. It was said of the woman who anointed Jesus, 'she wanted to give him all she had ... she has done what she could.' She was defended and commended by Jesus: 'wherever the gospel shall be preached, this woman must be preached about ... and this is a lesson to God's people.' However, 'some scholars believe she was a prostitute, but somehow she met Jesus, and Jesus delivered her from prostitution.' The biblical text used for this sermon was Mark 14, which does not specify that this woman was a prostitute. She is only described in Mark as 'a woman'. There seemed to be an assumption on the part of the preacher that this woman was a prostitute, as is the case in Luke 7. Thus, although the woman was preached about in a favourable light in terms of her anointing of Jesus, choices were made as to the negative rather than the positive aspects of this woman's life.

By contrast, within this same sermon, Solomon's lover was featured quite prominently as the one who rejected him. This narrative was preached in a very negative light. The woman was seen as lazy and complacent, since she would not get up for her lover and expected to meet him only when she was ready. The fact that he was not there when *she* wanted him was not considered as implying anything negative about the male character, illustrating the negative bias towards the female.

In one sermon, the woman of Samaria was seen as an outcast but became a missionary after meeting Jesus. However, she called only the '*men*' of the city to see Jesus. This sermon concluded with a list of five people whose lives had changed as a result of their encounter with Jesus, of which only one woman was mentioned. Another sermon also ended with a list of four people of faith, none of whom were women.

In contrast, Naomi and Ruth were positive role models in another sermon. They were seen as strong women, supporting each other. However, in general, women (when they were included) were deemed as helpless, diseased and in need of a cure. In comparison, the men were generally authoritative and on the whole shown in a more positive light. One sermon noted that the resurrection 'was so dramatic it completely changed 11 men's lives, so that all but one died a martyr's death ... After that he appeared to more than five hundred of the brothers.' This sermon implies that women were not included in the lives that were changed and Jesus subsequently did not appear to them either.

In another sermon, the word 'son' was mentioned twelve times, whereas no daughter was mentioned. The father was likened to God who was 'waiting for his son's return, last thing at night, first thing in the morning, thinking about the welfare of his son'. Women were totally missing in this sermon, although Mukti

Barton argues that the father's behaviour is more like the stereotypical action of a mother, suggesting that God has feminine characteristics, an insight not picked up in this sermon.[15]

On analysis, I found that men were generally respected, trustworthy and dependable. None needed to be cured of diseases. Although certain ones were blind and possessed with demons, these were not the major players. There was a certain amount of honesty in the sermon about Abraham: 'Abraham's family while he lived was a mishmash of unfaithfulness to his own wife, abuse of a slave girl, mistreatment of the child Abraham had with her, lying that his wife was his sister and more.' This was unusual, and potentially liberating for the hearers, whereas references to Abraham in other sermons saw him as a holy man called of God with very few faults. While some men were spoken of in less than favourable terms, it is interesting to note that, considering so many men were mentioned throughout the sermons, very few were preached about in a negative light.

Exclusive gender terms for God and Jesus – such as King, Lord, Father and Son, among others – were used on numerous occasions. Non-sexist God names were used to a lesser degree. Names such as Maker, Keeper, Almighty, Teacher, and so on were usually followed by male pronouns such as 'him' or 'he', indicating that God and Jesus were still seen as male, even though the names might suggest a gender-neutral perspective.

The Holy Spirit was referred to very infrequently but was always referred to in masculine terms, with one exception:

> ... although we universally have come to refer to the Holy Spirit as a He there is strong evidence that in early Christianity the Holy Spirit was considered feminine in gender ... But She, the Spirit, the Paraclete whom He will send to you, my Father, in my name, She will teach you everything; She will remind you of that which I have told you.

This was one of the most inclusive sermons (preached by a man) and the only time that the image of God as male was challenged.

Reflections

Taking the findings as a whole, my research established that women and their experiences were very rarely mentioned in the sermons preached in CoGoP churches and, when they were, they were generally referred to in negative terms. Women were usually included as they related to the male characters (for example, as mothers,

---

[15] Mukti Barton, 'Gender-Bender God: Masculine or Feminine?', *Black Theology: An International Journal* 7/2 (2009): 152.

wives, or disciples), rather than being regarded as actors in their own right.[16] This would make it difficult for women hearers to identify with the sermon. None of the sermons were really emancipatory for women hearers, and thus women were not being empowered to proclaim the gospel from their own perspectives.

Nancy Hardesty believes that gender-inclusive language is about justice. Women as well as men form the human race and should be included in preaching as a matter of course.[17] The injustices served within the sermons I analysed are quite blatant. Women are at best invisible – and encouraged to remain so – and at worst oppressed and disempowered. The highly exclusive language aids in the lack of self-worth and inferiority in women.

In her study, Cheryl Saunders concluded that women were twice as likely to use inclusive language in their preaching as men.[18] This was not borne out in my research, although it must be admitted that the total number of sermons preached by women was so small that it is difficult to generalize from my findings. It was, however, disappointing to find that the women preachers in my study used the same gender-exclusive language as men, appearing to have no awareness that this disempowered themselves as well as other women.[19]

Women were not seen in an authoritative light within these sermons and were generally regarded as appendages to male actors, important in relation to marriage; otherwise they were expendable.[20] The nursing child in one sermon was an important person; however, the only good the woman was said to perform was to provide a breast for the child to feed from ('God ... became a babe nursing on a woman's breast'). Even as a mother, she is not empowered but encouraged to stay in her place. There was no recognition that women create life, or that, as God is the ultimate creator, women could be seen as co-creators. The men, on the other hand, are by and large strong, upright characters and even their faults are generally overlooked. They are allowed to give guidance and set the example to follow.

Conclusion

From this admittedly small-scale study, my findings clearly indicate that the language used in preaching within the local branch of CoGoP is strongly androcentric. Elizabeth Smith says that 'people in the pew are in some sense

---

[16] Marjorie Procter-Smith, 'Images of Women in the Lectionary', in Elisabeth Schüssler Fiorenza and Mary Collins (eds), *Women – Invisible In Church and Theology* (Edinburgh, 1985), p. 57.
[17] Nancy A Hardesty, *Inclusive Language in the Church* (Atlanta, GA, 1987), p. 65.
[18] Saunders, 'The Woman As Preacher', p. 213.
[19] Clanton, *In Whose Image?*, pp. 75, 81.
[20] Procter-Smith, 'Images of Women in the Lectionary', p. 59.

preparing to speak the message of the sermon in the context of their own lives.'[21] To be relevant, sermons need to leave listeners with a sense of renewal, restoration and a feeling of empowerment to put into practice that which has been heard. The women within CoGoP cannot proclaim the sermon in their own context if they do not hear it from their own perspective, experience, or struggles.

From the evidence of these sermons, I conclude that gender-exclusive language in CoGoP is an issue that needs to be addressed. Women as well as men may not be discerning as to the harm that gender-exclusive language can have, but the results leave women predominantly voiceless and their experiences not expressed or valued. In addition, men are reinforced in a male-centred view of the world, and are not challenged to think differently.

With this in mind and for the Church to progress in this area, it is imperative that first, a gender-inclusive translation of the Bible be used; secondly, training be given about gender-exclusive language and the harm it can cause; third, constructive feedback be given to all preachers with a strong emphasis on language; and fourth, examples of good practice be made available in training sessions and in literature.

I end with the words of one preacher: 'But as she broke the box, just imagine the odour in the house, she changed the atmosphere ... yes, the atmosphere was changed. There was an odour of worship; there was an odour of true worship coming out of that woman.' After a sermon is preached, the atmosphere needs to be changed, changed to such a degree that women can identify themselves as authoritative and example setters. The positive language used in this narrative needs to be an experience that every woman enjoys as she hears the scripture expounded.

---

[21] Elizabeth J Smith, *Bearing Fruit in Due Season: Feminist Hermeneutics and the Bible in Worship* (Collegeville, MN, 1999), p.105.

PART IV
Women's Spiritual Practices, Beliefs and Attachments

Chapter 11
Broken Silence: Researching with Women to Find a Voice

Emma Rothwell

Introduction

Broken Silence was a small-scale piece of feminist action research which I conducted as part of an MA in Pastoral Theology. The study had a strong ethnographic component; I was living and working in the research locality as a vicar's wife, at the same time as training for ordained ministry in the Church of England, and I participated fully in the study. I was also heavily pregnant, experiencing the excitement and anticipation of new life, mingled and muddied with the fear of death that accompanies birthing a baby. This fusion of roles – birthing, training, mothering, leading and being a wife – are integral to the concerns of the research and my own approach to it.

My personal journey into this research illuminates the reality of local systems that still exist to repress the voices and experiences of women. As part of my vocational journey, I was asked to demonstrate my ability to manage motherhood, ministry and marriage to another clergy person. My capacity to juggle these areas would be ascertained before I would be ordained priest. As a woman leader within the Church, this precipitated a binding effect on my experience and freedom to speak about it. Much of my life, it seemed, needed literally to stay at home.

Women's silence as a theme in feminist literature is well documented,[1] but the process of trying to find a voice within the naturalized, hetero-patriarchal structures of middle-class rural English villages is very much still alive. In my personal research journal after an encounter with a woman from my local church, I wrote:

---

[1] Examples can be found in: Mary Field Belenky, Blythe McVicker Clinchy, Nancy Rule Goldberger and Jill Mattuck Tarule, *Women's Ways of Knowing: The Development of Self, Voice, and Mind* (New York, 1997); Zoë Bennett Moore, *Introducing Feminist Perspectives in Pastoral Theology* (London, 2002); Riet Bons-Storm, *The Incredible Woman: Listening to Women's Silences in Pastoral Care and Counseling* (Nashville, TN, 1996); Rita Nakashima Brock and Rebecca Ann Parker, *Proverbs of Ashes* (Boston, MA, 2001); Jeanne Stevenson-Moessner (ed.), *Through the Eyes of Women: Insights for Pastoral Care* (Minneapolis, MN, 1996); Nicola Slee, *Women's Faith Development: Patterns and Processes* (Aldershot, 2004).

Last week, I talked with Diana.[2] She is a feminist with a self-declared, mature faith, and as a member of the PCC [Parochial Church Council] she has a voice into our church system. Yet, she described aspects of her experience at church as 'alienating' and 'suppressing'. She said she often didn't feel part of the 'club'. Her sense of alienation has met my growing ambivalence about the patriarchal systems inherent in our church practices and precipitated a desire to explore further what local women's experiences of church are.[3]

This encounter revealed that there is still a wide gap between the understanding generated through feminist movements, and praxis in a local church. Diana and I were each struggling to find a voice that integrated our experience, our present sense of ourselves as women, and our capacity to contribute to the leadership of the Church. Equipped with knowledge of the systems that repress women, but without changes in church structures to accommodate women's growing roles, we were carrying a 'double-burden'.[4] The most profoundly spiritual and transformative experience that I would know during my training – the birth and early life of my second son – would be silenced as I felt pressure to prove my ability to manage roles within a patriarchal institution. Ironically, this is the same institution that calls its priests to 'watch for the signs of new creation', and 'tell the story of God's love'.[5] My encounter with Diana revealed that this kind of silencing was not an isolated experience; it brought vigour and life to the concepts underlying practical theology and formed the aims of this research. These were to create a safe space for women to break the silences of their experiences in the context of their faith, to explore women's perceptions of how their experiences have been received by Church and God, and to seek what helps faith to flourish in women and women to flourish in faith, thus creating possibilities for empowerment and transformation.

The Research Process

Broken Silence began with a period of prolonged engagement[6] with the life and heartbeat of a rural village of 3,500 people and its parish church. This offered insight into the context and presented opportunities to foster a sense of trust with participants. I kept a research journal to highlight significant moments and add depth

---

[2] Names were changed where requested.

[3] Memo 1, April 2008.

[4] Bonnie J. Miller-McLemore, *Also A Mother: Work and Family as a Theolgical Dilemma* (Nashville, TN, 1994), p. 94.

[5] Archbishops' Council, *The Ordination of Priests* <http://www.churchofengland.org/prayer-worship/worship/texts/ordinal/priests.aspx> accessed 20 July 2012.

[6] A method described by Catherine Marshall and Gretchen B. Rossman, *Designing Qualitative Research* (Thousand Oaks, CA, 2011), p. 139.

and reflexivity to the work. Some of these notes were written up as research memos and embedded as data in the study.

I chose a small, 'purposeful, homogenous cohort'[7] of five women ranging in age from 35 to 80. The homogeneity of the sample included factors such as the women's white British ethnicity, their locality and their similar socioeconomic backgrounds. The sample was purposeful in that it consisted of only five participants, all chosen for their willingness to participate. Confidences were maintained and data was member-checked at each stage of the research, incorporating transparency and validity. There was a corporate and reflexive nature to the research design, which embraced the concept of co-construction[8] of knowledge and understanding. This located the study within a feminist methodology, centralizing mutuality and shared power.[9]

The research participants met in a home environment as a focus group for two hours, fortnightly, over a period of ten weeks. We drew from art, film, scripture, current affairs, our own experience and academic papers to inform our discussion. Each meeting incorporated elements from a 'funnel of discussion'[10] guide, with opening questions to set the tone and build trust, followed by more specific, detailed discussion from which data was gathered using field notes and recording, and closing questions to aid transition from the group back into our personal contexts.

During this time of reflective sharing, we discussed the treatment of women locally and globally. We reflected on the use of androcentric language in society and in the Church and how this shapes our perception and imagery of God. We examined the use of scripture to legitimize violence and how this had affected our perceptions of self-worth. We talked openly about the liminal space between private and public, especially in relation to Church, discovering that much of our life experience was held silently in the public domain. The breaking of these silences was a painful and honest aspect of our pilgrimage through the research process. The metaphor of washing one another's feet became an explicit image of our sharing; we tended one another as we broke painful silences, and created space for sharing moments of flourishing and faith. It was cleansing and healing, and the research process itself began to be a vehicle for transformation.

Following the focus group meetings, each woman wrote an account of her personal journey of faith. This was an open-ended exercise, offering the possibility to re-member and re-create experience in light of the feminist perspectives we had begun to own in focus group meetings. Recreating understanding with a new hermeneutical lens was a painful and liberating part of the research process. The

---

[7] Sharlene Nagy Hesse-Biber and Patricia Leavy, *The Practice of Qualitative Research*, 2nd edn (Thousand Oaks, CA, 2011), pp. 45–6.

[8] Nigel King and Christine Horrocks, *Interviews in Qualitative Research* (London, 2010), p. 136.

[9] Bennett Moore, *Introducing Feminist Perspectives*, p. 15.

[10] A method suggested by Jerry W. Willis, *Foundations of Qualitative Research* (Thousand Oaks, CA, 2007), p. 143.

women collected images and artefacts to symbolize poignant moments of their story; through this process, alternative images of God began to emerge.

I interviewed each woman in her home, adding depth to the research and enriching the data yielded by group encounters. All the data collected was transcribed, and through detailed analysis, patterns and codes emerged from the text. Codes were clustered together and refined into the broader research categories; key among them were *silence*, and *alternative images and experiences*. Finally, excerpts from each woman's faith journey were collected and set alongside passages of (often challenging) scripture and photographs of the visuals they had chosen to represent each moment in their faithful journey. This document was reproduced into a booklet which recorded our collective 'human living document',[11] a text which uses for its data human experience recorded as poems, stories, and pictures.

This was a deliberately small-scale piece of qualitative research with a narrow sample, thus it is limited in its capacity 'to establish firm and general conclusions';[12] discussion and reflections drawn from it do not claim to be transferable to other contexts. Rather, it sought to generate themes and unearth trends to enrich discussion pertaining to the issues that women face locally, in the Church context, and in wider society. I acknowledge that my inquiry is deeply influenced by the values implicit in my own experience and I write to 'make sense of and shape that life experience'.[13]

Reflections on my Findings

Silence

Through focus group meetings, our small cohort of five local women developed relationships of deep trust and mutuality. Our shared ownership of the research created a sacred, safe holding space in which we heard one another with fresh attention. This offering of hospitable listening enabled silences about experience and faith to be broken, and gave new credibility to those experiences. *Broken Silence* revealed a plethora of issues or emergent codes that the women had held privately in the public domain and especially in the context of Church. *Silence* became the umbrella category for emerging issues such as loss and bereavement, self-sacrifice, violence and abuse, loss of identity and issues surrounding motherhood and birth. The breadth of experience, pain and determination to break into new ground was extraordinary and breathtaking within such a small group.

Mary talked with passion and lament about her marriage to John, an alcoholic: 'He was very controlling and jealous; he used to put cotton behind the door so he could see if I had been out.' With John's increasingly erratic and violent

---

[11] Elaine Graham, Heather Walton and Frances Ward, *Theological Reflection: Methods* (London, 2005), pp. 18–46.//
[12] Slee, *Women's Faith Development*, p. 11.//
[13] Ibid., p. 2.

behaviour, Mary suffered isolation from her local community. Her two small boys were bullied for their father's behaviour and in desperation she turned to her church. The pastoral care she received imposed on her a burdensome sense of duty to 'bear all things', leaving her not only un-embraced but further isolated and disempowered, and carrying the added weight of shame: 'It seemed to me at the time that the woman got blamed and was expected to cope; it was her duty. I don't think I realized how confined I was, I never spoke about any of this. Church wasn't a safe place, but I didn't stop praying.' Mary spoke of how her dreams to teach blew away as she cared for John until he died. She wept as she recalled the first thing she did, following his death: 'I went to get my nails done, he never let me. I felt so liberated and so lost.'

Mary's story exposed the deeply ingrained effect of imposed expectations regarding being the good mother and Christian woman on someone of her generation. Married, jobless and dependent, in a caring role of self-sacrifice and even self-abnegation, Mary was silenced and desperate for the increased public awareness that second-wave feminism would bring, a decade after John's death.

Eileen recounted the long and violent relationship she witnessed between her parents, and its tragic consequences for her mother. She described the covert assumption that no one would speak about the abuse her mother suffered: '(The) neighbours must have known, but no one did anything. It was only when I went to school, I realized my existence wasn't normal.' Eileen talked of her mother's paralysing mental health issues and broke her silence further as she wrote:

> My Mum did eventually divorce my Dad. She remarried. On one occasion, her new husband was violent to her; you could see the marks on her neck. I don't think she could face the abuse any longer, she was never allowed to be herself, to express herself, to find herself. After this incident, she committed suicide.

Eileen's story brought serious weight to the issues of compartmentalization for sufferers of experiences that are unresolved and unspoken. 'Splitting',[14] burn-out, breakdown and other mental health issues were apparent in many of the women's experiences where repressed pain lived long into their lives, rooted within inner conflicts which often still have no public narrative or voice.

In another meeting, Eileen discussed the pain surrounding the early death of her first daughter. After a long and traumatic labour, her daughter was born and immediately taken away from her: 'newly born and baptized, she was rushed off to Great Ormond Street Hospital, I hadn't even seen her. It was the most awful painful thing.' For Eileen it seemed that a religious rite of passage had replaced her womanly capacity to love and comfort her baby in the moments of her birth and death. Like Mary, in the midst of her pain and silenced by Church and society, Eileen did not stop praying: 'The God I encountered that day was an almighty, all-loving, non-judgemental, merciful God. I wasn't afraid of God.' Eileen and Mary

---

[14] Slee, *Women's Faith Development*, p. 92.

had been regular members of our local church for years, but we had no concept of the depth of pain they were carrying. As a group, our collective experience exposed that Church has not been a space where these issues were openly discussed.

Feminist literature has addressed issues of silence, and this research demonstrated that breaking the silence is still necessary, a rite of passage for women as they journey towards integration and flourishing. Amazingly, in the face of an unsympathetic Church, Eileen and Mary continued to pray. Their faith was immense. As a group, we began to consider aspects of God that women can connect with, and the traditional images that repress their faith.

As the lead researcher for *Broken Silence*, I was teetering on the edge of birthing my son. Previous losses and a long and traumatic labour with my first son had left me uncertain. The pain of Eileen's birth story had touched me and so had her faith. The actual process of research was a spiritual endeavour, imbued with mutuality and reciprocal care. As my pregnancy progressed, I was caught between contradictory expectations: my local church, which had struggled with my absence as I trained for ordination, validated me as I blossomed into a traditional vicar's wife. In contrast, the emphasis within my vocational pathway was placed on pressure to prove my ministerial capacity in spite of my motherhood. I wondered if I would ever find a comfortable and expressive voice of my own.

Alternative Images and Experiences

We discussed our feelings surrounding the maleness of God, acknowledging the ontological slippage as the 'human maleness of Jesus is transferred to God his Father'.[15] It was the first time some of us had considered this. Anna described imperceptibly imbibing paintings, images, language and teachings of the Church, which naturally invoked a male picture of God in her soul. She described the torment and violence surrounding her father's mental health issues and the binding effect of that as she prayed, too much in church, to 'Father God'. At eight years old, Anna had watched Christ's passion in Franco Zefirelli's 1977 film, *Jesus of Nazareth*: 'I was haunted by a man, dying and asking forgiveness for all those who silenced him. The next day, I made myself a cross and walked on holy ground as I re-enacted the crucifixion in my vest and knickers in our garden. This was my first encounter with God.' For our human living document, Anna chose to represent this first quiet encounter with an image of a Christa, a picture of herself on a cross in a garden, as she had re-enacted the scene at the age of eight. This was a powerful and moving visual image for all of us; a girl child reclaiming herself through the story of Christ, finding space to share her story and enter into faith. Anna explained that this was a private moment and had been held in silence for many years. She had not encountered imagery depicting the Christa in the public domain until recently.[16] The research process afforded her space to discuss the

---

[15] Bennett Moore, *Introducing Feminist Perspectives*, p. 34.
[16] Nicola Slee, *Seeking the Risen Christa* (London, 2011).

complicated issues of God as Father and tentatively to begin to own the flourishing potential of female aspects of God.

We shared many other images and experiences that reconnected us with the divine. Often these enshrined the beauty of nature and involved spacious places where, as Diana said, we learned 'peace and freedom to be'. Eileen was exuberant: 'an image of the divine?! A tree! I had a dream once that a tree grew in the middle of my house. It's something to do with the rootedness that makes it spiritual for me.' Mary shared an image of herself in an empty church. It was not the building that bound her spiritually: '[most] often, it was the people that occupied it.' This is typical of the beautiful expressions of faith found within a small group of local women dealing with deep uncertainty in their lives.

Conclusion

Broken Silence revealed that, whatever our experiences of birth, we had as mothers all found spirituality and transformation through it. Meriel wrote: 'I have met women who have been empowered and their lives strengthened and illuminated by a positive birth. It is the closest approximation to me of the divine.' The possibilities offered by birthing for accompanying, carrying, co-creating, and invoking a process of hope and promise were all aspects of holy endeavour for us. We also found that these values of birthing were deeply enriching aspects of researching together, and in this capacity *Broken Silence* was a birthing process, too.

Breaking silence still remains a risky business for women who have felt powerless to speak honestly in public. The reciprocal, reflective nature of our focus group generated a precious freedom to talk, by speaking into the liminal space between expectation and experience, or theory and practice. This breaking of silence brought a sense of healing and deeper understanding to each participant and thus a vocational and transformative aspect to the process of research.

Chapter 12
Integrating Ritual: An Exploration of Women's Responses to *Woman-Cross*

Susanna Gunner

Introduction

In the liturgical devotion known as the Stations of the Cross, Christians try to enter more fully into the suffering of Jesus. Traditionally, 14 stopping places or 'stations' around a church are offered, visual art at each stimulating prayer and reflection upon the road to crucifixion. It is an imaginative act. But the suffering journey of a first-century Jew to death but also beyond it can resonate powerfully with all who are treated unjustly and long to roll away the stone of dis-empowerment. There is much here which holds rich potential for re-imagining, potential which I claimed at a time when postgraduate study was sharpening my feminist sensibilities. How might this liturgy look when re-imagined from a feminist perspective? What sort of re-imagining would render the 'liturgical "truth"' of the Stations of the Cross, 'an engaged, embodied and particular truth'[1] for women in my own faith-community? In response to such questions, I created for Womenchurch[2] a liturgy called *Woman-Cross* and so found myself playing a part in the 'emerging sense of ritual empowerment on the part of women',[3] which has characterized the feminist liturgical development of recent decades.

---

[1] Marjorie Procter-Smith, *In Her Own Rite: Constructing Feminist Liturgical Tradition* (Nashville, TN, 1990), p. 13.

[2] Mary Hunt defines Womenchurch as 'a global, ecumenical movement of feminist base communities which gather in sacrament and solidarity to express their religious faith in egalitarian, democratic styles': in Lisa Isherwood and Dorothea McEwan (eds), *An A–Z of Feminist Theology* (Sheffield, 1996), p. 240.

[3] Susan A. Ross, 'Church and sacrament – community and worship', in Susan Frank Parsons (ed.), *Feminist Theology* (Cambridge, 2002), p. 225.

Writing *Woman-Cross*

Believing that the concept and rhythms of the Stations liturgy were 'open to being reclaimed',[4] I brought to them my own fresh conscientization to God-language as well as a commitment to the relationship between emancipation and worship, and to its shared, non-hierarchical delivery. In other words, I created for a gathered group of women a liturgy characterized by imaging of God radically different from that of traditional Christian worship, by a desire to reveal something of women's own story in Christianity's pivotal narrative, and by the expectation that participants would not only be actively engaged in delivering the liturgy but also transformed by it.

Because of the developed treatment each receives, five Stations only came under my spotlight. Stations 1 (Pilate condemns Jesus to death), 5 (The cross is laid on Simon of Cyrene), 8 (The women of Jerusalem weep for Jesus), and 11 (Jesus is nailed to the cross) were chosen for being fairly evenly spaced across the 14 but I knew that a feminist perspective – insisting upon the possibilities of hope and transformation – would support the growing tendency to add a 15th (The women find the empty tomb).

At each of these five, those participating, having aligned themselves into a cruciform shape,[5] first hear the relevant biblical text. One woman then gives voice to the feminist hermeneutic of deconstruction and reconstruction which weaves its way playfully throughout, by responding with poetry as the wives of Pilate or Simon from Cyrene, or as one of the women of Jerusalem, or Jesus' mother, or Mary Magdalene. These poetic responses to the biblical text often revolve around some symbolic action, the whole receiving insightful comment from a Chorus[6] before leading into concluding prayers.[7]

---

[4] Teresa Berger, *Fragments of Real Presence: Liturgical Traditions in the Hands of Women* (New York, 2005), p. 5

[5] Many strands of meaning are suggested by this ritual embodiment of the Cross. For example, it reinforces an identification with women everywhere who suffer their own (often gender-specific) crucifixions, while simultaneously affirming the bodies of women as valid vehicles for the expression of worship.

[6] Inspired by the masked choruses of ancient Greece, my use of the Chorus acknowledges both the frequent facelessness of women and the particularity of insights they offer.

[7] Parts of the liturgy are published in Margaret Rose, Jenny Te Paa, Jeanne Person and Abigail Nelson (eds), *Lifting Women's Voices* (Norwich, 2009), pp. 184–8.

Researching with *Woman-Cross*

The liturgy completed, I wanted to find out how women would respond to *Woman-Cross*, and what those responses might tell me about women's faithing,[8] about liturgy and about the relationship between the two.[9] So I gathered twelve women together[10] to embody and walk the journey of *Woman-Cross*. We spent four evenings together. The first served as an introduction both to the liturgy and to the feminist perspectives from which it was written; the second was our opportunity to plan its delivery; the third saw the *Woman-Cross* event itself, while the last provided a forum for reflecting upon this 'feminist reconfiguring of the liturgy and liturgical traditioning'.[11]

I have continued with that 'pressing task'[12] by returning again and again to the rich seams of the women's reflections tape-recorded in the fourth meeting, holding up to them the mirror of recent writing on women's faith development. In particular, I took Nicola Slee's *Women's Faith Development: Patterns and Processes* as my starting-point, and at the heart of this chapter is a brief reflective analysis of my project in the light of her work.

In what methodology would my action research be grounded? I would be a participant in my project, planning, delivering and reflecting upon the liturgy alongside the others, but I was the only one tasked to write a dissertation at the end of it! My role was therefore nuanced very differently from the others. I was also the creator of both concept and text, would invite the others to my home, would inevitably set the tone with what I said or didn't say. These were just a few threads in an intricate web of power differentials which needed, just as much as the women, to be 'heard into speech',[13] if 'non-hierarchical, non-manipulative research relationships'[14] were to flourish. Only with such relationships at its heart could the research process be not only about women, but also by and for women. What's more, this piece of qualitative research, however small-scale, was designed to engender a process of conscientization for us all, and it mattered deeply to me as both pastor and feminist research student that the women were not negatively affected. So, in addition to nurturing a project-culture which was

---

[8] Nicola Slee employs this word, in *Women's Faith Development: Patterns and Processes* (Aldershot, 2004), p. 61.

[9] For a full account of the research, see Susanna Gunner, 'Learning through Liturgy' (unpublished MA dissertation, Anglia Ruskin University, 2008).

[10] The group, as culturally and socially diverse as possible, ranged in age from 25 to 79.

[11] Teresa Berger (ed.), *Dissident Daughters: Feminist Liturgies in Global Context* (Louisville, KY, 2001), p. 221.

[12] Ibid.

[13] This phrase comes originally from Nelle Morton, *The Journey is Home* (Boston, MA, 1985), p. 202.

[14] Slee, *Women's Faith Development*, p. 44.

mutually supportive, empathic and empowering, I instinctively embraced the role of reflexivity: aware of how I, the researcher, was 'tangled up with (my) methods',[15] I listened not just to the responses of the other women but also to my own; as well as valuing their openness, I allowed the deepest part of myself to be open and responsive.

Preparing to embody *Woman-Cross*

As only one of the other women had had any contact with the feminist principles behind the theology, language, liturgical style and pedagogical approach of *Woman-Cross*, these were gently explored at our first meeting. Then we turned to the liturgy itself and the practical questions underlying its delivery. Keen to remain beyond Church, the women were adamant that it should be both prepared and delivered in my home, a decision which meant that my antennae would need to flap even more vigorously if corporate ownership of the process were to thrive.

An additional significant question remained. How were we to create the cross-shape at each station, forming the lines with our own bodies, *becoming* the cross as my liturgy requires? It was then that the first act of corporate creativity flashed out. We would each bring a scarf, tie them together in cruciform proportions and carry this cross of scarves from station to station setting it down on arrival and standing along its lines.

The rest of the first evening was spent with the liturgy itself, being introduced to the language and structures of *Woman-Cross*, and committing ourselves to re-reading both text and commentary before we met again, understanding that familiarity would free up further creative ideas – I had worked hard to communicate the vital fact that I was not 'delivering a product', but inviting them to be 'engaged in a process'.[16]

Creative preparation followed at our second meeting. First, from a huge pile of newspapers, we each selected one instance of injustice which inflamed us with compassion and anger. We would arrive next week with this article pinned to our clothing, the focus of our praying as the *Woman-Cross* journey moved constantly from Cross to contemporary crucifixion and the longing for deliverance.

Next, we turned to some new material for Station 11:

> I remember the blood of your birth,
> the straw
> slippery red,

---

[15] Rita Gross, *A Garland of Feminist Reflections: Forty Years of Religious Exploration* (Berkeley, CA, 2009), p. 96.

[16] Mary Field Belenky, Blythe McVicker Clinchy, Nancy Rule Goldberger and Jill Mattuck Tarule, *Women's Ways of Knowing: The Development of Self, Voice, and Mind* (New York, 1986), p. xxi.

wet with it;
sweat blinding,
reminding of your presence still,
your soon-to-be absence.
I remember the straining and panting,
the tearing of flesh;
my screams surprising the birds in the rafters.[17]

Hilary[18] spoke first: 'The words that jumped out to me', she said, 'were "the tearing of flesh".' She suggested that Mary the mother of Jesus should speak her opening paragraph accompanied by the brutal ripping of a red rose to symbolize the creativity of bloody birthing reversed.

That later wording of mutual absolution be accompanied by some sign or mark was then vigorously discussed. The group warmed to Alison's idea that, in pairs, we mark each other with a cross of red lipstick. This, it was felt, would speak both of blood and femininity, would, with two deft strokes, draw the repressive stereotype of the dizzy female into the cruciform shape of redemption.

We decided next who would read what and, keen to find ways of retaining the sense of journey within the confines of a house, where each station should be set. Lilian (having offered herself as Mrs Pilate) had the powerfully ironic idea of using the kitchen sink for the symbolic hand-washing action of Station 1. For Station 2 and its theme of global oppression epitomized in Simon of Cyrene, *Woman-Cross* would climb upstairs to a chair beneath a window framing our parish church beyond, a chair festooned in chains. Station 8 would be back downstairs, a bucket on a table for the tears of the women of Jerusalem. For Station 11 and the nailing of Jesus to the cross, we would go out into the night of the garden. We would stand on the hard tiles of the patio, saving soft grass and flickering lamps for the resurrection station. To this grass, as to each of the previous four settings, we practised moving, the knotted scarves we held keeping us cruciform.

Responding to *Woman-Cross*

Our *Woman-Cross* worship took place one raw April night and we came together some weeks later to reflect. It was integration – many different strands of integration – which undoubtedly had had the most impact, our collaborative method of delivery the most valued strand of all. Sheila said simply, 'It felt good. Everyone's bit was essential to the whole.' Lots of the women spoke movingly about how it had felt to form the cross and to journey together. Others spoke of the integration experienced with New Testament women, articulating the need identified by Wootton 'to enable congregations to bring their own living

---

[17] In Rose et al., *Lifting Women's Voices*, p. 185.
[18] All those quoted by name gave permission to do so.

experiences into a dynamic interaction with the experiences told in Scripture'.[19] Lesley noted how important for this integration had been the symbolic actions. As she placed the empty bucket on the table for our tears, she 'felt at that moment that I really became the woman at the well'.

Additional integration had come, then, through the way in which our intellectual engagement with words was illuminated by our physical engagement with ritual. The creative integration of words and action, always more than the sum of its parts, enabled us to think feelingly and to feel thinkingly and thereby offered us new ways of seeing.

In fact, the rose-ripping, the absolving with lipstick, and other such moments triggered episodes of striking theological reflection. As the chains of injustice had fallen from the chair, for example, Lesley had looked out beyond it and seen not just the darkness of an April evening but a world 'dark with injustice'; Helen had mused on how, looking in a mirror later that night, the lipstick cross on her forehead had smudged 'into a great wound'; Penny reflected that the scarves of our cross, for all their lightness, had been 'a terrible burden, especially when we were going upstairs'. Lesley, acknowledging that the curving staircase had sometimes forced us out of cross formation to walk alone, pondered movingly that 'we do each have to carry our own cross through life though others can walk alongside.' It was the physicality of our worship and its physical context (darkness, garden, kitchen sink, stairs, out-of-church-but-very-near-it, spring) which, more than anything, encouraged our minds to get to work. In other words, integrating our physical bodies with worship led to integration with our minds, an integration which touched the deepest, most tender parts of our humanity. It is impossible to untangle all these different threads of our being caught up by the hook of ritual drama.

The Power of Ritual

All this has helped me to identify an outcome which points up the difference between my study and Slee's. From her extensive programme of interviews, she identifies six 'faithing strategies' employed by women to 'shape and pattern their faith experience'.[20] As I listen to the recording of our final *Woman-Cross* evening, I am able to hear examples of all six strategies – conversational, metaphoric, narrative, personalized, conceptual and apophatic – in the ways in which we worked together and in our responses to the prayers and poems of *Woman-Cross*. But something is missing. A key strategy used by the *Woman-Cross* liturgy to help us pattern our faithing (and – apart from the relational aspects of all of the strategies – the one to which the women most warmly responded) was our engagement with symbolic action, the integration between our bodies and the liturgical expression

---

[19] Janet Wootton, *Introducing a Practical Feminist Theology of Worship* (Sheffield, 2000), p. 98.
[20] Slee, *Women's Faith Development*, p. 61.

of faith. At first, I wondered if this faithing strategy might be subsumed into one of Slee's faithing strategies, but the strength of Lesley's comment (about carrying our own crosses through life) helped me to realize that none of them does justice to the potency of the physical enactment of some metaphor or narrative or concept. Words to generate and explore the meaning of these actions were important, but it is very salutary that only one person initiated comment about the *words* of *Woman-Cross*. Much more than what we *said* together, it was what we *did* that counted.[21] It was *this* that took our faithing on to a different level.

Perhaps this was because the symbolic action was where the women had most creative power, both devising the action and resourcing any objects needed. And the actions were the more telling because they were concerned with the familiar and everyday. The women enthusiastically embraced the 'mundane sphere ... as the locus of the encounter with mystery, otherness and the presence of the divine'.[22] What Slee calls 'the sacrament of the everyday'[23] was deliberately sought (as with the sink and the lipsticks), was received without reservation and found to be profoundly nourishing. *Woman-Cross* had challenged us beyond chancing upon the holy in the ordinary, and we had intentionally and corporately set up the ordinary as a means of sacramental grace. There was little doubt in any of our twelve minds that 'the newest and most personalized ritual acts can speak the powerful language of the church's symbolic tradition.'[24]

To sum up, the fact that *Woman-Cross* revolves around a corporate performative experience in which meaning is deliberately sought using ordinary objects, led to a markedly greater emphasis on symbolic action than Slee's interviews reveal. So to Slee's six 'faithing strategies', I suggest that 'ritual faithing' be added. Repeatedly signalled by the women in my study as deeply important, it was a key component of the way in which we 'wrote the Body of Christ'.[25]

The sense of homecoming felt by us all during and after this collaborative liturgical process has prompted me to read other feminist liturgies and to see *Woman-Cross* in the context of a great global groundswell of liturgical re-imagining. Much of the material available and the research around it deals with ritual created to support individual women at significant times of transition. *Ritual Making Women*[26] is one example, the book's title itself endorsing my findings, both that women are often natural 'ritual experts',[27] and also that ritual supports their becoming. Though Berry's ritual-making contexts were different from mine,

---

[21] This is borne out strongly by several of the women of Berry's case studies: Jan Berry, *Ritual Making Women: Shaping Rites for Changing Lives* (London, 2009).
[22] Slee, *Women's Faith Development*, p. 152.
[23] Ibid.
[24] Elaine Ramshaw, *Ritual and Pastoral Care* (Philadelphia, PA, 1987), p. 64.
[25] Elaine Graham, Heather Walton and Frances Ward, *Theological Reflection: Methods* (London, 2005), Chapter 4.
[26] Berry, *Ritual Making Women*.
[27] Ross, 'Church and sacrament', p. 236.

everything she says about the performative power of ritual rings true with my study. It 'provides support' and 'builds community',[28] it 'shapes consciousness ... challenging power relations',[29] it does 'not simply express emotion or experience, but in some way construct(s) them'.[30] In sum, 'women's ritual making ... has transformative potential and power, shaping women's lives, actions and ... their encounter with the sacred.'[31]

Unlike Berry, my research was based upon a feminist re-imagining of a traditional Christian liturgy, and what Berger headlines the move 'From "Man's Liturgy" to Women's Rites'[32] took place within a subset of a confessional community. In *Woman-Cross*, we were not moving away from our common faith but embracing it more deeply. But while its embodied ritual offered us integration at all levels, it simultaneously raised an urgent question about it. How might experiences such as *Woman-Cross* be integrated into the broader worshipping life of faith communities and not kept apart in women's homes? The task now is for those who have become 'ritual experts' to integrate their expertise with others, restoring a common possession.

---

[28] Berry, *Ritual Making Women*, p. 176.
[29] Ibid., p. 188.
[30] Ibid., p. 217.
[31] Ibid., p. 129.
[32] Berger, *Dissident Daughters*, p. 3.

Chapter 13

Silent Gifts: An Exploration of Relationality in Contemporary Christian Women's Chosen Practices of Silence

Alison Woolley

Introduction

Silence has been a central practice in spiritual disciplines of religions in the East and West for thousands of years. Despite ongoing recognition of the importance of silence in expressions of Christian faith, references to specific *practices* of silence within theology are often superficial or insubstantial. Theological discourse has made little attempt to explore the meanings attached to the phrase 'practices of silence' as this is used by people to describe aspects of their individual spiritual practice.

Thirty years ago, Don Browning highlighted that Christians have often failed to reflect theologically on prevalent Christian practices because of their familiarity.[1] Since then, practical theology has played a fundamental role in addressing this failure to examine our understanding of Christian practices. Although practical theology has recognized the importance of recovering the transformational power of many meaningful traditional spiritual practices by engaging in a process of retrieval, critique and reconstruction,[2] practices of silence have still not received this attention.

In recent decades, the *silencing* of women has been extensively discussed by feminist theologians. They have exposed how men's voices have dominated scripture, liturgy, theological discourse and pastoral care, whilst women's voices have been omitted or subjugated: in effect, women, their voices and experiences have been silenced within faith communities. This has resulted in feminist theologians largely presenting silence as a pejorative. At the same time, feminist theology has privileged as desirable models of being antonymous to silencing: phrases like 'hearing to speech',[3] speaking truth to power, or finding authentic voice are common within feminist literature. The coalescence of these dialogues has been prominent in feminist theological discourse, and, consequently, its literature

---

[1] Don Browning, *Practical Theology* (San Francisco, CA, 1983), p. 6.
[2] Marie McCarthy, 'Spirituality in a Postmodern Era', in James Woodward and Stephen Pattison (eds), *The Blackwell Reader in Pastoral and Practical Theology* (Oxford, 2000), pp. 192–206.
[3] Nelle Morton, *The Journey Is Home* (Boston, MA, 1985), p. 210.

has made little enquiry into women's chosen practices of silence.[4] In effect, the dominant discourses of feminist theology have – however unintentionally – silenced discussion of the possible merits of chosen practices of silence in contemporary Christian women's experience. Within feminist theology's conversations, these practices remain a virtually forgotten and unexplored source of rich potential for women's spiritual journeys. That this has occurred within a discourse aiming to speak directly from and to women's experience is regrettable. By identifying this lacuna in practical and feminist theology's understanding of practices of silence, I suggest that their exploration is overdue.

Exploring Silence

Material presented here is drawn from in-depth, loosely structured interviews with twenty Christian women aged from their mid-twenties to early eighties.[5] They have long commitment in a broad range of Catholic, Protestant and nonconformist Christian traditions, including a small number of Quakers who also self-identify as Christians. Six of the women are ordained. One woman spent two years as a novice in a teaching religious order and one was a nun in a contemplative order. Both left their religious communities over two decades ago. Although not a prerequisite to participation, all have completed at least a first degree. Their participation in higher education may have contributed to their ability to be articulate at depth about experiences which are predominantly non-verbal and often portrayed as ineffable.[6]

Although practical and feminist theologies have highlighted the need to give attention to what is unspoken in any discourse, there is less recognition that pauses in speech can be sources of 'fat and rich information' which 'require our listening differently and to begin recognizing the richness in our own and others' silences.'[7] I gained a more nuanced understanding of the women's experiences of silence by paying attention to pauses in their speech, which were pointers to moments women were struggling for precision in their articulation, or suggested – often in association with non-verbal cues such as body language or facial expression – they were arriving at new comprehension or insight in our conversation. When transcribing interviews, I represented brief pauses and subsequent resumptions in speech by beginning a new line, annotating lengths of pauses longer than two seconds within round brackets. When presenting long quotations, I have retained this layout and annotation to offer some sense of pace and affect with which each woman's words were spoken, and to invite consideration of the unvoiced thinking

---

[4] Womanist theology (closely associated with, but distinct from black and feminist theologies) has identified choosing to remain silent as a form of protest.

[5] Conducted as part of my ongoing PhD research.

[6] Sara Maitland, *A Book of Silence* (London, 2009), p. 41.

[7] Lisa Mazzei, 'Inhabited Silences: In Pursuit of a Muffled Subtext', *Qualitative Inquiry* 9 (2003): 358.

occurring within pauses longer than would be expected in general conversation. In shorter quotations, pauses are indicated by a solidus (/).

Initial exploration of each woman's understanding of the word 'silence' revealed they broadly share an understanding of *external* silence as the cessation of extraneous noise outside of self.[8] Noises perceived as particularly intrusive into silence generally derive from human activity, occur unexpectedly, or have a rhythmic patterning which attracts the mind. Sounds from nature are considered relatively undisruptive of silence. Most women articulated some level of silence within self – *internal* silence – although their descriptions and depth of engagement with this are varied. All the women identified movement towards a sense of increased inner stillness, experienced in a slowing, diminishing number of thoughts. For a few, greater inner calm sometimes extends to short times of profound internal, contemplative silence, where thoughts greatly diminish or cease. Descriptions of what each woman perceives as part of her practice of silence were rich and varied, but space does not permit discussion of this here.

Silence and Presence

Despite variety in the women's individual understandings of internal and external silence, there is strong agreement with words about silence by feminist poet, Adrienne Rich, that it should not be confused 'with any kind of absence'.[9] They all resist or directly refute silence as emptiness, instead speaking of silence as a place of presence. Gaynor[10] said, emphatically, 'It's not absence of anything/it's a really full presence/the fullest presence I know!' Their understanding of individual silence as a place where presence is experienced challenges the frequent perception that silence is a place of solitude. Ali feels:

> it is the presence
> of something
> erm
> but (2.5)

---

[8] Throughout, 'self' refers to a woman's own being, while 'other' is used to refer to a person who is not self, apart from the person of God, who is referred to as God, or the Divine. The feminist theoretician, Jane Flax, writes, 'I believe a unitary self is unnecessary, impossible, and a dangerous illusion.' Sharing Flax's view and following the usage in some therapeutic literature, I have utilized 'self' and 'other' in preference to the more familiar convention of 'the self' and 'the other' to indicate that in my perception self and other are multiple and in a state of flux rather than singular. See Jane Flax, 'On the Contemporary Politics of Subjectivity', *Human Studies* 16/1–2 (1993): 33–49.

[9] Adrienne Rich, 'Cartographies of Silence', in *The Dream of a Common Language: Poems 1974–1977* (New York, 1978), p. 17.

[10] Some names are actual, others pseudonyms, at each woman's discretion. Quotations from interviews are used with consent.

it feels like (3)
ah
it feels like an encounter
it's
a sort of
a secret pleasure
a kind of sense of recognition ...
I don't have that presence other than
in silence ... (9.5)
it is silence that creates the awareness of the presence ...
you almost seem to touch it (4)
erm (8.5)
and it is alive. (4.5)

Their engagement in a discipline of silence is a deliberate decision to be open to this encounter.

The least surprising encounter in silence reported by the women is with God. This chapter will not pursue directly silence as a place of encounter with the Divine, this being the most familiar of the relational encounters identified within their narratives. Rather, I have chosen to focus on those which are, to differing degrees, more surprising.

The most unexpected encounter to emerge is every woman's perception of silence as a space where they encounter others. It is not difficult to appreciate how their understanding of silence as a place where others are encountered could arise from settings of *communal* silence. Consequently, encountering others in communal silence will also not be addressed here. More unexpected is their assertion that *individual* silence is a space where others are encountered. This will be discussed as the chapter continues.

The final presence the women spoke of encountering in silence is self. All vividly described experiences of relating to self in new ways as they engage in practices of silence. As I began to study their comments more carefully, it became clear that self encountered in silence is not only contemporary self. Instead, the women encounter self who has been, is, will become, or may eventually be. I describe encounters with self who changes over time as encounters with a temporally multiple self.

Silence and Relationality

Writing in the early 1980s, Carol Gilligan identified that, for many women, 'to see themselves as woman is to see themselves in a relationship of connection'.[11] Since then, relationality has been a significant concept around which much

---

[11] Carol Gilligan, *In a Different Voice: Psychological Theory and Women's Development* (Cambridge, MA, 1982), p. 171.

feminist thought has been organized.[12] As the place of relationality in women's development and decision making has been explored, the culturally engendered tendency of women to give greater consideration to the impact of their choices on others, and their relationships with them, than to their individual needs has often been acknowledged. For many women, enabling other(s) has frequently taken priority over their own enabling. Their ongoing exploration and development of self-identity can be inhibited by perceptions of societal requirements to privilege the imperatives of relationality over personal desires. In *The Exuberant Church*, Barbara Glasson emphasizes the possibility of relationality where the emergence of identity for some does not impede the growth of identity in others. She writes of relational search for identity where 'not only are others involved, but that one story points to another, so that the coming out of one person's identity enables and embodies the discovery of others'.[13] Here, enabling increased authenticity of selfhood in some does not hinder that of any who participate in its facilitation. Instead, the exploration of each individual is integral to the same process in other(s). They are woven together in a pattern that is dependent for its continuation on the ongoing interrelationship between each narrative. To encounter the presence of God, other, or temporally multiple self in silence is to be open to this profound relational experience. With its intertwining process of enabling between multiple participants, Glasson's image of relationality offers insights into women's chosen practices of silence as a place of transformational relational encounter, which will be developed as this chapter continues.

Individual Silence and Relationality with Self

The temporally multiple self encountered in silence is a changing, developing self known and experienced by the women and those they interact with in subtly different forms over many years. Aspects of each temporally multiple self can potentially be re- or newly encountered within silence.

The first of these selves is that currently being experienced: present self as known and experienced more consistently by the women and those with whom they interact. A second self is self who has been: in encounter with past self, they become aware of aspects of self that have been forgotten, lost, denied, repressed, or faded from memory, and can now be rediscovered. Third, silence is a space where many identified transition towards self who is becoming: new or previously forgotten aspects of self are developed and integrated within their identity. These aspects of a becoming self may also be recognized from the past or seen as 'new' by those who know the women well. Finally, some detected a glimmer of self they hope or dream

---

[12] See Christie Cozad Neuger, 'Women and Relationality', in Bonnie J. Miller-McLemore and Brita L. Gill-Austern (eds), *Feminist and Womanist Pastoral Theology* (Nashville, TN, 1999), pp. 113–32.

[13] Barbara Glasson, *The Exuberant Church: Listening to the Prophetic People of God* (London, 2011), p. 48.

they may be some day. Here silence is a space, not so much to encounter but to see, a brief glimpse on the horizon of seeds of potential future self.

For many of the women, individual silence is valued as a place to pause in their busy lives and allow self space simply to be. Silence gives them a temporary respite from the expectations of self and others, and allows the pace and number of thoughts to decrease. In this calmer space, they have opportunity to shed what leaves them feeling 'jammed up', begin to reconnect with self, gather up bits of self that have been dispersed or forgotten, and put self back together. As a result, they describe being more in touch with thoughts, feelings and needs, recognizing this increases their self-awareness. Lynne's words echo those of many: 'to/get in touch with my/self/and what I really think feel experience ... there has to be [silence].'

Silence facilitates greater awareness of self in the present moment. This frequently leads to the women discovering that in silence they can explore the truth of who they are more honestly. Similarly, silence offers space in which aspects of self from the past can be acknowledged. The truths about past and current self are not always comfortable to acknowledge, either to self, or in encounter with God. For Dawn silence is 'a time when/I am truthful with my God ... this is the absolute truth ... this is/what I thought ... what I said ... this is/how I think.' Silence can reveal self-delusions, leading to significant change in self-perceptions and impacting on future interactions with others. Many identified that as they begin more fully to own the truth of self – past and present – they also discover that the truth of their former and current identities is unconditionally accepted by God. They spoke of silence as a place where self-exposure to God is not crushing: as Claire said, 'you can stand there naked/and survive.' In turn, knowing God's acceptance of the truth of self helps them to come to a new place of self-acceptance.

Silence also offers an essential transitional space for self who is becoming, giving the women freedom to develop aspects of self that were perhaps acknowledged as existing, but remained partially hidden or undeveloped. Most identified this readily within their own narrative, but a small number initially refuted any self-development in silence, before returning to this later in our conversation as something they *were* now able to articulate: the opportunity to tell their narrative, and my attentive silence, enabled new recognition of where self-development had been overlooked. Silence is also known as a place where unexpected new aspects of self emerge to consciousness. For Sian: 'silence/has enabled at least a recognition of/new blossoms of me/that might emerge.'

As new aspects of self emerge, silence offers the women space to explore changing self-narratives. Previous self-perceptions undergo change as self 'expands' to encompass new self-knowledge. As self-narrative develops, they also expressed differing levels of awareness of new voice emerging. In silence, Gaynor felt she found her voice, stating 'I wouldn't have a damn thing to say if I/didn't start in silence!' Silence is valued by many because it is an accepting, safe, or comfortable space where they can explore emerging voice. A small number also articulated that silence enabled recognition of increasing authenticity of voice as different aspects of their expanding narrative are integrated into their lives and begin to be articulated in different contexts.

A few of the women recognize that changes in self-identity occurring in silence as a result of a deeper encounter with their temporally multiple selves allows them to live lives which increasingly reflect their individuality. This was most explicitly stated by Gaynor, whose experience is that silence 'fuels/I believe/a more true expression of the/unique little thing I was made to be ... so I can be more true to myself because of that practice'.

Individual Silence and Relationality with Other

The women also perceive that times of individual silence have significance for their relationships with others. Silence is experienced both as space where relational encounter with other is explored with God, and also where they can rest from the demands of relationality. Although these statements verge on paradox, the latter gradually enables them to consider relationships with increased honesty and composure.

Silence offers a space where the majority of the women experience liberation from judgements of others. Loretta spoke of spending

> most of my life being hurt
> and angry
> and [*sighs*] ...
> I didn't know
> that there was a way of living
> where I wasn't
> feeling where I wouldn't feel criticized
> all the time
> and silence is what's
> brought me to that (24).

As a result, in silence they feel greater freedom to be entirely themselves without self being constrained by external perceptions of who they are, and they also experience healing of self-perceptions that have been damaged by relationships. Similarly, engaging in silence also enables a separation from expectations that originate externally to self, particularly those associated with being a partner, mother, or carer. In vivid language portraying the blows to self that others' expectations can inflict in life, Elizabeth values that in silence she doesn't have to be 'knocked into/shape by/ expectations from elsewhere'. In silence, they begin recovery from pain caused by expectations of relationality requiring the sublimation of their own needs. A small number identified that this healing has included experiencing deeper forgiveness towards those with whom relationships have been painful.

Virtually all the women acknowledged that time spent in individual silence improves the quality of their interpersonal interactions: silence is crucial in facilitating their ability to connect with other. When Julay's practice of silence is in a regular rhythm:

> I enjoy being with people more and
> sort of (3)
> I feel
> I feel I'm more able to kind of
> more warmly connect with people somehow (5)
> ... when I'm
> practising
> I feel (3)
> much less defensive
> about people
> less defensive
> less likely to ...
> take offence or
> erm (4.5)
> or feel nervous feel shy ...
> I feel
> able to
> enjoy people more [laughs]
> ... it just seems to kind of facilitate
> connection I think (11).

The personal nourishment found in silence enables them to be more fully present and real in interactions. They experience relationships becoming more satisfying and enjoyable, often engaging in these at greater depth. However, some recalled experiences when their need for time alone in silence has been perceived as rejection, with little understanding that, as Barbara said, 'in order to *be* with you/I need to do this first.'

Experiences in silence develop the women's self-worth, diminishing their need to seek approval from others. Some described feeling more 'grounded' or 'steadier' personally and socially. Many also understood that changes in self-perception have a positive impact on how they relate: they manage relationships better, resist retaliating or ranting, and are more likely to contain difficult relational encounters rather than contribute to these escalating. As well as expressing ways in which engaging in silence is constructive for relationality, almost all identified that temporarily suspending their engagement with regular practices of silence has negative impacts on relationships.

The women's perceived safety in silence makes it a space where conflict can be addressed more directly. Most spoke of silence as where they intentionally reflect on and explore relationship difficulties by developing new insights from the viewpoint of others involved. Mary feels that silence allows her to 'take a step or two/back' and gives her 'a bit more perspective', balancing her understanding of a situation with that of others. Comments relating to silence as where the women became able to recognize their own imperfections in relationships were frequent: silence is a place where they acknowledge a need to speak Jesus' words from the cross –'Father, forgive' – for their behaviour towards others at least as frequently as for treatment they have received.

Many of the women identified silence as a place bypassing any time differential, where they feel aware of connection to others across time and space. When engaged in some practices of silence, a few felt connected to other people they knew, locally or globally, who would be praying at some point that day. This web of connection through prayer transcending time was echoed by some who also feel a sense of deep connection with those who have prayed in the same location – usually a church or other sacred site – over many hundreds of years. A small number spoke of silence as a place of deep connection with loved ones who have died. For others, this was extended to awareness of the presence of the Communion of Saints during times of silence. Several find in silence a connection with emerging life: attending Quaker Meeting whilst pregnant, Alison experienced profound connection to her unborn child, giving her new insight into how she exists in God:

> sitting there
> actually wi [incomplete] with life inside you
> and just all the imagery
> about
> y'know in
> God in whom we 'live and move and have our being'[14] and that you actually have a
> y'know a being
> inside you doing that
> and of course when you actually start to feel movements! ...
> the freedom to move [*laughs*]
> and yet
> and yet held in love.

Una insists there can be no place where we are alone with God. Her words encapsulate understandings of both a traditional perception of silence as solitude with God and a clear recognition of individual silence as experience of relational encounter:

> 'sit in your cell and your cell will teach you everything'[15] – it's perfectly true
> but it's the difficulty of sitting in that cell where you are and not where

---

[14] Acts 17:28. NRSV continues, 'For we too are his offspring'.

[15] A widely quoted saying of the Desert Mothers and Fathers, as found, for example, in Thomas Merton, *The Wisdom of the Desert: Sayings of the Desert Fathers of the Fourth Century* (New York, 1960).

where you would like to be or in some romantic wonderful
erm
tower
ivory tower [*laughs*] where you can be 'alone with God' [*said with affected piety, laughs*]
because when you get to God everybody else is there [*long, loud laughter*]
what is this aloneness with God?

Individual silence as a place of encounter with God, self and other was most succinctly expressed by Michaela: 'in silence I connect more/than in anything else ... with other people/with myself/with the divine/yes ... if I'm doing it alone or with other people.' It is to relationality with the tangible, visible presence of other in silence that I now turn.

The Gift of Silence in Encounter

The women spoke of receiving silence, and the changes that occur within it through encounter with God, self and other, as gift. Recognizing the potential of silence to facilitate change and growth, some explicitly articulate offering their own silence as a deliberate, active presence in their interactions with others.

The terms 'listening' or 'hearing' are usually applied to being present with others in silence while attending to what they communicate. Both of these words were used by the women in speaking of offering silence in their interactions. But they do not perceive their silence as only listening to, or hearing other. Instead, relating to other in silence was identified as belonging to their intentional practices of silence. They hope offering a deliberately focused silence to other, where self is fully, attentively present, will be experienced by other as valuable gift.

Some of the women articulate that silence offered to other is grounded in the personal acceptance and safety they encounter with God in silence. From their own experience, they recognize the need, particularly for women, to have space where it is safe to acknowledge truths of self, assured that self will be accepted. It is central to their practice of offering silence that other experiences being deeply and unconditionally heard. Alison, speaking of her work within the NHS, demonstrates the naming of deep listening as part of her deliberate practices of silence:

> by one definition it isn't
> silence
> 'cause somebody's talking
> but in fact if I'm silent
> erm
> and fully listening to the other person
> and
> and not just listening with my ears but
> you know

trying to take in every
every bit ...
that deep listening to another person ...
my listening is much deeper than it ever used to be
because of my own ... experience.

Some identified awareness that offered silence is a space where other and self experience deeper relational connection. For Sally, this is 'quite a/uniting/ experience', while Claire feels 'the quality of a relationship/I can partly monitor by the quality of the silence/that I can rest in with that person.'

There are occasions when profound encounter with other in silence is experienced as sacred. For Lynne, a counsellor, 'there's this/silence which is/ it's about connecting with the other person/about the person knowing they're understood/and that feels a very spiritual/moment.' Some women deliberately seek God's presence in silence offered to other, listening for what God might be saying as well as to what is expressed by the person to whom they give silence. Two women also explicitly expressed a desire that in the silence they offer, other might also encounter God for themselves.

Many recognize that busyness of life can leave people with little time to process experiences. Having experienced increasingly authentic self emerging in individual silence, the women are aware that silence in their interactions can offer processing time to others, facilitating similar opportunities for greater self-awareness, authentic identity and new insights. Rhona said it is in 'allowing silence/that sometimes can feel quite uncomfortable/that actually ... the moment of/awakening/comes for folk.' The silence offered gives space and permission to do this. The importance of offering silence to those who are experiencing internal conflict or conflict in relationships was implied by several women. It was explicitly addressed by Una, who, after many years offering spiritual accompaniment, is convinced no words she utters can resolve conflicts for other: 'it's actually not you ... it's/the people who resolve it/because/of the silence/because they experience resolution within the silence ... it's not us ... it's the presence and the silence.'

Several spoke of the importance of attending to their intuitive selves as they offer silence. They see intuition as particularly significant in discerning when their gift of silence is needed by other because at that time words would be inappropriate. Many are aware of numerous instances where they recognize feminist theologians' exposition of women having been silenced. The women know their words have power to silence, and seek to avoid treating people in this way. As Lynne said, 'if you speak too soon then you silence something/so you close things down and you/ shut people up.'

Words were recognized as only one way of communicating, which alone can be inadequate. Elizabeth, a professional wordsmith, says words 'can be lazy ... a sort of shorthand ... one can listen to ... and not attend so/to what else is happening.' Often maintaining silence and responding non-verbally is perceived as a more appropriate response than using words. The women value the ways that offered silence can give space for different ways of knowing and responding in relationship when words are too solid or narrow to carry meaning. Many have experienced for themselves that silence can be profoundly supportive when words *will not* comfort. They recognize there are times when silently being able to hear and bear the agony of other is the most effective support they can offer.

A small number of women realize that words which may need to be spoken in response to other cannot yet be received. Their intuition and careful attention tells them that the one to whom they are listening needs to give voice to what they express, and receive acknowledgement these words have been heard and understood. Although they identify misperceptions or inaccuracies in others' words, they may deliberately refrain from any verbal challenge: in that moment, their silence may be challenge enough.

Finally, silence is considered an important signifier of what cannot be expressed verbally. Across the interviews, 'mystery' was often used to refer to something – or someone – the women encounter in silence. Lynne said: 'there's a mystery/which/silence kind of catches/so to be silent is to/say that words are not enough/or … there are no words for this.' In the women's experience, silence often signifies the ineffable in relational encounter, whether with self, other or the Divine.

Conclusion

For the women participants in my research, chosen silence is not a place of absence or solitude. It is full of presence, a place of relational encounter. In individual silence, they encounter God as one who assures them of acceptance. Silence is a liminal place where identity undergoes gradual transformation as growing self-acceptance in turn enables them to encounter the truth of their identity in all the temporal multiplicity of self. Individual silence also offers a space where they can safely begin to explore the encounter between their own self-narratives and those of others.

Silence is greatly valued by the women, and along with its fruits, is perceived as gift. Their personal withholding of speech and fully attentive presence to other is not designated 'hearing' or 'listening', but named a deliberate practice of silence. This silence is offered as gift to enable change and growth in those with whom they find themselves in relationship, reflecting the women's personal experience of relational encounter with God in individual silence.

In this interplay of giving and receiving silence, we see the outworking of Barbara Glasson's depiction of relationality, where the emergence of identity in one story enables discovery of identity for others. What the women value in individual silence is closely mirrored in what they hope other will receive in the gift of silence offered to them.

Yet what is experienced of other in silence, and self's awareness of internal response to this, may further challenge self's own perception. In a reflective, cyclical process, insights into self and self's relationality with other emerging from this encounter may be engaged with in future times of silence. And so, the gift of silence offered to facilitate change for other has potential to be transformed within that encounter into new, unexpected gift in the life of the giver. It is in such giving we continue to receive.

Chapter 14
Patterns of Women's Religious Attachments

Eun Sim Joung

Introduction

This chapter[1] describes patterns of women's religious attachments which emerged from a qualitative study of women's affective and relational aspects of faith experiences. Attachment is recognized as one of the distinctive qualities and characteristics of women, although the importance of attachment in their affective and relational life, particularly in relation to faith experiences, has been less valued in existing, cognitively based, faith development theories. The aim of my research study was to find a way to describe women's manner of faith experiences, hoping to provide a coherent and convincing account of the roots and characteristics of women's faith experiences.

First, I will discuss the importance of attachment in women's development and its connection to faith experiences; a literature review on the dynamics of religious attachment will follow. Then, after delineating the methodology of the research, I will describe the similarities and differences of attachment-related religious phenomena that the women commonly displayed as they recounted their personal faith journey.

Attachment in Women's Faith Experiences

Women are generally thought to be adapted to attachment and develop their identity in a context of constantly building attachments and affiliations with others. Women's experiences come from 'the most emotionally moving relationships that help constitute our daily lives',[2] where 'the presence of the object becomes related to a sense of well-being, security, and need gratification.'[3] Women's moral

---

[1] A more detailed account of the research on which this chapter is based can be found in Eun Sim Joung, 'An Attachment Theoretical Approach to Women's Faith Development' (unpublished PhD dissertation, University of Birmingham, 2007), and *Religious Attachment: Women's Faith Development in Psychodynamic Perspective* (Newcastle upon Tyne, 2008).

[2] Nancy Chodorow, *Feminism and Psychoanalytic Theory* (New Haven, CT, 1989), p. 2.

[3] Janet L. Surrey, 'The Self-in-Relation: A Theory of Women's Development', in Judith V. Jordan, Alexandra G. Kaplan, Irene P. Stiver, Janet. L. Surrey, Jean B. Miller

choices and voices are also distinctively relational, as their identity is defined through attachment.[4]

Attachment theorists provide a greater depth of understanding of women's attachments. Attachment researchers support the idea that the differing value that the genders place on attachment is displayed in the differing gender tendencies towards patterns of attachment.[5] This explains why women in general seem to display a greater tendency towards attachments.

Attachment is one of the important aspects which influence women's ways of thinking, feeling and acting, and is of particular significance in their religious experience and commitment. Faith is not just cognitive knowing but is 'being aware of God in the affective domain', having a relationship with God, and encompassing of one's commitments and values.[6] Women's distinctive qualities and characteristics should be properly recognized and valued and, as Nicola Slee points out, relational and psychodynamic theories could offer 'interpretative frameworks for analysing the function of the symbolic and affective realm'.[7]

Dynamics of Religious Attachments

To describe how religious attachment forms and functions, attachment theory offers fundamental information. An attachment system is established during infancy and little change in structure is expected throughout a lifetime unless severe changes occur in circumstances. With repeated experience of interaction with the attachment figures, the child develops beliefs and expectations about the availability and responsiveness of the attachment figures, as a goal-corrected system, which influence the child's cognitive, emotional and behavioural responses when new relationships are established. These are called internal 'working models' of attachment. In adulthood, working models are expected to be much more complex and intertwined, and at the same time, each model is supposed to be separated and flexible to adapt and satisfy the individual's attachment needs.[8]

(eds), *Women's Growth in Connection: Writings from the Stone Center* (New York, 1991), p. 61.

[4] Carol Gilligan, *In a Different Voice: Psychological Theory and Women's Development* (Cambridge, MA, 1982), pp. 8, 14.

[5] Judith A. Feeney and Patricia Noller, *Adult Attachment* (Thousand Oaks, CA, 1996), pp. 122–6.

[6] V. Bailey Gillespie, *The Experience of Faith* (Birmingham, AL, 1988), p. 31.

[7] Nicola Slee, *Women's Faith Development: Patterns and Processes* (Aldershot, 2004), p. 165.

[8] Nancy L. Collins and Stephen J. Read, 'Cognitive Representations of Attachment: The Structure and Function of Working Models', in Kim Bartholomew and Daniel Perlman (eds), *Advances in Personal Relationships* (London, 1994), vol. 5, p. 57.

The network size of the working models and their density may also impact the quality of religious attachment.[9] The characteristics of religious attachment are very much influenced by other attachment relationships. In other words, the representations of the self and God are closely related to the representations of the mother, father and partner figures in particular. Conversely, religious attachment also impacts on general representations of the self and others. Peter Hammersley is convinced that 'the character of the person's God representation and their pattern of relating to their religious community provide a significant litmus test for the pattern of object relations which operate in other areas of life.'[10]

Religious attachment has always been an element of religious experience, although most academics have not specifically named it. In his research on attachment in the religious domain, drawing out the relationship between human attachment and religious attachment, Lee Kirkpatrick postulates the experience of faith as an attachment to God and the process of the experience as an attachment process.[11] He outlines two hypotheses: the compensation hypothesis and the correspondence hypothesis. The compensation hypothesis explains that God can be a substitute attachment figure where human attachment is insecure, whereas the correspondence hypothesis explains that the pattern of attachment relationship with God can be predicted based on an individual's human attachment relationships.[12] According to Nancy Collins and Stephen Read, each attachment relationship shares four interrelated components: first, memories of attachment-related experience; second, beliefs, attitudes, and expectations about self and others in relation to attachment; third, attachment-related goals and needs, and fourth, strategies and plans associated with achieving attachment goals.[13] Along with Kirkpatrick's hypotheses, Collins and Read's four interrelated components are important elements when we explore religious attachments.

Methodology

This research study emerged out of my own experience and commitment as a Korean Christian woman. One motivation was to bring visibility to Korean women's faith lives, since the women's grassroots experiences have not been much heard and valued by either academics or the public. The experiences of growing up

---

[9] Ibid., p. 59.
[10] Peter Hammersley, 'Adult Learning Problems and the Experience of Loss: A Study of Religious Rigidity' (unpublished PhD dissertation, University of Birmingham, 1997), p. 55.
[11] Lee A. Kirkpatrick, 'Attachment Theory and Religious Experience', in Ralph W. Hood, Jr. (ed.), *Handbook of Religious Experience* (Birmingham, AL, 1995), pp. 446–75.
[12] Lee A. Kirkpatrick, 'An Attachment-theory Approach to the Psychology of Religion', *International Journal for the Psychology of Religion* 2/1 (1992): 16–19.
[13] Collins and Read, 'Cognitive Representations', p. 61.

as a woman and a Christian are largely influenced by centuries of internalization of the ideologies of patriarchy and gender hierarchy embedded not only in the family but also in the church system. The research study is characterized by a phenomenological and hermeneutic approach, since it seeks attachment-related religious phenomena in the women's narrative discourse. It also follows the principles of qualitative studies as it pursues quality in the depth of the women's accounts; the findings demonstrate patterns between and within them.

The research employed autobiographical narrative in-depth interviews with ten Korean Christian women living in Birmingham, UK, at the time they were interviewed. In open-ended, loosely structured interviews, the women were asked about their present understanding of faith and about influential people and significant events in their faith journey from childhood onwards. Notes and full transcriptions of each interview were made and used for initial analyses. A series of analyses was carried out whilst the representations of each attachment figure were sought on the basis of each component of attachment.[14]

Three patterns of women's religious attachments emerged: distant–avoidant, anxious–ambivalent and secure–interdependent. The patterns are distinguished from one another based on the women's ways of holding faith, such as beliefs and attitudes towards religious issues, the goals of having faith and representations of self and God. The process of the interview as well as the content of the narrative was considered since both indicate the characteristics of the patterns.

Descriptions of Women's Religious Attachments

Distant–Avoidant Religious Attachment

The distant–avoidant pattern of religious attachment is focused on an inability to have an intimate personal relationship with God. In terms of the contents and forms of their interviews, two women showed the characteristic of this pattern. They saw this as stagnation which was an expression of their faith that they were unable to move forward in their faith journey; stuck in the situation, they could not fit in where they used to, should, or wanted to. This image is similar to other images presented by previous scholars who have highlighted women's experiences of disconnection with self, others and God, and the inability to integrate. Slee identifies this phenomenon as 'alienation',[15] which is an experience of 'nothingness' for Carol Christ,[16] and 'deep sleep' for Sue Monk Kidd.[17]

---

[14] For more information, see Joung, 'An Attachment Theoretical Approach to Women's Faith Development', pp. 282–92.

[15] Slee, *Women's Faith Development*, p. 86.

[16] Carol Christ, *Diving Deep and Surfacing: Women Writers on Spiritual Quest*, 2nd edn (Boston, MA, 1986), p. 13.

[17] Sue Monk Kidd, *The Dance of the Dissident Daughter* (New York, 1996), p. 18.

The women with this pattern showed strikingly dejected self-images. Having been wandering around to look for the meaning of life, Laura[18] described her feeling as 'an unsettled outsider' to Christianity, although she was always on the boundary of Christianity. Rachel saw herself as 'a victim of a religious family', as she experienced isolation when growing up in a busy minister's family and also being misunderstood and hurt by other ministers and their family members. These distant–avoidant self-images intertwined with identity and intimacy issues as they entered adulthood. Laura's account particularly demonstrates this well:

> The situation is that I am not married, having no job, no career or living no purposeful life, too much [p] my life was false [p]. ... I do not know what I want to do. ... the worst enemy for me was the sense of falsehood that I did not know the reason to live my life. ... if I died, just this pain would be ended.[19]

The pain and the sense of falsehood of becoming adult are powerfully presented. Yearning for a purposeful life and wanting to resist all the feelings of entrapment in conformity from society is a typical image of a woman growing up in an androcentric society like Korea. As Jean Baker Miller suggests, this is also affected by feelings of inefficiency as carers in the human relationships rather than by a misinterpreted notion of women's dependency.[20]

In the same manner, the women's representations of God also demonstrate patterns of distance and avoidance. Laura's account shows an imageless, depersonalized, un-relational image of God: 'I did not assume that the being might have a personality ... . Although we say "a being" which notes a person, I thought, "there is a thing and we [p] exist".'

Rachel displayed her distress, feeling disconnection with an abstract, conventional image of God: 'I thought I had known God but in fact, I didn't know the character of God and the attribute of God. I realized that I didn't know the God I used to think he was.'

Both women spoke of 'Father God' as an expression of their hidden, unavailable and undependable image of God:

> For me, God is in heaven, yet. I want to have 'father God', 'my God'... God is not yet my God, real father God for me. (Laura)

> Then, uh [p] God [*hesitantly*], indeed, father, these two are the same word, aren't they? There were times when I really felt good although I only said the word 'father'. (Rachel)

---

[18] The names of the interviewees used throughout this chapter are pseudonyms.

[19] Throughout this chapter, [P] was used for relatively long pauses and [p] for short pauses in the excerpts.

[20] Jean B. Miller, 'The Development of Women's Sense of Self', in Jordan et al., *Women's Growth in Connection*, p. 15.

The striking representations of self and God are revealed in their distant and avoidant faith styles, in which the characteristic features of their goals and strategies for gaining God attachment are explored. Laura particularly showed a tendency to deny, hide, or minimize her desire for intimacy with God with denouncing, cynical and sceptical expressions: 'Paradoxically, I had been thinking that I wanted to be a Christian. I don't know where it came from'; I wanted to do creative work ... I might have a good-deed illness.'

Rachel repeatedly used the strategy of negativity, passivity and contradiction: 'It is not easy ...'; 'I don't really know what to answer ...'; 'If there is no faith, there is no purpose of life ... there was no special moment for me.'

Difficulties in recalling or verbalizing the experience of God and lack of hope were evident, particularly in Rachel's account which often ended with long pauses, hesitations, remaining in deep silence, conducted in a small and fading-away voice. The following two excerpts show this well:

> I have never doubted the existence of God [*with a small voice, very long pause and remaining in deep silence*].
>
> I sometimes wonder when this stagnation will end ... I don't know when my faith will rise up again. I am not sure if there will be a moment ... [*with empty laughs, remaining in silence*].

Rachel and Laura could only express their desire for God in these ways. Rachel was trying to find a way to appreciate her old meaning of faith, which was a very private and precious experience, but had not yet found a new meaning since undergoing a traumatic experience which contradicted her old faith meaning. Living a meaningful life was Laura's long-standing desire, yet she couldn't find it from Christian faith. The strategies these women employed seem negative and in some way similar to 'apophatic faithing', which Slee suggests as one of the styles of women's faithing, 'typified by its negative, denunciatory or contradictory quality'. That is, the experience of God can only be 'named as "not this, not that" or through a series of paradoxical and apparently contradictory images and symbols'.[21]

This experience of dark night and vulnerability can, however, be one of the ways of discovering the deepest self and of longing for God, which paradoxically leads women to transform themselves in their own time and own way, although this has not been much appreciated as a way of faithing. Pamela Cooper-White also asserts that 'the persistent inner sense of emptiness, fraud, self-doubt, shame, and incipient depression associated with these experiences are often missed out from considerations of the developmental issues.'[22] Thus, it is important to encourage

---

[21] Slee, *Women's Faith Development*, p. 76.

[22] Pamela Cooper-White, 'Opening the Eyes: Understanding the Impact of Trauma on Development', in Jeanne Stevenson-Moessner (ed.), *In Her Own Time: Women and Developmental Issues in Pastoral Care* (Minneapolis, MN, 2000), p. 100.

women to be imaginative, to see these experiences as 'a sign of life, of growth, of development'.[23]

Anxious–Ambivalent Religious Attachment

The key point in this pattern of religious attachment is that God's work is recognized in the individual's life, while ambivalence still exists in the person's way of relating to God. Six out of ten women showed anxiety and ambivalence in their attachment relationship with God. Anxious–ambivalent feelings and attitudes are another way of responding to our desire for attachment relationship. Anxiety and ambivalence are displayed when individuals desire extreme intimacy in the relationship with God, but they feel unfulfilled and frustrated as a result of a lack of autonomy. Anxious–ambivalent individuals are, however, more sensitive to their emotional reactions and more distressed than other groups.[24] Although women in general tend to display ambivalence, it is a matter of the level of anxiety and ambivalence that distinguishes this pattern from others. There is a positive side of this pattern as the women recognize their own desire for God and God's work in their life, even though they are still struggling with doubt and ambivalence. Women academics regard the phenomenon as an awakening,[25] listening to the deepest self,[26] and listening to their own longings.[27]

Some of the self-images shared by the women with this pattern include speaking of themselves as 'imperfect' and 'improper' (Janet and Nancy), 'obedient' and 'obliged' (Cynthia and Hannah), 'lonely' (Libby), while 'wounded' was a self-description used by all the women with this pattern. The pattern is evident in their narratives, which are long and extensive, using conspicuous recurring words and phrases with anxious tones and nuances. Nancy's account shows this very well. She wanted to serve God as a pastor's wife, but she was told that she was improper or imperfect for the role: 'After she [a pastor's wife] prayed for me, she said that I was not such such such person to properly become a pastor's wife, pastor's wife. Then, [p] she prayed prayed prayed and said that I just seemed to serve for the church [as a lay person].'

The women's self-images are expressed in relation to their parental images: images of the mothers as excessive and dominant and at the same time flawless and perfect, while the fathers as less dominant, largely absent, irresponsible and

---

[23] Constance FitzGerald, 'Impasse and Dark Night', in Joann W. Conn (ed.), *Women's Spirituality: Resources for Christian Development*, 2nd edn (Mahwah, NJ, 1996), p. 414.

[24] Feeney and Noller, *Adult Attachment*, pp. 99, 101.

[25] Christ, *Diving Deep*, pp. 18–19.

[26] Kathleen Fischer, *Women at the Well: Feminist Perspectives on Spiritual Direction* (London, 1995), pp. 114–17.

[27] Patricia O. Killen, *Finding Our Voices: Women, Wisdom, and Faith* (New York, 1997), pp. 34–51.

weak. In many cases, as Irene Stiver points out,[28] the dependence and autonomy issues in the mother–daughter relationships in their adult life were important factors in the women's development and faith journey. In particular, the mothers' styles of rearing their daughters could perhaps be influenced by the experience of discrimination against women and their own struggles to hold their thoughts together on how to become whole in a largely patriarchal society like Korea.

In the same way, the feeling of ambivalence towards the mother is reflected in the women's dual and split images of God, which they all shared: God was both connected and interfering (or controlling), both benevolent and strict, giving both blessings and judgement. For example, Joan expressed a dual image of God using the metaphor 'fine thread': 'There is a fine thread and it is invisible but does not let go of me [p] indeed [p]. It seems to me I am connected all the time. I think God gives a way to return by holding and pulling us with his thread.'

It is very interesting to see the similarity in these women's language as they express God's love for them and their feeling of ambivalence, although the words and metaphors are different from woman to woman.

Another representation of God they frequently expressed was an absolute image such as 'the only one', or absolute power and authority. The next excerpt from Libby's narrative shows both images:

> God, eternity, everlasting [P] um [p] a sovereign [P] transcends [p] omniscience [p] my protector [p] and [p] uh [P] [*long silence*]. [*Started again*] um [p] the one who always [p] follows me [p] so [p] accepts my [p] my cry, the one who can accept my cry and my sigh. Yeh, the only one on whom I can lean and the only one on whom I can rest.

Her tones here changed from theological and conceptual terms to personal and emotional ones, and more frequent use of 'my' instead of 'a (an)' as her narrative goes on. The women's use of this image is based on their beliefs and experiences that God is the only one who cares and listens to them and who has the power and authority to resolve all the problems they have, in contrast to their previous experiences where nobody cared or understood them properly. This is reminiscent of such phrases as 'the exalted one' and 'a stronger and wiser' used for the image of an attachment figure (suggested in attachment theory). In fact, this also explains that God could become a substitute attachment figure for them in the experience of conversion or perhaps in the compensation process according to Kirkpatrick.[29]

The women's goals for attachment are focused on their emotional needs for comfort, acceptance, or recognition. They are very aware of their emotional

---

[28] Irene P. Stiver, 'Work Inhibitions in Women', in Jordan et al., *Women's Growth in Connection*, p. 232.

[29] Lee A. Kirkpatrick, 'Attachment and Religious Representations and Behavior', in Jude Cassidy and Philip R. Shaver (eds), *Handbook of Attachment: Theory, Research, and Clinical Applications* (New York, 1999), pp. 803–22.

reactions and tend to engage in displays of distress to get a response from God. Their strategies for religious attachment are also shown accordingly. They seek intensively and value regular activities such as prayer, Bible reading and attending worship services in order to get God's attention (or that of the religious community). Some particular words and phrases come up intrusively and repetitively in their narratives, as they are confused by their entrapment between autonomy and intimacy issues with their attachment figures.

This pattern appeared in women who had experienced emotional conflicts which are still not completely resolved, remaining as a scar or wound in their mind. This is a result of struggling to sustain the women in the social norm or tradition where discrimination against women is apparent and damages women's self-esteem. As Patricia Killen asserts, many women are anxious and ambivalent about whether God cares for them, particularly when they face difficult times in relationships, power-dominant social structures and traditional gender expectations.[30] Although the women's strategies were not entirely positive, their desire to become, as well as resistance to becoming, 'proper' and 'whole' are powerfully presented in the interviews. For these women, getting through the pain and emotional turmoil and discovering who God is for them is a way of having a faith which leads to revitalization and empowerment. Listening to one's deepest feelings and desires is a capacity which 'evokes an act of faith'[31] and 'is, rather, a goal of spiritual direction'.[32] The journey towards listening to the deepest self and awakening is 'neither pain-free nor risk-free'.[33] Thus, it is important to encourage the women's capacity to listen to their own longing and deal with the pain, which will paradoxically be followed by awakening whilst holding onto their hope for wholeness.

Secure–Interdependent Religious Attachment

Security and interdependence are important qualities which signify psychological and spiritual health. They indicate the capacity to be autonomous, to be intimate and to overcome the ambivalence between them. Women's connectedness and interdependence are similarly understood by many feminist scholars as qualities of mature spirituality. According to Slee, relationality involves qualities such as seeking connectedness through empathy, finding the sacredness in ordinary everyday life experiences and working towards integration: seeking 'to hold all in a balance and interconnectedness not fully graspable by the intellect but intuited by faith.'[34]

Security and interdependence enabled the women in my study to become relational and tolerant beings. Two women, Jean and Ruth, showed confidence and competence in their attachment relationships and presented their narratives

---

[30] Killen, *Finding our Voices*, p. 31.
[31] Ibid., p. 38.
[32] Fischer, *Women at the Well*, p. 115.
[33] Slee, *Women's Faith Development*, p. 112.
[34] Ibid., p. 149.

about attachment issues with relevant evidence in a succinct and truthful manner. Their self-images are presented with a quality of empathy toward others which flourished out of security and confidence in relationships as they could tolerate the differences between 'I' and 'you', and between 'ideal' and 'reality'. Since they could identify their own selves and reflect the feelings of others, the women could consequently develop the capacity to integrate autonomy and intimacy issues.

In the same sense, for both women, their secure self-images were reflected in their representations of God; they saw themselves as 'a child of loving God', being 'a carer like loving God' and 'one of God's people'. In the relational context, they spoke uniquely of God's love and care, and his fairness. Jean's account expresses this well: 'Even if the parent seems to do a favour for one child to the other ... the heart goes equally to every child to be well. So I think that God's heart for us would be the same even if God gives a test to one and a sweet to the other.'

All the women in the study quite commonly used parental metaphors to express God's love, care and fairness, yet each group differed, according to their parental attachment relationships. In this third pattern, secure attachment relationships with parents, particularly with their fathers, reflected significantly on their representation of God. Perhaps a secure attachment relationship with the father is a critical element for women's development, particularly in Korean society where many kinds of discrimination against women still exist. Security and interdependence in the attachment relationship with God also enabled them to reach out to people in need. When Ruth voluntarily provided health care for the isolated using her acupuncture skills and when Jean delivered the gospel message to her Buddhist husband, they both thought that they were God's mission partners.

Generally in the research, the women exhibited their strategies for religious attachment through the way they described prayer and their prayer lives. The women with secure religious attachments showed a distinctive tolerance towards what they prayed for and what they expected from God, as they recognized God's authority and fairness towards his people. Confidence and competence in the issue is well presented in Jean's account: 'It was like that the child phones and visits to see its parents. If there is a trial ... I interpreted it in the same manner, if I did something wrong, my parents would be upset and unhappy.'

It is interesting to see that, for them, prayer is an ordinary activity like seeing one's parents, as they believe God is both available and responsive. Attachment theory supports this and suggests that secure individuals deal with a distressing situation relatively well and in a constructive way; their anxiety level is relatively lower than other groups.[35]

As such, the most distinctive and important quality of the women with this pattern is their ability continually to refine their mental model and maintain a secure image of God. Susannah Izzard suggests a healthy spirituality is the capacity to 'constantly refine and elaborate internal objects' and the capacity 'to

---

[35] Collins and Read, 'Cognitive Representations', pp. 64–6; Feeney and Noller, *Adult Attachment*, pp. 97–100.

encounter a God who is more than the God we carry around'.[36] Having a secure representation of God is continuously to refine one's mental models of the self and God. This enables an individual to obtain self-esteem and to tolerate the difference between the old self and the new self, the tension between the need of the self and that of others, and the variation between the world you can see and the world you cannot see. It is an ability to live life in a connected and integrated way. This is a significant quality for becoming an adult, becoming whole and becoming a secure Christian, which should be nurtured in every educational and pastoral context.

Conclusion

Exploring religious attachment is one way to describe patterns of women's faith experiences and may both enhance and challenge existing accounts of women's religious lives. Viewing faith experiences through the attachment perspective enables us to see faith as a dynamic system of a person's whole life experience. With this perspective, we can fill the gaps to which cognitively oriented faith development theories have paid less attention.

An attachment perspective provides a valuable theoretical basis and interpretational tool for relational and affective dimensions of faith. It particularly enables us to recognize and value women's characteristic capacity for religious attachments. The three patterns of religious attachments have been described in terms both of the content and form of the women's narratives about faith experiences. The descriptions indicate the women's spiritual health and relational maturity. The women's pain, resistance, anxiety and ambivalence are also recognized as one of the ways in which they experience their faith journey.

This chapter has tried to deliver the stories of some Korean Christian women who are largely separated from their familiar religious community and temporarily living in the UK. Undoubtedly the outcome would be different in other contexts. Whilst I do not attempt to represent all Korean Christian women, it is important to realize the significance of the Korean context for the research: a largely male-dominated context in which women seek to become adults, Christians and whole persons. It is also important to recognize the women as those who both share common ground and yet also possess many differences in the ways in which they experience faith. In particular, my hope is that the grassroots experience of Korean women's faith attachments may be heard and given greater value, as a result of my research.

---

[36] Susannah Izzard, 'Holding Contradictions Together: an Object-relational View of Healthy Spirituality', *Contact* 140 (2003): 5.

Chapter 15

Boundaries and Beyond: Weaving Women's Experiences of Spiritual Accompaniment

Caroline Kitcatt

In the Beginning

This chapter is based on my doctoral research,[1] the aim of which was to explore the training, experience and knowledge necessary for the work of spiritual accompaniment. 'Spiritual direction' is the commonly used term for the activity of accompanying another in a formal way in their spiritual journey, but I favour 'accompaniment' as a better description. Whilst the term 'director' implies a power differential, 'accompanist' does not entirely fit and 'companion' conveys an intimacy that risks bordering too closely on friendship. No one term is entirely satisfactory.[2] In this chapter, as in my thesis, I have used the terms interchangeably, reflecting common usage. I wished to research this topic in relation to women, since historically women have been invisible in many religious faiths, their voices unheard, and their stories unwritten. It was important to me to research this from the perspective of the seeker, rather than the accompanist, as most of the material I had read was written by spiritual directors, from the perspective of their experience, and I wanted the seekers' voices to be heard.

I approached the interviews with a genuine curiosity to discover what the participants felt was important in the spiritual direction relationship. I interviewed 13 women, recruited via an email network and word of mouth.[3] As the interviews progressed, it became clear that a key focus of concern related to the nature of the relationship with the spiritual director or companion, and an important aspect of that was the boundary with friendship.

What is spiritual direction? Kathleen Fischer, writing from a Christian feminist perspective, defines it very simply: 'The goal of spiritual guidance is openness and responsiveness to God's presence in our lives. Spiritual direction is a conversation

---

[1] Caroline A. Kitcatt, 'Dancing Barefoot: An Exploration of Women's Experience of the Spiritual Accompaniment/Direction Relationship' (unpublished EdD thesis, University of East Anglia, 2010).
[2] See Kitcatt, 'Dancing Barefoot' for a more detailed discussion of definitions.
[3] Six of the women were companions as well as directees.

in which a person gives expression to her experience of faith and discerns its movement.'[4]

A wider and more inclusive definition of 'interfaith spiritual guidance' is offered by Beverly Lanzetta:

> The ancient art of soul guidance – often called 'spiritual direction' in the Christian tradition – is considered an essential dimension of a person's spiritual life. It is the process whereby a person is assisted in developing his or her relationship with God, Ultimate Reality, or the Holy, however named or defined. The primary focus of spiritual direction is on religious experience, not ideas, and how this experience touches the most profound level of the person. It is concerned with the inner life – that dimension of existence that deals with the heart, and the deep feeling states that arise from the closeness of the person to his or her divine source.[5]

A Textured Canvas

In looking for an appropriate method I felt it needed to be, in the words of Carol Wolter-Gustafson, 'a dialogical, person-centred research method'.[6] Like Wolter-Gustafson, I needed a method that would 'involve my whole being, including intellect, intuition, feelings and spirit. To honor and reclaim as strengths my emotions, sensitivity, and creativity [is] to claim my wholeness as a researcher.'[7]

In the process of considering the research methodology, I became interested in organic inquiry/research. Jennifer Clements, Dorothy Ettling, Dianne Jenett and Lisa Shields describe how they met out of a desire to 'find a personal and sacred voice in [their] individual research projects'.[8] Informed by transpersonal psychology[9] and a feminist approach, they felt that feminist methodologies did not

---

[4] Kathleen Fischer, *Women at the Well: Feminist Perspectives on Spiritual Direction* (London, 1989), p. 5.

[5] Beverly Lanzetta, *Spiritual Vocations in a Multireligious World* (2008) <http://www.beverlylanzetta.net/writings/86-spiritual-vocations-multireligious-world> accessed 28 January 2013.

[6] Carol Wolter-Gustafson, 'Women's Lived Experience of Wholeness' (unpublished EdD dissertation, Boston University, 1984), p. 15.

[7] Carol Wolter-Gustafson, 'How Person-Centered Theory Informed My Qualitative Research on Women's Lived-Experience of Wholeness', *Person-Centered Review* 5 (1990): 222.

[8] Jennifer Clements, Dorothy Ettling, Dianne Jenett and Lisa Shields, 'Organic Research: Feminine Spirituality Meets Transpersonal Research', in William Braud and Rosemarie Anderson (eds), *Transpersonal Research Methods for the Social Sciences* (Thousand Oaks, CA, 1998), pp. 114–27.

[9] For an explanation of transpersonal psychology, see Rosemarie Anderson, 'Introduction', in Braud and Anderson, *Transpersonal Research Methods*, p. xxi.

'carry the idea of the sacred',[10] and furthermore that even feminist researchers set out to prove something, rather than letting knowledge emerge:

> Instead of providing the researcher with a set of processes or procedures, organic research offers ways the researcher might position herself or himself to harvest the information that becomes available both from her or his own psyche and from the stories of the co-researchers and the context of the research.[11]

They use the metaphor of growing a healthy, productive tree to describe the process:

> The gardener must first prepare the ground by loosening and preparing the soil. Then the seed can be planted. Underground, a complex root system develops. The tree sends up a shoot, and branches develop. Finally, the tree bears fruit, which contains tomorrow's seeds. We use this metaphor to describe the five characteristics of organic research.
>
> *Sacred*: Preparing the soil
> *Personal*: Planting the seed
> *Chthonic*: The roots emerge
> *Relational*: Growing the tree
> *Transformative*: Harvesting the fruit.[12]

A metaphor for research process that has become particularly significant for me is of weaving a tapestry. It is as if I have chosen the canvas, and the women and I in our conversations have produced multicoloured threads, fabrics of all hues and textures, shiny beads of all sizes, and glittering pieces of precious metals. As I have worked with these, I have begun to see shared threads and colours, perhaps with slight variations in colour or texture. Woven into each other and onto the canvas, they produce a picture, a vision perhaps, of this relationship we call 'spiritual direction' or 'companionship'. This approach to research enabled me to let the information emerge rather than imposing my own agenda, and was therefore congruent with the person-centred approach which is my underlying theoretical base.[13]

---

[10] Clements, 'Organic Research', p. 116.

[11] Ibid., p. 123.

[12] Ibid., pp. 116–17.

[13] I was trained and work as a person-centred therapist, an approach characterized by the development of increasing empathic understanding, acceptance and congruence. See Dave Mearns and Brian Thorne, *Person-Centred Counselling in Action*, 3rd edn (London, 2007).

Weaving the Tapestry

It emerged from the interviews that it is very important to these women seekers to find a relationship which is separate from day-to-day life, with a person who is not from their circle of acquaintance. They do not want to feel responsible for their spiritual director/companion and they do not want to know more about the companion than they need to know in order to assure themselves of the companion's ability to stay alongside them where they are, accept them, and provide a space where they can feel safe to explore more deeply into their relationship with God or the sacred. This person is not a friend in the social sense, but is someone who is warm, caring and committed to the relationship. At the same time, it is not a reciprocal relationship; it is one where the needs of the seeker are central.

This is a relationship which allows the seeker to be where they are, in contrast to the institutional Church which so often seems to require people to be where they are not. These seekers need to feel that they can explore and question and not simply believe what they are told to believe. It is most often a relationship which supplements or complements the relationship with a religious institution, and one which provides a sense of connection.

These findings demonstrate aspects of the dynamics of power in relation to the boundaries of the relationship, and it is important from this perspective to have an understanding of issues of power. Feminist literature has much to offer here, and equally important to me is an understanding of the contribution of the person-centred approach in respect of its insistence on collaborative power in relationships, which allows equal voice to everyone, something which women, among others, have lacked historically.

The person-centred approach was developed by Carl Rogers initially in his work with counselling clients, but it has many applications outside therapy and has been used, for example, in education and conflict resolution. The relationship offered by the spiritual companion would, in terms of person-centred theory, be one in which the spiritual capacity of the person would develop or actualize, although there is a difference in the purpose of the relationship and also in the psychological state of the seeker, compared with therapy. Rogers states:

> The politics of the person-centred approach is a conscious renunciation and avoidance by the therapist of all control over, and decision making for, the client. It is the facilitation of self-ownership by the client and the strategies by which this can be achieved; the placing of the locus of decision making and the responsibility for the effects of these decisions. It is politically centred in the client.[14]

---

[14] Carl Ransom Rogers, *Carl Rogers on Personal Power: Inner Strength and Its Revolutionary Impact* (London, 1978), p. 14.

There is a boundary somewhere here, where the relationship becomes less about one person accompanying another, and more about the intrusion into the relationship of the other person's needs.

But what is a boundary? Perhaps it is a place where things change from being one thing to being another. But whilst the boundary between my cup and my desk can be seen, the boundary between friendship and spiritual direction is less clear. Relationships are fluid, not static, they must change or they will stagnate; perhaps some change is necessary, whilst other changes threaten the integrity of the relationship. If the boundaries dissolve, what happens? My findings suggest it depends on which boundaries, and how they dissolve or change.

It was the transgressing of the boundary between friend and spiritual director that emerged as the most significant concern of the seekers. The spiritual director's self-disclosure and taking up of space in the relationship was not helpful, and some of the participants ended up feeling a sense of responsibility for their director. Sarah[15] commented:

> Very quickly we ended up with her talking as much as I was, so I would go to her place and have three quarters of an hour, an hour, and then she started telling me all her stuff, well not all of it, but quite a lot of it. It kind of made me feel responsible to her, for her, to some extent, and that's fine in a friendship, but that's not what this is about, and for me it's quite important to have the formal differences.

The relationship transgressed a boundary for Sarah, between friendship and the relationship she wanted and expected. The nature of the transgression was the difference between being able to bring her needs to someone who held them for her and responded to her, and someone who imposed their own needs onto this relationship. There are many aspects of the spiritual direction relationship which are close to friendship, and this raises the question as to how professional should the spiritual direction relationship be. What happens when we confine relationships within professional boundaries?

Joanne is clear that her spiritual director's self-disclosure was only in response to her direct questions in the early stages; her sessions are always about her and that is what she wants.

One of the key things, Barbara feels, of spiritual accompaniment

> [is] the discernment of what and when and how, isn't it? It's a basic thing ... with my present director, we do walk alongside, I feel that ... I think he is extraordinarily open with me, without any confidentiality being breached, about how he sees things and what people are encountering and how he feels about it,

---

[15] Names have been changed to protect confidentiality and permission was given to publish the data.

and indeed how he feels about me and … I feel in a way there is a friendship there, so much so that it's caused me to think is this the right way to be?

At the same time, Barbara values warmth in the spiritual direction relationship:

> There's a very human aspect to, as far as my experience is of spiritual direction, accompaniment, verging on the kind of friendship, warmth, relationship, all that to me is important, which is another way of saying that some of the stuff I've read about spiritual direction sounds to me so clinical and unfeeling and I wouldn't want to be seen within 100 miles of it because I just don't think it actually treats people with the respect that they're due.

There is a boundary here, where the relationship becomes less about one person accompanying another, and more about the intrusion into it of the other person's needs. What seems interesting in this situation is that Barbara is finding herself having to consider raising the issue, but her director seems unaware that there might be a problem.

As mentioned earlier, Sarah found herself in a similar situation when she saw her first spiritual director. However,

> as a result of that [spiritual] direction relationship I took one or two important steps in my life, which were right to have done, but I wouldn't have done without that, so I'm very, very grateful to her, but we both acknowledged that we should stop having that form of relationship.

In this case, Sarah was able to discuss it with her director, and move on, but she was clear about the impact it had had on her.

So again, the spiritual director's self-disclosure and taking up of space in the relationship was not helpful, either for Barbara or for Sarah. Both ended up feeling a sense of responsibility for their director. Fiona, however, felt that she had benefited greatly from the relationship before it drifted into friendship and should not question the friendship offered, even though it was very difficult for her to manage the shift of relationship:

> [It was] really fantastic, absolutely wonderful, for many years, in that she really taught me, I suppose about quarterly meetings, all with some sort of food at the beginning or the end, and always some sort of chat at the beginning or the end, but in the middle of it a deep hearing of wherever I was, an affirming of me, and that went very well for quite a long time. It became more difficult when my life at last began to get its act together in terms of priesthood and a happy relationship life and I thought then we started in some ways to become more friends, and I found that very difficult.

This relationship transgressed the boundary between spiritual direction and friendship by becoming a social relationship, leading to the breakdown of meetings confined to a specific time, place and purpose. With her current spiritual director, Fiona was very clear about what she didn't want, and is pleased that this relationship is

> much more boundaried, we use a room at a centre, and even though the offer was of going to her home, because her home's quite near mine, I told her very clearly why I really didn't want that to happen this time and that it was really helpful for me to be in a room like off a library, rather than a home. She was very accepting of that.

For Fiona there is something about the location which helps to hold the boundary between friendship and spiritual companionship.

In this concern about the relationship straying into friendship, there is a feeling of wanting the relationship to be separate from everyday life, but yet of there being warmth, a sense of being cared for and connection. Tilden Edwards explores the issue of boundaries:

> The basic question concerning boundaries in the spiritual direction relationship I believe is this: What boundaries will support our mutual freedom for God in the direction session? Our answers will likely be a bit different with each directee. *We especially need to respect the boundaries that each directee sets in the relationship. We may see these changing somewhat over time, as trust between you and the directee grows.* [emphasis added][16]

Here it is the directee, or seeker, who sets boundaries, although they may change as trust grows. Adaptability and flexibility are therefore required of the director, and confidence on the part of the seeker.

For the women I interviewed, the relationships which became friendships seem to have followed an evolutionary path for one person, the companion, which was not desired by the seeker, and it may be difficult to address this, particularly when the companion seems vulnerable, as Barbara's was, or unaware, as Fiona's was. It may also be difficult to address if there is a sense that the seeker gains something from the change in relationship, for example, if they actually desire the friendship. Then there may be an issue of needing to seek another companion, as Barbara was considering.

In their chapter entitled 'Boundaries: Protecting the Vulnerable or Perpetuating a Bad Idea',[17] Carter Heyward and Beverly Wildung Harrison build on the argument

---

[16] Tilden Edwards, *Spiritual Director, Spiritual Companion* (New York, 2001), p. 124.
[17] Carter Heyward and Beverly Wildung Harrison, 'Boundaries: Protecting the Vulnerable or Perpetuating a Bad Idea', in Katherine Hancock Ragsdale (ed.), *Boundary Wars: Intimacy and Distance in Healing Relationships* (Cleveland, OH, 1996), pp. 111–28.

Heyward put forward in her book *When Boundaries Betray Us*,[18] challenging the standard approach to boundaries in therapeutic discourse. They argue that by regarding good boundaries as the solution to the problem, there is a danger that the issue of abuse of power is then not dealt with effectively; it becomes concealed and the therapeutic relationship merely treats the symptoms of a sick society rather than the underlying cause. They are concerned that 'this is what the boundary discourse does amongst contemporary feminists: it helps us *feel* safe in a violent and abusive world.'[19]

Peggy Natiello, a person-centred therapist, writes:

> Power over others, or authoritarian power, is still the primary political orientation in the world. This orientation is, I believe, inappropriate and ineffective in addressing the issues that challenge us at this point in human history. The radically different view of power subscribed to in the person-centred approach offers a map to the facilitation of egalitarianism, adaptability, and interconnectedness – qualities that seem essential in confronting the crises we face today.[20]

One of the themes of Heyward and Harrison's argument is that 'the psychological structure undergirding the current enthusiasm for boundaries among feminist therapists, clergy, and other helping professionals is the dynamic of "transference".'[21] They see this as a block to mutuality, and the theory and practice of the person-centred approach would support this. Transference exists, but is not the focus of the work.[22] A further theme in Heyward and Harrison's exploration of the damaging effect of boundaries is the nature of vulnerability. They argue that when vulnerability is seen as weakness, it can be treated as pathological and in need of cure.

A different perspective is put forward by Karen Lebacqz and Ronald G. Barton in their chapter in the same book, in which they explore 'Boundaries, Mutuality, and Professional Ethics'.[23] Whilst agreeing that mutuality and friendship are important in relationships, and that an examination of issues of power is necessary, they believe that there are other forms of relationship more appropriate to professional helpers, that professional boundaries need not be abusive, and that failure to

---

[18] Carter Heyward, *When Boundaries Betray Us: Beyond Illusions of What is Ethical in Therapy and Life* (San Francisco, CA, 1993).

[19] Heyward and Harrison, 'Boundaries', p. 113.

[20] Peggy Natiello, *The Person-Centred Approach: A Passionate Presence* (Ross-on-Wye, 2001), p. 59.

[21] Heyward and Harrison, 'Boundaries', p. 115.

[22] Transference in this context means relating to one person as if they were someone else, for example, relating to your female boss as if she were your mother, or your therapist as if they were another person in your life.

[23] Karen Lebacqz and Ronald G. Barton, 'Boundaries, Mutuality, and Professional Ethics' in Ragsdale, *Boundary Wars*, pp. 96–110.

maintain professional boundaries is 'abusive and unethical'.[24] They argue that professional power must be seen as a more complex issue than simply 'power over':

> there are alternatives to 'power over' other than simple mutuality, equal vulnerability, and friendship. In the counselling context, one person remains the helper and the other the help seeker. Yet this does not mean they are in a hierarchical relationship. There is a kind of mutuality in which one receives support from the other, yet each respects the role and personhood of the other.[25]

I suggest this also applies in the spiritual direction relationship, and perhaps more so in that the seeker is seeking a companion rather than a therapist. The director/companion is putting themselves at the service of the seeker, in that they are making time and space available for the purpose of accompanying the seeker, and of helping the seeker to find their way to grow spiritually. The quality of the space is created between the two, but the director/companion has a responsibility to foster that quality in their way of being, their way of listening and responding, and their presence. A degree of transparency and mutuality may evolve, depending on the ability of both parties to be honest in the relationship and requiring quite a high degree of self-awareness and trust.

Janet Ruffing[26] believes that mutuality in the spiritual direction relationship can emerge if the relationship is sustained over a long enough time. The growing maturity of the directee will enable mutuality to emerge. By mutuality she means 'a mutuality of attitude in which the other is accepted as a peer'.[27] Perhaps in the relationships described by Fiona, Sarah and Barbara, this mutuality had not had time to emerge, or perhaps it is more the expectation of professionalism and the need for professional boundaries which creates the differences between these seekers and their companions. Maybe there is a particular need for women to feel they will have their needs met in this relationship, and not be required to be giving of themselves to the other, something which they may do in the rest of their lives. Certainly most of the women I interviewed were in caring roles of one kind or another, and they did not expect to be caring for their spiritual director or companion. The key here, I suggest, is to remember that this is a relationship which is for their benefit, not that of others.

It is important to note that the converse is also a possibility, where the seeker is actually looking for a friend or substitute parent; this is something which needs to be resisted. Teresa spoke about someone who came to her for spiritual direction seeking friendship: 'I met someone who started direction with me but in fact I

---

[24] Ibid., p. 98.

[25] Ibid., pp. 101–2.

[26] Janet K. Ruffing, 'Spiritual Direction: An Instance of Christian Friendship or a Therapeutic Relationship', *Studia Mystica* XII (1989): 64–73.

[27] Ibid., pp. 66–7.

think she needed more a friend than a director. I offered to meet her from time to time just to have a cup of tea and chat because she needed to talk. She wasn't ready to do the work of reflecting on her relationship with God.'

In this instance, it is important for the spiritual director to be able to hold appropriate boundaries and to be self-aware in order to avoid being drawn into a friendship or parental role when that is not appropriate. Training and supervision are important to help recognize the potential for this.

It is very clear, from all the interviews, how significant the spiritual accompaniment relationship was for the women, and whilst it was important to hold the boundaries and not let the relationship turn into something else, several of the women felt a sense of close connection to their spiritual director, and reflected on the nature of this. For Mary, the difference between her relationship with her spiritual director and with a friend is to do with the responsibility towards a friend of being regularly in touch and maintaining the relationship, which she does not feel obliged to do with her director. There is something here about a lack of possessiveness, and a clearer sense of the limits of her obligation towards her spiritual companion.

This issue of the boundary with friendship is complex, and those who are exploring their spirituality may also need to venture into unexplored territory. While that territory may not be identical to that which therapists encounter (although it could be), the spiritual companion needs to be discerning in when the boundaries are held, and when they may, in discussion with the seeker, be allowed to change to accommodate the needs of the seeker. One important way in which self-awareness can be raised is through the companion's own supervision processes. Sarah, who had the experience of a spiritual director disclosing and using the relationship for her own ends, pondered:

> One of the questions I have ... is about how ... supervision or support for directors, you know, and especially newer directors ...can help people set the tone right and maintain the right kind of relationship, and make sure that it's reviewed from time to time ... because I think that's quite important, to be able to feel you can stop a relationship, without it being seen as a criticism of the director.

Joanne felt reassured that her spiritual director had supervision, as well as working on his continuing development, and felt that she benefited from it:

> I know that my spiritual director has supervision and I know he does things like retreats and stuff and I think those are important things as well, I think that the spiritual director does need support and ongoing training in what they're doing. But they also need to be looking after their own spiritual life in whatever way is appropriate for them, I do think I get the benefit of him doing that.

It is clear that supervision, whether in a peer group, supervised group, or through individual supervision, is an important source of support and insight and is to be recommended, not just in training, but on an ongoing basis. However, if the spiritual director is unaware or chooses not to explore an issue, the supervisor cannot help with it.

Training is another important area and several of the women who were also accompanists spoke about their training when I interviewed them. Susan reflected:

> It's very helpful because you get to, you know, part of the session would be, you will direct, someone will come and bring something with them, for you to talk about and you direct them for twenty minutes and then you swap and someone else does it and everyone else in the small group will watch and reflect and give positive feedback and growing points and more positive feedback! It's a very nurturing environment to do that ... it's good because it gives you a 360-degree view and feedback of what's happening, because all those people feed back, the tutor feeds back, your directee feeds back and then you can feed back your experience of it so I think that's just a very, very helpful way of learning.

The importance of this in raising self-awareness and in providing challenge to assumptions was apparent and they all felt it had been valuable whilst having had varied experiences.

Gathering the Threads Together

I was surprised how important the boundary issues were for these women, because although I understood their importance in therapy, I saw spiritual accompaniment as a more fluid relationship which could be negotiated. However, negotiation requires awareness and confidence, and a damaging sequence of events involving a friend of mine and her spiritual director, where the boundary with friendship was transgressed, brought home to me the importance of training and supervision around boundary issues.

The subtleties of the inappropriate use of power are often difficult to detect, can be open to defensive justification, or denied completely. It is a life's work in developing self-awareness for the spiritual director to be able to engage openly and honestly with their own use of power, as they uncover new challenges to their ability to be alongside someone all the time. Those accompanying seekers need to be aware of the issues raised by this research, and whilst spiritual directors may argue about professionalization, or the influence of therapy and its 'norms', the women in my study have stated their expectations, in particular around boundary issues.

This research indicates that it is essential that spiritual directors discuss boundaries with those who seek their companionship. It is important for both parties to be clear what is being offered and what is being sought, and how the boundaries will be managed. Trainers need to ensure that those they are training are aware of the need to hold boundaries appropriately, and of the risks of using the relationship to meet their own needs. Supervision relationships must be sufficiently open and honest to enable spiritual directors to voice their experience and concerns. Supervisors need to be alert to the possibility of boundaries being transgressed, and support must be available for both parties when things go wrong.

I believe that this research makes a valuable contribution to knowledge about the spiritual direction relationship in respect of expectations, the problems encountered, and in particular the issue of ethics and boundaries, especially in respect of the boundary with friendship. Whether this is a specific gender issue cannot be stated with any certainty, but the concerns around boundaries and my understanding of issues of power suggest to me that it is, and that further research in this area is necessary.

Chapter 16
Understanding Jesus Christ: Women Explore Liberating and Empowering Christologies

Francesca Rhys

Introduction

As a minister in the Methodist Church, I am expected to espouse historic doctrines while also being encouraged to reflect theologically, bringing tradition into dialogue with experience. Hence, I have been exploring the character and nature of Jesus Christ, attributing my need to examine inherited understandings of Jesus Christ mainly to my growing awareness that men's leadership has defined language and doctrine. Classical Christology has over the centuries over-emphasized and exploited the male gender of Jesus, and this has taken place in order to bolster male power in the churches.[1] In the research summarized in this chapter, I investigated whether other women from different Christian traditions have questioned doctrine and language about Jesus Christ as a result of this patriarchal context, and record how ten women whom I interviewed accommodated such questioning into their faith and practice, especially through the use of liberatory rather than oppressive metaphors for Christ. I document these women's understandings of Jesus Christ and what resources helped them shape their ideas.[2]

I was interested to explore models of Jesus Christ which can be liberatory and empowering for women.[3] Women make up the majority in Christian congregations but historically have been under-represented in leadership roles. Are the understandings of Jesus Christ being used in churches liberatory for women or, on the contrary, disempowering? The limited qualitative research from across the denominations notes that women are increasingly rejecting the

---

[1] Historically, the Methodist Church has been inclusive of women in leadership roles and of women's experiences. Nevertheless, theology and leadership structures remain weighted towards male experience and contributions.

[2] This chapter is based on Francesca Rhys, 'Figure of Faith, Human Example, Secondary to God: Some Women's Understandings of Jesus Christ' (unpublished MA thesis, University of Birmingham, 2007).

[3] Jacquelyn Grant, for example, analyses different responses in feminist theology to the figure of Jesus Christ, and models which effect liberation and empowerment: *White Women's Christ and Black Women's Jesus* (Atlanta, GA, 1989).

Church,[4] and although Brown attributes this largely to cultural changes,[5] the oppression of women by the predominantly male leadership of the churches is a contributory factor in this trend. From the Roman Catholic Church, Dyckman, Garvin and Liebert describe how credal language emphasizes exclusively the maleness of Christ; drawing on the writing of Johnson, they recognize that theologically maleness is not normative in Christ, and advocate that women are helped to develop this consciousness so that Jesus' male gender 'does not become an obstacle to a woman's ability to grow in the knowledge of Christ, loving more deeply and following more closely in discipleship'.[6] Predominant male imagery retards women's Christian discipleship, so that Ruether's question, 'Can a male saviour save women?'[7] remains extremely pertinent.

In my reading on Christology, there was little qualitative research into women's understandings of Jesus Christ from feminist perspectives, even though feminist and womanist theologians have reflected extensively on Christology.[8] In her documentation of women's faith narratives, Slee also includes only minimal reference to Jesus Christ.[9] Christie's research documents and analyses qualitative Christological 'answers from the pews', although the research is not from a feminist perspective.[10] Clark-King brings the issue of the maleness of Jesus Christ into her research when she interviewed Christian women in the north-east of England and documented their quasi-erotic devotion to Jesus Christ, interestingly as something positive yet limiting. She observes how 'they are still left ... with a male figure at the centre of the universe and not encouraged to see fulfilment within their own image.'[11]

---

[4] Marcella Althaus-Reid, 'Response to Claire Herbert, "Who is God for You?"', *Feminist Theology* 23/1 (2000): 34.

[5] Callum Brown, *The Death of Christian Britain: Understanding Secularisation 1800–2000* (London and New York, 2009).

[6] Katherine Dyckman, Mary Garvin and Elizabeth Liebert, *The Spiritual Exercises Reclaimed: Uncovering Liberating Possibilities for Women* (New York and Mahwah, NJ, 2001), pp. 185–6; Elizabeth Johnson, 'The maleness of Christ' in Anne Carr and Elizabeth Schüssler Fiorenza (eds), *The Special Nature of Women?* (London, 1991).

[7] Rosemary Radford Ruether, *Sexism and God-Talk: Towards a Feminist Theology* (London, 1983), p. 116.

[8] For example, Lisa Isherwood, *Introducing Feminist Christologies* (Sheffield, 2001), and Muriel Orevillo-Montenegro, *The Jesus of Asian Women* (New York, 2006).

[9] Nicola Slee, *Women's Faith Development: Patterns and Processes* (Aldershot, 2004), pp. 140–146 is a section of reflection on narratives that do make reference to Jesus Christ as God or the Other.

[10] Ann Christie, *Ordinary Christology: Who Do You Say I Am? Answers from the Pews* (Aldershot, 2012), pp. 33–62.

[11] Ellen Clark-King, *Theology by Heart; Women, the Church and God* (Peterborough, 2004), p. 74.

In this chapter, the name and title 'Jesus Christ' are both used as a way of encompassing the historical Jesus of Nazareth and the Christ of faith. While the Christ of faith holds greater scope for theological exploration, continual reference must be made back to the Jesus of history for purposes of historical accuracy. However, not all the women interviewed made a theological differentiation between the historical Jesus and the theological concept or mystical experience of Christ. This lack of differentiation highlights how doctrinal and lived understandings can be at variance, how our heads and our hearts can respond differently, and demonstrates some ambiguity about our understandings. Sometimes in this chapter, I need to emphasize the differentiation and so refer to either Jesus or Christ.

Understanding Jesus Christ

The ten women interviewed were chosen intentionally because in a preparatory questionnaire they expressed a preference for using arguably non-traditional understandings of Jesus Christ, including one suppressed in the past as heretical by the Church's hierarchy. The majority of the women interviewed were 40–65 years of age. Most had undertaken formal theological education to first or higher degree level and three of the ten came from minority ethnic backgrounds.

These women did not consider themselves alienated from Jesus Christ even though, for some of the women interviewed, the fact that Jesus was historically male had been or still was a stumbling block. The women focused more on the inheritance of patriarchal church history as a problem rather than Jesus' male gender. Many felt that father-son images were not helpful, since this traditional Trinitarian language excludes women's experience. Where the women had little issue with Jesus' maleness was in the idea that Jesus was culturally progressive for his time and had surpassed his biology and identity. In the words of Christine,[12] one of the interviewees, he was 'aware of his cultural bias, and was dealing with it'.

The women accommodated their questions about Jesus Christ in a number of ways. They downplayed Jesus' gender by using inclusive language such as 'person', 'human being', 'it', and by avoiding using 'he', in order to assist their identification with the historical figure and the Christ of faith. Two of the women, who had a mainly Christ-centred faith, seemed to have a particularly gender-inclusive sense of Christ; they believed that Christ encompasses male and female,[13] and that male and female persons could both embody Christ.[14] All the women used a wide variety of metaphors for Jesus Christ, including some female

---

[12] I have changed the women's names: all gave permission for their interviews to be used here.

[13] Galatians 3:28.

[14] Kelly Brown Douglas, *The Black Christ* (Maryknoll, NY, 1994), p. 110 posits how Christ appears to us today in the guise of other people, both male and female, especially among those struggling to withstand oppression.

imagery such as Wisdom incarnate or Christa, a female representation of Christ,[15] as a way of counteracting disempowering imagery, such as the dominant model of the individual male hero.

Liberatory Metaphors

Among the women's responses, I identified four models or understandings of Jesus Christ which they found liberating. Some held more than one view. First, Christ was a figure of faith, for whom they often used alternative metaphors to the fourth-century credal language of Father, Son and Spirit. Secondly, Christ was secondary to God, arguably an Arian understanding. Third, a co-equal Trinitarian Christ was seen in divine community, and lastly, Christ was a human example, as liberator from oppression. Within these models they used a range of different language or metaphors.

In what follows, I quote the women's observations about these models and elaborate the type of questioning these models represent. I trace how they have accommodated their own questioning and exploration about Jesus Christ to their faith and practice.

Figure of Faith

Most of the women understood Jesus Christ as a figure of faith or as divine in some way. Some of them felt this much more strongly than others, who demonstrated greater ambiguity through some contradictory statements, yet these latter women retained openness to Christ as faith-figure or divine. Hilary, who had a Christ-centred rather than a God-centred or Trinitarian faith, referred to 'a presence' or 'a being' of Christ 'that's always been there'. 'Jesus Christ', she said, 'comes from outside us, but becomes a part of us and changes us.' Jennifer talked about Christ as a figure of faith being more flexible, and therefore more liberating than relating to the (male) historical Jesus. Some found the metaphor of Jesus Christ as co-sufferer pertinent to their experience. Said Kate of her hospital chaplaincy: 'in quite critical pastoral situations ... Christ is present ... and in some deeply painful places ... often in deep agony as well.' As one of the women who expressed more ambiguity about the nature of Jesus Christ, Pat claimed 'the divinity of Christ I have problems with', and yet after receiving communion she was able to use the anonymous fourteenth-century 'Anima Christi' prayer which speaks of Christ's eternal (divine) presence.[16] Debbie was alone in specifically denying Jesus Christ's divinity. She attributed this understanding to her background of biblically literalist

---

[15] Nicola Slee describes how female Christa representations are consistent with Christian tradition in *Seeking the Risen Christa* (London, 2011), pp. 3–15.

[16] See, for example, <www.preces-latinae.org/thesaurus/PostMissam/AnimaChristi.html> accessed 26 January 13.

church teaching and to patriarchal church history and theology. The alienation she experienced in both contexts had together contributed to her loss of faith. Yet she continued to teach religious studies and she retained an openness to regaining a God-centred or divine spirituality.

Secondary to God

Some of the women put great emphasis on God as a primary concept, similar to an Arian understanding; Christ's divine nature was therefore open to question. 'Arian' refers to the understanding of the church leader, Arius, and arguably up to half of those at the ecumenical Council of Nicaea in AD 325. They understood Jesus Christ as secondary, or an intermediary, to God (the Father) and queried whether Jesus was divine and in what ways. The Arian question has recurred at different points in history and, as both Wiles and Christie demonstrate, is still a live issue for Christian faith.[17]

Christine, for example, said: 'I don't pray to Jesus. I pray to God through the Holy Spirit.' However, earlier, she had said: 'I've always had a sense of Christ's presence as a child, but I've never really seen Christ as God, so I've always had problems with the notion of God incarnate. Even today I don't see Jesus as God.' Jennifer spoke of contact as a teenager with Jesus-centred evangelical Christianity, but concluded: 'I think my concept was still God, rather than Jesus, and Jesus was secondary.' She went on: 'And God is easy because it's a very primal concept, and it's common to other great faiths.' Hilary and Kate both spoke affirmatively about relating to Christ, but their inter-faith contexts also led them to emphasize God, rather than Christ. 'God as a person without sex, or of both sexes, is somebody that is easier to relate to [than Jesus],' said Jennifer, yet she also stated: 'I view Jesus very much as God, in a specific time, location, and place, rather than as a separate person sent by God.' Pat likewise claimed: 'I'm more [into] God than Jesus Christ.' Huang Fu mentioned four times that Jesus Christ was 'a great figure of religious teaching or religious values', perhaps reflecting both her East Asian cultural background which emphasizes philosophical teaching and her current Quaker membership which allows doctrinal space to query Christ's divine nature. These reflections express an ease in relating to God, but ambiguity over the person of Christ, suggesting clear links with Arianism. Christie's interviews offered some similar findings among the majority of her interviewees.[18]

---

[17] Maurice Wiles, *Archetypal Heresy, Arianism Through the Centuries* (Oxford, 1996), pp. 2–24; Christie, *Ordinary Christology*, pp. 55–7.

[18] Christie, *Ordinary Christology*, pp. 33–62.

Christ in Divine Community

Other women emphasized the dynamic, relational image of the three persons of the Trinity, as described by Moltmann.[19] They also re-imagined the different persons of the Trinity in order to move away from exclusive father-son imagery. This re-imagining was accomplished in a number of ways. Kate used androgynous visual imagery such as in the Rublev icon of the Trinity. Vandana preferred to use Greek or Hebrew female nouns, *Sophia* or *Chokmah* for Jesus Christ as Wisdom incarnate.[20] Christ as the embodiment of Wisdom is believed to have been a key understanding in the early centuries.[21] In addition, Vandana used non gender-specific or plural Hebrew terms for all three persons (*Yahweh* or *Elohim*, *Chokmah*, *Ruach*). Judith mentioned knowledge of *Sophia* but mainly adopted a more domestic approach, describing the Trinity as a family of three favourite uncles over the telephone. However, this retained male imagery.

These two contrasting views of Christ as subordinate to God, and Christ in trinitarian community, echo two of the predominant understandings of Jesus Christ, God (the Father), and the Holy Spirit debated at the Council of Nicaea: Arian and Trinitarian.

Human Example, as Liberator of Oppression

Many women had a strong sense of Jesus as having been human, like themselves, who experienced similar emotions and went through some experiences like theirs. Elizabeth felt Jesus' solidarity as he wept in the face of loss. They valued Jesus' witness as a liberator of women within the context of his time and of those disadvantaged and oppressed, for example, Christine described his breaking of taboos. In this assessment of Jesus, the women interviewed were more generous towards Jesus than are some feminist theologians.[22] Debbie described one of her remaining understandings of Jesus as 'a revolutionary Jewish man of the first century with very unusual and different ideas'. Jesus Christ was specifically described as an example to learn from, a pattern or a teacher who challenged unjust structures and practices. Vandana described how as a mission partner she 'held conferences and travelled to meetings in other parts of Asia, where other women were also doing liberational theology. So Jesus was the liberator.' Vandana

---

[19] Jürgen Moltmann, *The Trinity and the Kingdom of God: the Doctrine of God* (London, 1981), p. 172.

[20] Wisdom (Hebrew *Chokmah*, and Greek *Sophia*, both female nouns) is described in Scripture as being present with God from the start of creation (Genesis 1:26, Proverbs 8:30).

[21] John Macquarrie, *Christology Revisited* (London, 1998), p. 131.

[22] Hampson points out that the parables of Jesus never challenge male privilege of his day: Nicola Slee, *Faith and Feminism, An Introduction to Christian Feminist Theology* (London, 2003), p. 50.

'think[s] about Jesus every day' and described how she took Jesus Christ as 'the main centre of my life', understanding Jesus Christ as relevant for collective life and not just for individual salvation. Kate was aware of Christ alongside the poorest and 'very much in the struggle towards the healing of the nations'. She linked his activity in his day with what is experienced by those in liberation struggles today. Jennifer regretted Jesus did not undergo a woman's biological experiences such as childbearing, since this emphasized the difference between her life and his. The metaphor of Jesus Christ as friend was favoured by Elizabeth who described how 'Jesus to me is a friend, and we do chat.'

Resources for Change

For all the woman interviewed, their contact with feminist, liberation, contextual and other theologies had led to in-depth reflection on their assumptions and beliefs about the nature and character of Jesus Christ. Whether they had undertaken formal theological training or not, the women all made reference to different Christian resources which had stimulated change in their outlooks and lives. Those who had not undertaken formal theological study had attended a variety of programmes, such as those of the Iona Community and the public lectures of the Queen's Foundation for Ecumenical Theological Education; these had helped stimulate their reflection and practice. I traced how these women had traversed a process of self-determination where they were 'remove[ing] the exclusive, perfect god–man Jesus Christ from the center of our Christian commitment to allow[s] us to claim ourselves and, then, to reclaim the historical Jesus and Jesus Christ'.[23]

Conclusion

I have documented the understandings of Jesus Christ of some women who have dared to validate their own experience by questioning historically entrenched doctrine and language. Some women sit uneasily with inherited understandings and imagery for Jesus Christ that they consider are confining. When Jesus Christ is repeatedly named by church leaders in hymns and liturgy as 'only son of the father' (or variations on that theme), women are consciously or unconsciously excluded. What is at stake is women's empowerment within Christian theology. This research has shown that women are empowered by inclusive Trinitarian imagery, by the example of Jesus as a liberator of oppressed and marginalized people, and by the Jesus of history who challenged repressive but accepted orthodoxies. Instead of being polarizing, the Trinitarian/Arian debate allows women to explore issues around their experience of Jesus Christ's divinity and humanity.

---

[23] Rita Nakashima Brock, 'The Feminist Redemption of Christ', in Judith L. Weidman, *Christian Feminism: Vision of a New Humanity* (New York, 1984), p. 68.

What can the Methodist Church and its ecumenical partners learn from listening to the views of these women? We can encourage exploration of different understandings of Christ, human and divine, including those beyond church orthodoxy, through preaching, liturgy, art and hymnody; we can offer women avenues and space to do this, and create more opportunities for liberating and contextual theological education for all ages, for the continued flourishing of the Church and its people.

PART V
Experiences of Liminality in Women's Faith Lives

Chapter 17

The Relevance of a Theology of Natality for a Theology of Death and Dying and Pastoral Care: Some Initial Reflections

Jennifer Hurd

Introduction

In 1993, I began in ministry as a presbyter within the British Methodist Church. Not least among the changes in attitudes and practices within church and society in the years since are those concerning death and dying. As the twenty-first century unfolded, for example, I became aware that funeral services were different from those with which I had been involved before. My training had prepared me to officiate at a rite of passage but, more often than not, families were not seeking traditional funerals but services of thanksgiving or memorial for their loved ones. A greater personalization was expected, emphasizing celebration of the individual life of the person rather than locating him or her within the wider 'communion of saints', and less about commending the dead to God to more of commending the living to God's ongoing keeping and care. I responded to the pastoral needs of such changes as best I could, but felt the lack of a coherent theological foundation for them. I became aware that I was ministering in a situation which called for 'new kinds of observance ... a belief which links life to death', so that 'a great positive [may] come out of [the] great negative' of dying,[1] and that I was needing new theological expressions to support this taking place.

In 2007, at a pastoral training day on death and bereavement, I found myself wondering if there had been any formal research into the pastoral and theological relationships between birth and death. Were there understandings relating to the former that could inform theology and pastoral care for the latter, and vice versa? I was curious whether, given the changing nature of human life in which endings contain beginnings and beginnings necessitate endings, these liminal, 'threshold' experiences had mutual relevance that would speak to the changes I discerned in attitudes towards death and dying. Although I had experienced birth and death with others, I had never been pregnant myself or experienced a close bereavement in

---

[1] Michael Young and Michelle Cullen, *A Good Death: Conversations with East Londoners* (London, 1996), p. 204.

adulthood.[2] In midlife, however, and in the midst of ministry, I started to contemplate these two phenomena more deeply and to consider a comparative study.

To pursue this, I searched for theological literature, but found little. However, the Internet yielded Giles Fraser's December 2003 *Face to Faith* column in *The Guardian* newspaper, 'Birth – the ultimate miracle'. In this Christmas reflection, Fraser refers to natality, the conceptual opposite of mortality, as found in the work of philosopher Hannah Arendt:

> What, she asks, if human beings were to see themselves first and foremost not as mortals but as natals? What if we were to prioritize birth rather than death in our cultural imagination? Or – to give this a seasonal twist – what if Christians were to think of the birth of Christ at Christmas as more fundamental than his death at Easter? Like all important ideas, it is both simple and brilliant.[3]

He also mentions 'the feminist theologian Grace Jantzen, who has done most to develop a theology of natality'.[4] The relationship between theologies of natality and mortality intrigued me and when, independently, a friend with whom I had shared my thoughts showed me Jantzen's essay, 'The Womb and the Tomb: Health and Flourishing in Medieval Mystical Literature',[5] I felt I had found what I was looking for. I am now undertaking postgraduate research exploring the relevance of a theology of natality for a theology of death and dying and pastoral care. This chapter presents some initial reflections arising out of the related pilot study, reached by engaging the data in dialogue with the scholarship of Grace Jantzen.

Jantzen and Natality

When she died in 2006, Professor Grace Jantzen was working on an intended six-volume project entitled *Death and the Displacement of Beauty*. In its initial Preface,[6] she sets out her aim of demonstrating that a 'symbolic' characterized by violence and death (termed 'necrophilia') has been the predominant choice of western civilization from Graeco-Roman times to the postmodern age. She asserts that this is still found deep within society, with disastrous consequences of destructiveness, a fascination with other worlds to the detriment of this one, and antipathy to the body and sexuality. Resulting from this has been the oppression of

---

[2] Although my father died when I was four, my present concern is with adults' experiences.

[3] Reprinted in Giles Fraser, *Christianity With Attitude* (London, 2007), p. 7.

[4] Ibid., p. 9.

[5] Grace Jantzen, 'The Womb and the Tomb: Health and Flourishing in Medieval Mystical Literature', in Jonathan Baxter (ed.), *Wounds that Heal: Theology, Imagination and Health* (London, 2007), pp. 149–77.

[6] Grace Jantzen, *Foundations of Violence* (London, 2004), pp. vii–viii.

those who are 'other', different to the masculine ruling elite, particularly women. Taking a deconstructionist approach, her intention was therefore to contribute towards a change in contemporary consciousness by presenting a constructive alternative, a 'symbolic' to displace necrophilia. This would be characterized by beauty, creativity, new beginnings, flourishing and love of life itself. The term Jantzen applied to this symbolic was 'natality', drawing on the work of Hannah Arendt. As a concept, her exploration of natality had already begun in her book *Becoming Divine: Towards a Feminist Philosophy of Religion*.[7]

Although linguistically, natality is to birth as mortality is to death, Jantzen was clear that it is not synonymous with birth but rather, that it encompasses birth and all that makes for life and creativity, health and wholeness. In contrast to how human beings have been defined philosophically as mortals, that is, by our death and endings, Jantzen proposed that we should be defined as natals, those who have been born and have the potential to make new beginnings.[8] This replacement of the deadly necrophilia at the heart of western civilization would bring allied 'features', such as valuing human physicality and the material, gender justice and equality, our relationality as humans and with the whole of creation, thereby making for hope through new possibilities, creativity and beauty.[9] Jantzen's project was ambitious but, as the twenty-first century began, she believed humanity to be in need of 'the healing of the western psyche so that instead of its death-dealing structures the present may be redeemed and the earth and its people may flourish.'[10]

While Jantzen's philosophy/theology of natality has already been applied to themes such as women's priesthood,[11] disability and impairment,[12] and the faith development of girls,[13] no exploration has yet been made of the theological and pastoral relevance of natality for death as a natural phenomenon. Jantzen acknowledged that death per se is part of being human,[14] but her work specifically addresses death which is necrophilial, violent and untimely. Natality is undoubtedly a powerful response to such death. However, for many, death comes as an intrinsic, natural part of human life. If our natality belongs at least as much to our being human as our mortality, we may expect there to be value in exploring theology and pastoral practice which is related to and inspired by it. Its relevance may

---

[7] Grace Jantzen, *Becoming Divine: Towards a Feminist Philosophy of Religion* (Bloomington, IN and Manchester, 1999).

[8] Ibid., p. 127.

[9] Jantzen, *Foundations of Violence*, pp. 36–8.

[10] Ibid., p. 5.

[11] Ali Green, *A Theology of Women's Priesthood* (London, 2009).

[12] Mary Grey, 'Natality and Flourishing in Contexts of Disability and Impairment', in Elaine Graham (ed.), *Grace Jantzen: Redeeming the Present* (Farnham, 2009), pp. 197–211.

[13] Anne Phillips, *The Faith of Girls: Children's Spirituality and Transition to Adulthood* (Farnham, 2011).

[14] Jantzen, *Becoming Divine*, p. 141.

then be assessed alongside existing understandings in this field, and alternative approaches suggested accordingly.

Research Methodology and Methods

As a minister of religion engaged in pastoral care, the paradigm of practical theology is my dominant methodological approach. According to Elaine Graham, Heather Walton and Frances Ward, all theology is practical theology:[15] our beliefs inform our practice and vice versa. This understanding is important to me, personally and as a pastoral practitioner. As a woman, I am also drawn to the approach of feminist research methodology. I find a significant degree of similarity between this methodology and practical theology, for example, in the shared importance placed on mutuality between researcher and subjects in the research process. To me, these methodological approaches are complementary, and so I am drawing on elements of both for my research project.

A researcher's methodology reflects a 'perspective or frame', while a method is 'a technique for doing research, for gathering evidence, for collecting data'.[16] It is therefore helpful to make a distinction between the broad methodology within which my study is being conducted, and the discrete research methods employed. In terms of the overarching methodology, I am drawing on both feminist practical theology and the qualitative paradigm of social science research. The methodological emphasis of feminist practical theology is on 'context, collaboration and diversity', utilizing 'a critical correlational method of relating feminist/gender studies, social studies, and theological studies'.[17] Its methods are praxis orientated, seeing practice and reflection upon it as primary to the development of knowledge.[18] Thus theory and practice are regarded simultaneously for the constant renewal of *phronêsis*, practical wisdom.[19] Similarly, the methodological approach of social science qualitative research is 'interactionist', generating data which 'gives an authentic insight into people's lives'.[20] It is flexible in the methods used to draw data from the perspectives of those being studied and their diversity, and it values

---

[15] Elaine Graham, Heather Walton and Frances Ward, *Theological Reflection: Methods* (London, 2005), p. 8.

[16] Gayle Letherby, *Feminist Research in Theory and Practice* (Buckingham, 2003), p. 5.

[17] Bonnie J. Miller-McLemore and Brita L. Gill-Austern, *Feminist and Womanist Pastoral Theology* (Nashville, TN, 1999), pp. 45, 104.

[18] Zoë Bennett Moore, *Introducing Feminist Perspectives on Pastoral Theology* (London, 2002), p. 22.

[19] Elaine Graham, *Transforming Practice: Pastoral Theology in an Age of Uncertainty* (London, 1996), p. 90.

[20] David Silverman, *Qualitative Research: Theory, Method and Practice* (London, 1997), p. 100.

the reflexivity of the researcher as well as its subjects. The researcher's own reflections therefore become part of the data.[21] It has an 'emancipatory potential'[22] as it addresses understandings and their resulting actions. In this respect, it shares the concern of feminist practical theology for social and personal transformation.

My Research Question

In Chapter 4 of the first volume of *Death and the Displacement of Beauty*, Jantzen sets out four main 'features' of natality. These are: first, 'natality entails embodiment'; second, 'all natals are engendered'; third, 'to be natal means to be part of a web of relationships', and fourth, natality 'allows for hope'.[23] The promotion within Christianity of such natal characteristics over the necrophilial is a natural approach for Christian feminists. Relationality, a positive attitude towards embodiment and engenderment, and hopefulness belong also to feminist theology, affirming life over death and creativity over destruction. However, all human beings die, as surely as we are born: our lives had a physical beginning and will have a physical end. In spite of this, death, dying and bereavement have not received much attention from feminist theologians. There are exceptions,[24] but often, feminist theology has responded to the necrophilia of patriarchal church and society by declining to address death. Jantzen herself acknowledged death as part of life, but effectively passed over the matter, emphasizing love of life and this world above concern about our physical end. However, by giving at least as much weight to birth as to death, natality reminds us that these are both 'threshold' experiences. The question arises for me whether this shared liminal character may indicate understandings in theology and pastoral care relating to birth which could have a bearing for death, dying and bereavement. This underpins my exploration of the relevance of a theology of natality for a theology of death and dying and pastoral care in the Church.

---

[21] Uwe Flick, *An Introduction to Qualitative Research,* 2nd edn (London, 2002), pp. 5–6.

[22] Colin Robson, *Real World Research: A Resource for Social Scientists and Practitioner-Researchers*, 2nd edn (Oxford, 2002), p. 41.

[23] Jantzen, *Foundations of Violence*, pp. 36–8.

[24] For example, Elizabeth Stuart, 'Elizabeth Stuart Phelps: A Good Feminist Woman Doing Bad Theology?', *Feminist Theology*, 9 (2001): 70–82; *idem*, 'Exploding Mystery: Feminist Theology and the Sacramental', *Feminist Theology*, 12 (2004): 228–35; Bonnie J. Miller-McLemore, *Death, Sin and the Moral Life* (Atlanta, GA, 1988); Melanie A. May, *A Body Knows: Towards a Theopoetics of Death and Resurrection* (New York, 1995).

Reflecting on Four Pilot Interviews

In order to discern the relevance of the concept of natality for those nearing the end of life, those close to them, those who care for them and those who have been bereaved, my research involves conducting semi-structured interviews with people in these situations. Such interviews are of a sensitive nature, requiring a high level of ethical and pastoral awareness and reflexivity from the interviewer, in keeping with my methodological approach described above. The piloting of the process was therefore of great importance. During 2010, I conducted pilot interviews around the subject area with three women and one man, here referred to pseudonymously as S, C, M and G,[25] who spoke openly about birth and death in their lives. I recorded, transcribed and reflected upon these interviews, initially in the light of the four characteristics outlined above which, according to Jantzen, are pre-eminent in natality: embodiment, engenderment, relationality and hope. None of these attributes is discrete, and each has further, related aspects, such as the value of our shared uniqueness, our potential for flourishing within the web of humanity and creation, and beauty, creativity and love. Jantzen's main features of natality therefore provided the first level of coding, and further categories appeared with deeper readings of the texts.

Jantzen's Main Characteristics of Natality within the Pilot Interview Data

Within each pilot interview, it was clear that relationality was the most prominent of Jantzen's main characteristics. The respondents spoke frequently of life-affirming relationships with loved ones and within wider human society. S referred to a multi-layered example when, as a palliative care chaplain, she offered support to a woman who had had a stillborn baby at a time, some years ago, when such occurrences went unacknowledged. The woman was unable to respond effectively to physical pain relief until S helped her find peace in her 'emotional and spiritual pain'. In S's words, 'Eventually, what we agreed would be helpful was that we would have a *service* around the bed with her family, in order to enable her to say goodbye and to allow that child, at last, to be given over into God's hands, so she knew it was at peace.' The service effectively 'reinstated' the child within the family. S commented that: 'Her pain carried on because her disease was advanced but the pain relief was much more effective. She was much less agitated and much more able to rest. There was a very deep healing ... and that was what enabled her to find the peace she needed to die.'

For C, too, it was important to maintain family relationships beyond death. Referring to her son, J, and her father-in-law, T, nicknamed 'Big Bad T', she said: 'J's middle name is T, and in the card T sent when he was born, he put, "Welcome to Little T from Big Bad T!" which has become a lovely thing that we do refer to,

---

[25] All have consented to the use of their data in this chapter.

so J knows about his granddad.' For her, the ongoing nature of the relationship was clearly symbolized by the link between J and his grandfather, even after T's death, through the family nickname. The importance she placed on relationality was also shown in being present with her husband at T's death: 'I was very glad to be there ... We were holding his hand, all three of us, holding hands together, talking to T. I felt very sad, but I felt this is a real – this is *real*.' In this experience of relationality, she saw a similarity between birth and death, saying, in both, 'that *this* is stripping away everything that's a veneer and everything that's sort of made up in our lives, that we surround ourselves with, then you're just down to something *real*. So I was glad to be there.'

In a less intense but no less significant way, M spoke of the importance of relationality beyond the family context when caring for her terminally ill mother:

> I can remember she was in such pain, and we hadn't a telephone. So I, in the night, went to the square, to the telephone, phoned the doctor, and he said, 'Give her two paracetamols.' I *was* really cross about that. And the next day, they sent a locum, and he was a *older* man, and he sat and talked with her for ages and gave her some Omnipol ... Why couldn't that doctor have *done* that?

For M, the way in which the locum demonstrated relationality by taking time to talk bore significance similar to his giving of medicinal pain relief: 'He did come and respond and made her more comfortable, the locum, whom we'd *never* seen *before*. And they *talked*.'

Likewise, for G, the practical expression of human relationality became very important during the period of time of the terminal illness and death of his son: 'We had tremendous support from individuals, from organizations, and that did help ... You need that. You certainly need that. When you get to the situation we're in, you need support, end of story. You can't do it on your own; there is no way you're going to do it on your own.'

As well as the support of Christian friends who prayed for the family, G valued supportive communication received through various media:

> I will tell you this now – a phone call, and a written letter! – took on a meaning that I never could possibly have imagined before! A hand-written letter is so very meaningful. And when someone has sat and taken the trouble today – not an email, not a quick one! – sat, and thought about it, and perhaps poured out their heart to you, and you can always tell, those are meaningful, and far more meaningful.

The significance of this tangible, physical expression of support links to the second most prominent of Jantzen's main features of natality to feature within my pilot interview data: embodiment. This was a factor strongly affirmed by all four respondents. G, a funeral director by profession, spoke holistically of preparing his son for transfer from the family home, where he died, to the funeral parlour:

'I washed him and put him in his pyjamas – clean pyjamas – and just made sure he was OK.' The value G placed on the physical, embodied nature of his son was echoed in the value he placed on physical contact for himself:

> Squeezing wasn't enough: hugs had to be full on, from the heart, yes. Hugs became very important. You feel the warmth and strength of somebody, don't you, with a hug? ... I mean, for instance, now, when I've been upset at night ... all my anxiety, all my grief could be settled in one swift hug – that's the hug you can't have.

For M, the significance of embodiment was expressed in the imperative of physical pain relief. Coming from a nursing background in her youth, and remembering her own dying mother, she said:

> I'm all for it! This – what do you call it? – slow release, you know. I think it's *wonderful*, because you're not exactly giving someone a big dose that puts them out, and pain is kept at a minimum ... But people have had to push for it! I do believe! There's so many people who are against something new, or they think it's wrong to do it. Why is it so *wrong* ... to help somebody through something that they're going through, you know? I mean, it affects other people as well, doesn't it? – to sit and watch somebody in such *pain* – it's bad all round!

M's comment reflects the relational nature of embodiment: within the web of human relationships, pain is shared and experienced by others, beyond the individual who suffers.

Data from C reflected the potential proximity of embodied death to the profoundest of natal contexts, as she spoke of her experiences of giving birth. Referring to her difficult labour and Caesarean section with her first child, she said,

> I remember looking at my body the next morning ... and thinking, 'That's *my* body,' but feeling a strange detachment from it, because it was *so* bruised and so battered. I remember thinking, 'I look as though I've been in a war zone or I've been assaulted.' ... I'd had a morphine drip and I'd had a blood transfusion ... even my feet were bruised. My arms; obviously my stomach was swollen. I looked down and thought, 'Gosh! That *was* a *trauma!*'

While the imagery used by C may relate more in common usage to necrophilia than to natality, it indicates the essential embodiment of both birth and death.

While she was working in maternity hospital chaplaincy, S encountered a number of occasions when birth and death coincided. Valuing the embodied humanity of the babies was particularly important at such times. S found herself

> as a chaplain, taking a lot of funerals for babies, which is quite hard, but so important for people, and ... so much work has been done probably over the past

fifteen years in helping people to do that, how they say goodbye to their baby, and photographs, and memories ... which didn't used to be the case.

Significantly, it was the use of a photograph of the stillborn baby, produced for the bedside service by the husband, which enabled the woman with whom S had worked while serving in palliative care, as mentioned before, to move towards the peace she needed to die. Such physical representations demonstrate the importance of embodiment.

While I have paid closest attention here to Jantzen's natal characteristics of relationality and embodiment, her further features of engenderment and hope were also significant for the respondents. These were sometimes found in conjunction with the stronger characteristics considered above. For example, gender was held as important in family relationships. For C, the matrilineal relationships within her family held a particular significance. Speaking of her daughter, she said,

> I look at O, and I do think, 'When I was your age, I didn't have a mum.' I'd lost my mum three years before. So I thought, yes, when she was ten, 'I'm still here ... I'm still here. I'm still here, my children still have a mother' ... O has reached a stage of development that, you know, I didn't have a mum and she does, and I'm very glad for them that they do.

With regard to the fourth of Jantzen's natal characteristics, hope for new beginnings often came for the interview participants from using their own experiences of bereavement to support others. As S expressed it,

> I had been involved in those issues partly through experiences in my own life of fracture and brokenness and moving and working through that, and finding in those difficult times, or dark times, that even when one felt that one was falling through the abyss, you could never reach the bottom and God was always there. That sounds a bit glib but, I mean, that was the kind of fruit of that experience at the time.

For S, as for others, the divine was found to be present in the tomb-like abyss, which in turn became a womb-like place of natal flourishing, not only for her but also for those with whom she worked in her pastoral ministry.

Further Observations from the Pilot Interview Data

Much additional material was gathered in my pilot interviews, but I will refer here in particular to the impact of the respondents' experiences on their Christian faith and living, and its relevance to another aspect of natality which, in a term inspired by Luce Irigaray, Jantzen named as 'becoming divine'.

Speaking of his son's terminal diagnosis, G said: 'We realized that it had gone out of our hands completely and it was truly in God's hands and we all believed that, yes.' In that belief, he prayed for his son to be 'spared', but 'We are control freaks today and we want everything our way. But life's not like that, of course, is it? No.' Consequently, G drew strength and comfort from the anointing of his son, P, by a prayer group:

> And they came, and they anointed P, and I'd never seen that done before, and I thought that was a strange thing, particularly as he was taken from us, and I thought, 'Well, he was anointed.' And that again was meaningful ... It was as though he was saying, 'Now, look, I'm going to take your son, but I'm going to anoint him in front of you.' That's getting towards the ultimate, isn't it?

Perhaps 'the ultimate' may be understood as the affirmation of P's right to share in the divine nature. For Jantzen, becoming divine is our birthright as natals, as we recognize the divine image in ourselves and others, and live accordingly. Certainly, G observed that, as his son's physical condition deteriorated, 'his faith had grown and had a tremendous influence on all of us as a family', and 'It isn't as though the situation was in vain or nothing came out of it, because I know a lot of people were touched by him and I think we were given strength, from what went on.'

For M, faith was a kind of *habitus*,[26] a way of being that sustained her through multiple bereavements. Referring to a conversation with her sister, she said, 'I think I must have said to her, "But I'm *all right*, because I have faith," ... it's just something that's there.' Of attending church within her practice of faith, she said, 'I feel you get kind of regenerated.' Regeneration implies rebirth, and so this may be understood as natal participation in the process of 'becoming divine'. For M, her faith meant this could still be possible, even in the midst of grief and bereavement.

C echoed this *habitus* when she spoke of faith as 'not what you believe, not a set of beliefs but a way to live', acknowledging herself as one who sees 'the divine in the everyday'. For her, 'nature, and the beauties of nature, and the order of things ... that is an embodiment – it's telling me about something else as well.' To experience both birth and death, then, for C, was to be 'at the very core of life'. In the 'realness' of such situations, 'in some sense you're touching something more real in yourself, and I think that's connected with my faith ... because it's about what it is to be human ... it's something like you feel you're more than human at those times.' The being 'more than human' may also be seen as a 'becoming divine', through the sharing of birth and death as integral to life.

---

[26] A *habitus* may be defined as a way of being developed from an individual's or a community's experience, acquired to such a depth that it becomes an almost automatic or unconscious mode of living, a way of being in which the individual or community may be said to *dwell*.

S spoke of how her faith 'deepened' through her work with dying and bereaved people and her own experiences of 'fracture and brokenness'. These experiences were integral to her vocation to healthcare chaplaincy, enabling her to '*be*' with others, embodying the presence of God for them:

> I encountered, inevitably, a *huge* variety of human suffering, but in terms of my faith, I never went through a time of feeling, 'Where is God in all this?' because in being with other people, I suppose, existentially, I maintained that sense that even if I could not see, even if it was a very broken place, that somehow, I had faith that in my being there with and for that other person, there was God in that place, too.

In this, it may be seen that S herself was 'becoming divine', recognizing God's image within her and demonstrating the presence of God with suffering, dying and bereaved people.

Conclusion

Undoubtedly, natal elements have always been a major part of Christian theology and pastoral care. Equally, attitudes towards death and dying in the West may be seen as becoming more natal in the twenty-first century, influenced by, for example, the hospice movement and growing ecological awareness. Nevertheless, the influence of dualistic, sexist, anti-relational and negative ways of thinking and acting remains strong: its destructive effects are still seen in church, society, the natural world and the lives of individuals. The data gathered from my pilot interview project provides only a small sample of human experience, but I believe it indicates certain natal approaches for theology and pastoral care in death, dying and bereavement. These include the mutuality of 'becoming divine' for one another, for example, and the practice of continued relationality, contrasting with the 'letting go' which is sometimes part of pastoral care in bereavement. In the light of this, I believe my exploration of the relevance of a theology of natality for a theology of death, dying and pastoral care in the Church is worth pursuing. I am grateful to those who shared their lived human experiences with me as part of my research, and hope that, in time, it may contribute towards 'new kinds of observance ... a belief which links life to death' so that 'a great positive (may) come out of (the) great negative' of dying.[27]

---

[27] Young and Cullen, *A Good Death*, p. 204.

Chapter 18

The Liminal Space in Motherhood: Spiritual Experiences of First-time Mothers

Noelia Molina

Introduction

The transition from womanhood to motherhood is a profound psychological, cultural, social and physical event in the life of a woman. The last decade has seen the emergence within nursing and midwifery of the study of spirituality in the transition to motherhood.[1] These researchers believe that a question such as 'Do you have any spiritual beliefs that will help us better care for you?' should be routine in assessments of hospital admission for childbearing. More than two decades ago, one of the first ethnographic studies that focused on the sacred dimensions of pregnancy and birth was undertaken.[2] This academic interest seems to have increased at the beginning of the twenty-first century. Childbearing is now recognized as a context within which spirituality is often enriched or deepened, or it is a possible occasion for spiritual awakening.[3] Extensive cross-cultural research on birth narratives has revealed that childbearing is often regarded as a spiritual experience.[4]

In this pilot study, I interviewed four first-time mothers regarding their experiences of birth, the transition to motherhood and the postnatal period as a time of awakening to an expanded, spiritual consciousness of life. When I approached them, at least a year had passed since the birth of their babies. Thus, these women have had an 'engagement' with motherhood, a period identified as central to the first year of motherhood in the maternal literature.[5] This first year leads to a 'transformation' in the women's social, cultural, physical and emotional contexts.

---

[1] See Jennifer Hall, *Midwifery Mind and Spirit: Emerging Issues of Care* (Oxford, 2001), and Jennifer Parrat, 'Territories of the Self and Spiritual Practices during Childbirth', in K. Fahy (ed.), *Birth Territory and Midwifery Guardianship* (Oxford, 2008), pp. 39–54.

[2] Jane Balin, 'The Sacred Dimensions of Pregnancy and Birth', *Qualitative Sociology* 11/4 (1988): 275–301.

[3] Lisa Miller, 'Spiritual Awakening through the Motherhood Journey', *Journal of the Association for Research on Mothering* 7/1 (2005): 17–31.

[4] Lynn Callister, 'Spirituality in Childbearing Women', *Journal of Perinatal Education* 19/2 (2010): 16–24.

[5] Constance Barlow, 'Mothering as a Psychological Experience: A Grounded Theory Exploration', *Canadian Journal of Counselling* 31/3 (1997): 232–7.

The aim of this pilot study was to explore the spiritually transforming experiences that occurred at the liminal space in the transition to motherhood. The three themes that emerged from the data – 'crisis', 'embodiment' and 'transformation' – are perceived by the author to be intrinsically related to spirituality, since spiritual well-being is understood to be intertwined with the physical, social and emotional needs of the mother.

A liminal space arises in a context of a breakthrough and often out of a crisis. It is in this marginal terrain that the new mother often encounters major transformation at all levels of her life. A meaning-making mechanism is necessary to integrate, support and adjust to the new role she has assumed as a mother. Spirituality intrinsically involves the quest for meaning, purpose and values within life.[6] The study of the transition to motherhood through the lens of authentic meaning-making can open the door to recognize the distinct place that spirituality plays in the crisis and in the transformation that occurs in the event of becoming a mother.

The cultural and historical dimensions of motherhood are challenging and contradictory. Most women feel unassisted and unsupported in this journey and many research studies show the high risk of maternal psychological maladjustment.[7] The conceptualization of spirituality which informs this investigation of the mothering experience aims at uncovering the types of spiritual awareness in a mother that can be socially, culturally, economically and politically transformative.

Liminality, Spirituality and Motherhood

The last decades have witnessed an emergence of research in the study of spiritual experience, with most scholars recognizing that spirituality needs to be researched broadly throughout the population.[8] Nevertheless, there is a lack of research into the spirituality of birthing women, and the academic literature seems to be at an embryonic stage in relation to spirituality and motherhood.

The method of my study is interdisciplinary, engaging disciplines such as sociology, psychology and cultural studies to investigate spiritual phenomena. I draw on humanistic, transpersonal and anthropological perspectives to inform my understanding of spirituality. The humanistic approach investigates human beings in terms of the meaning, values, freedom, potential and spirituality of the individual. Humanistic spirituality refers to the fundamental capacities in human beings variously described as human spiritual nature, capacity for transcendence and self-

---

[6] John Swinton, *Spirituality in Mental Health Care: Rediscovering a Forgotten Dimension* (London, 2001).

[7] Pranee Liamputtong, 'When giving life starts to take the life out of you: Women's experiences of depression after Childbirth', *Midwifery* 23 (2007): 77–91.

[8] Annick Hedlund-de Wit, 'The rising culture and worldview of contemporary spirituality: A sociological study of potentials and pitfalls for sustainable development', *Ecological Economics* 70 (2011): 1057–65.

transcendence. Humanists also emphasize the lived reality of these capacities and the ways in which they shape life.[9] The transpersonal approach recognizes that human behaviour is influenced by forces outside the individual, at the same time as studying consciousness within the individual.[10] Transpersonal is concerned with the study of humanity's highest potential, and with the recognition, understanding and realization of unitive, spiritual and transcendent states of consciousness.[11]

The anthropological approach seeks to understand essential characteristics of human beings and how those impact on and mould culture and beliefs. Like the other two approaches, this one also values the capacity for spirituality in every individual as an innate capacity. Theorists such as Bernard Lonergan and Daniel Helminiak[12] argue that human beings engage in a range of experiences in life in order to establish normative values, reasoned judgement and self-determination, and in search of authentic truth. Each of these approaches embraces the significance of cross-cultural, religious and non-religious contexts for their capacity to awaken spiritual awareness in the individual. Describing spirituality in these terms will be a common reality for most people.

In this study, liminality is also understood within an anthropological framework. 'Liminality' comes from the Latin, meaning 'a threshold'. Motherhood is one of the major life transitions experienced by women. Pregnancy, birth and the transition to motherhood have been found to create conditions that are ritualistic in nature.[13] Anthropologically, being on the 'threshold' is to exist within two existential planes, a rite of passage. Anthropologist Arnold Van Gennep observed three basic stages within rites of passage: the pre-liminal rites that served to separate the participant from his or her previous world, the liminal or threshold rites, and the post-liminal ceremonies of incorporation into a new world.[14] In motherhood, the prenatal stage can be considered pre-liminal as it assists the woman into the threshold, and the postpartum as the post-liminal rite. Women in this study reported mostly on experiences which correspond to the second stage of the rite of passage: the liminal space. In this space, there are frequently feelings of loss, challenges and

---

[9] David Perrin, *Studying Christian Spirituality* (London, 2007), pp. 35–44.

[10] Frances Vaughan, 'What is Spiritual Intelligence?', *Journal of Humanistic Psychology* 42/2 (2002): 16–33.

[11] Lajoie Shapiro, 'Definitions of transpersonal psychology: the first twenty-three years', *Journal of Transpersonal Psychology* 24 (1992): 79–98.

[12] Bernard Lonergan, *Insight: A Study of Human Understanding* (Toronto, 1957), p. 13; Daniel Helminiak, 'Neurology, Psychology, and Extraordinary Religious Experiences', *Journal of Religion and Health* 23/1 (1984): 33–44.

[13] Gregg Lahood, 'Rumour of Angels and Heavenly Midwives: Anthropology of Transpersonal Events and Childbirth', *Women and Birth* 20/7 (2007): 3–10.

[14] Arnold Van Gennep, *The Rites of Passage* (London, 2004), p. 21.

disruptions of the existing structure.[15] Three themes were of particular significance for spirituality, and in what follows I turn to examine these themes.

Research Findings

The Descent into the Underworld: Spiritual Crisis in Motherhood

> There is a natural time after childbearing when a woman is considered to be of the *underworld*. She is dusted with its dust, watered by its water, having seen into the mystery of life/death/pain/joy during her labour. So, for a time she is '*not here*' but rather still '*there*'. [my emphasis][16]

Mythically and archetypally, the descent into the underworld is characterized by a psycho-spiritual initiation. In this study, liminality, the underworld and the unconscious are interchangeable terms used to denote a personal space in which the individual faces a deep challenge, undergoes a growth experience, enters a transpersonal/sacred space, undergoes an identity crisis and has a sense of being an outsider.[17]

In this liminal phase between the unconscious and conscious stages, the woman is struggling with ambiguity, paradox and opposing feelings. The initiation and emergence have been described by anthropologists as a breakthrough that is often painful, acute and dramatic and which happens on all levels, material, spiritual and bodily.[18] Once the darkness of the symbolic and archetypal unconscious has been entered, a deconstruction of identity occurs. In some maternal studies, this experience is identified as a personal crisis and a type of identity disintegration which can threaten the women's sense of self.[19] All participants in my study described feelings of 'entering the unknown' and an intense conflict with identity:

---

[15] Victor Turner, *The Ritual Process: Structure and Anti-Structure* (New York, 1991), p. 80.

[16] Clarissa Pinkola Estes, *Women Who Run With the Wolves* (New York, 1996), p. 164.

[17] Rozz Carroll, 'At the Border between Chaos and Order', in Jenny Corigall and Heward Wilkinson (eds), *Revolutionary Connections: Psychotherapy and Neuroscience* (New York, 2003), pp. 191–211.

[18] David Steindl-Rast, cited in Emma Bragdon, *A Sourcebook for Helping People with Spiritual Problems* (Woodstock, VT, 2006), p. 18.

[19] Ruth Darvill, 'Psychological Factors that Impact on Women's Experiences of First Time Motherhood: a Qualitative study of the Transition' *Midwifery*, 26 (2010): 357–66.

I just had no idea what was going on, what was coming, you know, it sounds great but you just don't know what you are getting yourself into and then here: that's a baby. (Interviewee 4)[20]

Yeah, sometimes it was teary-eyed how hard this is. How am I going to do this? How long is this going to last? Where is my life gone? I actually found that very difficult. My own needs not be met. Where am I in this? What is happening? (Interviewee 1)

Maternal identity is suspended between the opposites of subjectivity and objectivity and does not wholly inhabit either. In the paradoxical nature of liminality, death coexists with birth. In a recent study into birth, women described their experiences of becoming a mother in terms of 'facing death' and of 'survival'.[21] In this paradoxical place, the transcendent function of the self helps to bridge or remove the gap between subject and object.[22] There is a symbolic dialogue with the unconscious that the new mother needs to dare. This dialogue is a form of spiritual emergence, an awakening and a step to a more expansive way of being, in which there is a development of a more profound consciousness.[23] In this stage, the awareness of the women's value system is tested by the vulnerability of her newborn. In the fog of this process, she seeks to comprehend what is meaningful in order to make adjustments.

A spiritual crisis has been defined as a drastic change in the individual's meaning system.[24] A recent maternal study concluded that the transformation, growth and transition into motherhood are usually mediated by reflective self-acceptance, spiritual perception and increased self-awareness.[25] Openness to change and letting go of the old self are foundational factors for integrating a spiritual experience.[26] Mothers often struggle with change versus rigidity. Feelings of control and perfectionism in the face of the new realities of motherhood were repeatedly related at length in the interviews. Mothers felt that they no longer had control over anything in life and the inclination was to rigidify their experiences:

---

[20] All participants consented the use of their data for this article. I have chosen not to use pseudonyms but to allocate numbers to the four interviewees.

[21] Jennifer Parrat, 'A Feminist Critique of Foundational Nursing Research and Theory on Transition to Motherhood', *Midwifer*, 27/4 (2010): 445–51.

[22] Jeffrey Miller, *The Transcendent Function: Jung's Model of Psychological Growth through a Dialogue with the Unconscious* (New York, 2004), pp. 100–110.

[23] Ken Wilber, *The Atman Project: A Transpersonal View of Human Development* (Wheaton, IL, 1980), p. 204.

[24] Stanislaw Grof and Christina Grof, *Spiritual Emergency: When Personal Transformation Becomes a Crisis* (Los Angeles, CA, 1989).

[25] Kristin Akerjordet, 'Being in Charge – New Mothers' Perceptions of Reflective Leadership and Motherhood', *Journal of Nursing Management* 18/4 (2010): 409–17.

[26] Bragdon, *Sourcebook*, pp. 43–76.

> I don't know. I suppose I had a bit of fear of losing control or not being able to cope or do something. I just started to feel really like I wasn't coping. It wasn't that I was trying to be a perfect mother or anything. I don't know what it was. I was just too determined to do things the way I thought I wanted to do it. (Interviewee 1)

Psychologically, control is one of the mechanisms that the ego uses to counteract persecutory anxiety.[27] Maternal anxiety was also a common and recurrent theme within the narratives of the new mothers in this study. They discussed how they had tried to understand this anxiety and the feelings that it provoked:

> There is the anxiety in there as well. I am trying to figure out why I am so anxious. I don't understand this, where is this anxiety coming from? (Interviewee 1)

> That is the one that I am most afraid of [*laughs*]. I hate it. That is the one that has come up. I feel that I am questioning what this anxiety is. I haven't quite worked it out yet. It is a very difficult job being a mother and I don't think our society supports it. I don't think it is held up to be supported. (Interviewee 2)

> It is hard, especially if you are feeling anxious. The baby is just sitting there or he is asleep, if you know what I mean. Then he will get periods of crying and you don't know why. It is hard and very intense. (Interviewee 3)

> Then it started to escalate and I really didn't want to be left on my own with the baby. I was just really – very, very anxious. (Interviewee 4)

This anxiety was not only at a cognitive level, but existed symbiotically with the 'unconscious suffering' that the mother needed to tolerate during the life-altering transition. This is a very difficult act to juggle and mothers are often overcome by a profound struggle within themselves. Maternal ambivalence is a direct consequence of this constant conflict in the liminal space. Out of this ambivalence, intense feelings erupt: anger, joy, love, shame, guilt, loneliness and sadness.

Most of the women interviewed felt or described the intensity of such feelings:

> There is that sense of loss and sometimes you feel a bit bad about what you are just thinking. (Interviewee 1)

> Because how can you feel lonely if you have a child here? The loneliness is in my soul and that is important to me. (Interviewee 2)

---

[27] Harold Searles, *Collected Works on Schizophrenia and Related Subjects* (London, 1965), p. 46.

It is too much, yes. You just kind of didn't want to be responsible for somebody's life completely. (Interviewee 3)

Specifically I just feel much more deeply. It is like my experience of life is a lot more intense. There is more fear, love and joy. (Interviewee 4)

This pattern of psycho-spiritual liminality has been understood as a form of psychological renewal and new birth through the activation of a central archetype. It is a period where archetypes and symbols may be significant for interpreting the profound experience that the mother undergoes in the transition to motherhood.[28] Maternal ambivalence often arises because of the powerful, central archetype that is awakening in women at this liminal level: mother as both creator and destroyer.[29] All archetypal images necessarily have a dual nature and, as the transpersonal psychologist Hillman has noted: 'You cannot have a good side without the other. The moment motherhood is constellated both sides are constellated. Nor is it possible to convert the negative into the positive.'[30]

In the coexistence of ambivalence, conflicts and dualities in the mother, insights into truth and wisdom strive to be born. New ideas may emerge as barely explicit or 'half-hinted' consciousness.[31] The unified and integrative self is often glimpsed 'in-between' consciousness and unconsciousness. Some mothers have described it as learning to legislate for two states, and to secure the border between them.[32] The crisis that the transition to motherhood provokes and the journey into liminality have been described as a profound quest for wholeness and authentic integrity.[33]

---

[28] Christina Grof and Stanislav Grof, 'Spiritual Emergency: The Understanding and Treatment of Transpersonal Crises', *ReVision* 8/2 (1986): 7–20. The Grofs named eight patterns in the process of spiritual emergence: Awakening of the Serpent Power (Kundalini), Shamanic journey, Psychological renewal through activation of the central archetype, Psychic opening, Emergence of a karmic pattern, Possession states, Encounters with extra-terrestrials, and Inner-life and other mystical experiences.

[29] Rozsika Parker, *The Experience of Maternal Ambivalence: Torn in two* (London, 1995), pp. 212–20.

[30] James Hillman, 'The Bad Mother, an Archetypal Approach', in Patricia Berry (ed.), *Fathers and Mothers* (Dallas, TX, 1990), p. 107.

[31] Antonio Damasio, *The Feeling of What Happens: Body and Emotion in the Making of Consciousness* (New York, 1999), p. 183.

[32] Rachel Cusk, *A Life's Work: On Becoming a Mother* (London, 2001).

[33] Naomi Lombardi, 'Dancing in the Underworld: the Quest for Wholeness', in Annette L. Williams, Karen N. Villanueva and Lucia C. Birnbaum (eds), *She is Everywhere! Vol. 2: An Anthology of Writings in Womanist / Feminist Spirituality* (Indiana, 2008), pp. 337–50.

Embodiment: The Conundrum of Motherhood

The second theme that emerges in this study of expanded consciousness through the transition to motherhood is embodiment. The close link between spirituality and the material human body[34] has become more widely recognized in recent decades. A spiritual sense of embodiment includes body-based self-understanding, self-esteem manifested in the embrace of the body, self-acceptance of embodied identity and awareness of the bodily manifestation of affection and sexuality. The experience of embodied power is also at the core of our bodily health.[35] Women voiced the experience of connections with their bodies and their maternal identities in numerous ways. The various sub-themes revolved around pain, empowerment, change, sexuality, exhaustion and trust.

Women's bodies were viewed historically as unpredictable and chaotic. In particular, the maternal body has been governed and ordered by religious institutions, as well as by the state and medical sciences.[36] Tyler described her unmapped, unthinkable pregnant body in terms which vividly convey this sense of the liminality of the maternal body: 'My body, my massive pregnant body ... Am I inappropriate? Monstrous? Am I obscene? Am I representable as an "I"? Am I?'[37]

In such experience, the dichotomy of subject and object is called into question. Subjectivity resides in the liminal space of consciousness arising from the autonomous life processes in the body.[38] The relationship of subject and object in the self assumes new forms, some of which cannot be articulated or even understood in 'higher cortex' mode, but exist within body-state changes.[39]

All the women interviewed in this study spoke about the intense bodily connection with their baby and the unique feelings that this provoked:

> I passed him through between my legs. He was so slippy, I couldn't hold him. It was always so beautiful. This little baby has come out and you are connected to him. It is just so incredible. I held him in my arms for a while and then he fed. (Interviewee 1)

---

[34] Meredith McGuire, 'Why Bodies Matter: A Sociological Reflection on Spirituality and Materiality' *Spiritus*, 3 (2003): 1–18.

[35] Joan Timmerman, 'Body and Spirituality', in Philip Sheldrake (ed.), *The New Westminster Dictionary of Christian Spirituality* (London, 2005), pp. 153–5.

[36] Rebecca Kukla, 'Introduction: Maternal Bodies', *Hypatia* 21/1 (2006): 7–9.

[37] Imogen Tyler, 'Reframing Pregnant Embodiment', in Sara Ahmed, Jane Kilby, Celia Lury, Maureen McNeil and Beverley Skeggs (eds), *Transformations: Thinking through Feminism* (London, 2000), p. 290.

[38] Maurice Merleau-Ponty, *The Phenomenology of Perception* (New York, 1962), p. 121.

[39] Suzanne Langer, *Philosophy in a new key: A Study in the Symbolism of Reason, Rite, and Art* (New York, 1948).

When you see them, it is really exciting. It is certainly quite overwhelming. There is a protective, a fierce protection and a love, a fierce love but it is fiercer than I would have expected. (Interviewee 3)

Yeah. I don't want to lose those feelings because they are so precious. They are just incredible. I could hold him then and just the feeling and the connection. (Interviewee 4)

Maternal holding and connection includes not only the physical holding, but also a psychic holding that provides ego-coverage for the infant. Thus, it has been argued that the mother and infant relationship is a chiasmic, embodied experience.[40] This embodied relationship challenges the boundaries of the woman's body as the relationship between the self and the infant is profoundly symbiotic. The boundaries between self and environment also become altered. In particular, the mother's kinetic experience of the newfound clumsiness, slowness, delay and viscosity of the life she lives with her newborn results in a range of heightened sensations that mothers very often report.[41] Women in my study described this kinetic experience:

I wasn't able to have a shower. I couldn't speak to other people. I couldn't go to the loo. Having a shower was like luxury. Being able to text someone or check your emails or just be able to have a cup of tea [*laughs*]. To finish having a cup of tea; I get to now. It took months before I was able to have a cup of tea and get to the bottom of the mug. (Interviewee 1)

I always say you can tell how busy you are with babies by how many full cups of tea you have thrown down the sink because you never get a chance to drink them. *There is always something happening.* You don't really get a chance. I remember when I went back to work and I had a cup of tea and just going – I am sitting here having a cup of tea and I don't have to jump up. (Interviewee 3) [emphasis added]

One recurrent topic that all the women in this study discussed was the relationship between maternal embodiment and sexuality. Research has shown that in the transition to motherhood, women encounter new restrictions on their sexuality.[42] In most cultures, the desexualized mother is an important cultural construct in the

---

[40] Francine Wynn, 'The Embodied Chiasmic Relationship of Mother and Infant', *Human Studies* 19 (1997): 253–70.

[41] Lisa Baraitser, *Maternal Encounters: An Ethic of Interruption* (London, 2009), pp. 126–9.

[42] Ariella Friedman, 'Sexuality and Motherhood: Mutually Exclusive in Perception of Women', *Sex Roles: A Journal of Research* 38/20 (1998): 781–800.

discourse regarding what is to be a 'woman'.[43] Rich asserted that the experience of motherhood is stereotypically characterized by a move in the woman towards an emphasis on femininity and nurturance, and a concomitant decreasing emphasis on woman as sexual being. She believes that the biblical command to 'be fruitful and multiply' (Genesis 1:28) is an entirely patriarchal one and pointed towards the biological potential of women. Culturally, this characterization reveals the oppressive institutionalization of motherhood.[44]

Women's sexuality is placed on 'standby' in the liminal transition to motherhood. Two women in the study expressed this as follows:

> I think it is hilarious. I think it is separating something. In one way it is great because you are bringing sexuality into motherhood and you are not sexual anymore because you are a mother. (Interviewee 2)

> Yeah. There are two desires. There is desire about being desired, wanting to be desired and putting yourself out there well. Mothers are very much put into a box. You are not sexual anymore. I think you are definitely on a standby. I think this whole yummy mummy thing. (Interviewee 1)

Participants acknowledged the sexual transformation that had happened for them while becoming a mother:

> For me sexuality as a mother has been completely deepened in me and it is intensified hugely which is amazing. I have moved from child to woman, very much so, and that is what it feels like. If I can connect with that and stay connected with that, it is lovely. (Interviewee 3)

> For me, it is about being a woman and what it means to be a woman and how I can express that and how I can embody that. (Interviewee 1)

Forming a deeper connection with sexual energy also alleviated symptoms of anxiety that one mother was experiencing:

> I feel disembodied most days. I was very breathless for the first few months. However, the more I connect in with my sexuality as a woman and what it means to me to be a woman, the less anxious I am. (Interviewee 1)

This account may indicate how an empowered sexual identity could have a transformative effect on anxiety, if the mother is able to accept the necessary challenge to differentiate inherited conflicted sexual feelings from the spiritual

---

[43] Rita Jones, 'Sexuality and Mothering', in Andrea O'Reilly (ed.), *Encyclopedia of Motherhood* (Thousand Oaks, CA, 2010), pp. 1114–6.

[44] Adrienne Rich, *Of Woman Born* (New York, 1986), pp. 119–27.

resource of her own creative energy. Research has shown how difficult a journey this may be, as culturally and historically, mothers have been displayed as undesiring, non-sexual beings.[45]

Rich has suggested that, in order for women to have access to their innate potential for wisdom, they need to understand the power and powerlessness inscribed in the state of motherhood in patriarchal culture. Two participants in this study made a link between their own power and the embodied experience of motherhood as follows:

> I have realized how important being embodied is in my life because it gives me a sense of power, it is an empowerment. (Interviewee 1)

> Whereas, if I am conscious of my body, I am very much in the present and very much in the moment and I feel much more empowered. (Interviewee 3)

A consciousness of empowerment engenders feelings of transformation. Women in the study described this transformation in terms of acquiring a deeper consciousness, more inner growth, a great sense of mutual responsibility and an enriching sense of achievement in life.

The Liminal Space of Maternal Transformation

At the beginning of this essay, I described how the post-liminal nature of birth requires women to incorporate into a new world. The new mother needs to transcend from the underworld into a ground-breaking adjustment and acceptance of her new self. The diverse emotions, desires, beliefs and values that were noted above as endemic to the crisis of motherhood are the fertile soil that will assist the growth of the mother's transformed self-awareness. This changed self-awareness is essential for developing spiritual maturity.[46] Women need the capacity to reflect on the complexity of the conscious and unconscious thoughts and behaviours that are distinctive to the task of forming a maternal identity.

Self-reflection practices can be of assistance in increasing the reflective process and allow healing, self-acceptance and, ultimately, transformation to mark this stage.[47] The mother starts accepting her responsibilities and reflecting on how these are changing her and her relationships. Most of the mothers in this study talked about the sense of growth and maturation through motherhood:

---

[45] Andrea O'Reilly, 'Mothering, sex and sexuality', *Journal of the Association for Research on Mothering* 4/1 (2002), 150–238.

[46] Ken Wilber, *Sex, Ecology, Spirituality: The Spirit of Evolution* (Boston, MA, 2011), pp. 313–17.

[47] Daniel Siegel, *Mindsight: The New Science of Personal Transformation* (New York, 2010), pp. 25–37.

> It was a real milestone in your life. To become a parent, it does make you feel that bit more mature and older. I would never have thought about it before. I don't know if people see me differently. (Interviewee 4)

They also reported the changes that motherhood made in their relationships with their partners:

> We would have had full-blown arguments and we would have been shouting and you just can't do that. We have had to learn to negotiate differently, communicate differently and grow up. (Interviewee 1)

> Basically we have had to; it has been tough and very strenuous. We have had to grow up for one because you can't act out the way you used to act out in relationships. That has been incredibly trying. There is a huge amount of learning. (Interviewee 2)

The mode of responsibility assumed in motherhood is closely linked to beliefs and core values that are important for the woman's sense of identity.[48] A sense of achievement and reflective leadership may emerge for the woman in her newfound ability to manage difficult emotions. Another study has shown that this reflective leadership is anchored in love:[49]

> There was such a rush of love. It is like the best drug ever. It was like wow! It is indescribable the feeling of achievement because we worked so hard at this. (Interviewee 1)

> I am not sure. I think lately – and it has taken me years – you do feel that your life is a little bit more complete. You do feel that it is a bit of an achievement. Like I said earlier, when people say, 'have you got any children?' I am always really glad when I can say, 'yeah I do, I have one'. Sometimes I wish I could say I have two or three. (Interviewee 4)

The development of self-awareness through self-reflection, along with the motivation and receptivity to engage with the unconscious processes that motherhood provokes, will decide how far this transformation can be canalized in the life of the mother.[50] Speaking of this transformative dynamic, mothers in

---

[48] Mary Looman, 'Reflective leadership: strategic planning from heart and soul', *Consulting Psychology Journal Practice and Research* 55/4 (2003): 215–21.

[49] Otto Scharmer, *Theory U: Leading from the Future as it Emerges. Open Mind, Open Heart, Open Will. The Social Technology of Presencing* (San Francisco, CA, 2009), pp. 111–19.

[50] Ethel Person, *Feeling Strong. How Power Issues Affect our Ability to Direct our Own Lives* (New York, 2002), pp. 260–82.

this study recognized that the profound experience they had gone through, when processed over time, had helped them to construct a transformed self to engage the new realities of life.

> Yeah. I can probably bring my own experience to it and my own depth of experience and what it means. I can bring my own spirituality to it and that is probably enough. However, I am looking more to connect. I want to help women to feel less alone. (Interviewee 1)

> To be honest with you, it took a good couple of years – it did take a good two years before day by day I felt better and I started to feel more able. (Interviewee 3)

Motherhood is not only linked with biological birth or culturally learned patterns of mothering, then, but also heralds spiritual insights into human experience.[51] One of the mothers in this study expressed it in this way:

> There is very little meaning in the Church these days. I am debating whether to christen him at all. I think spirituality; there is empowerment in spirituality, of course, and I think it gives you a sense of self and a sense of identity. That identity is fundamental. (Interviewee 1)

Here it is recognized that spirituality is embedded in the dynamic, transformative quality of the lived experience of becoming a mother. Implicitly spirituality here is linked to bodiliness, to nature and to relationships with others and society. According to Canadian philosopher-theologian Lonergan,[52] through engaging in a varied range of life experiences, human beings establish normative values, reasoned judgement and self-determination in the quest for authentic truth. My research suggests that this process is taking place for mothers through their transition to motherhood.

Conclusion

This study shows the courage that every new mother needs in order to birth herself in the subjectivity blur which occurs in the experience of maternal liminality. Motherhood is a time in the life of a woman when the encounter and struggle with opposite dualities in the self is at its peak. Heraclitus wrote, 'Change is the constant

---

[51] Ursula King, *The Search for Spirituality: Our Global Quest for a Spiritual Life* (New York, 2011).
[52] Tad Dunne, *Lonergan and Spirituality: Towards a Spiritual Integration* (Chicago, IL, 1985).

conflict of opposites and the universal logos of human nature.'[53] There is a real potential for deep spiritual transformation in motherhood, even as we must also recognize the potential for stagnation, depression and giving up. Deeper research into these dual spiritual dynamics and more discussion of the conceptualization of spirituality in the context to motherhood will assist women on the journey into motherhood, and will support them to encounter the occasion as a moment of life-giving potential. This pilot study therefore raises important questions about the resources needed to deepen further the transition into motherhood. Much research is needed to identify the different spiritual capacities that are called forth in the maternal spiritual journey and for which appropriate supports need to be developed. The main argument of this chapter has been to suggest that a more holistic awareness, authentic self-acceptance and expansion into new layers of empowering consciousness can be spiritual gifts from the liminal space entered by the transition into motherhood.

---

[53] Edward Hussey, 'Epistemology and Meaning in Heraclitus', in Malcolm Schofield and Martha C. Nussbaum (eds), *Language and Logos: Studies in Ancient Greek Philosophy presented to G.E.L. Owen* (Cambridge, 1982), pp. 33–59.

Chapter 19
How Survivors of Abuse Relate to God: A Qualitative Study

Susan Shooter

Introduction: Challenging the 'Narratives of Harm'

By the age of 18, around 25 per cent of girls and 10 per cent of boys have been victims of sexual abuse.[1] Despite this alarming statistic found across the literature, qualitative research on spirituality and abuse is sparse in the field of pastoral theology, where literature is focused on ministry *to* the abused. Christie Neuger argues that giving theological attention solely to pastoral responses to suffering is inadequate for safeguarding the vulnerable and for supporting healthy relationships. Rather, fundamental core narratives which are the seedbed for abusive behaviour must be deconstructed and actively resisted.[2] Giving the abused a voice necessarily means challenging 'narratives of harm',[3] notably the patriarchal gender-based discourses that underlie Christian theology and practice. The basic research question addressed in this chapter, which introduces a qualitative study of nine Christian women survivors, is: What do abused people, who have profound faith, reveal about God that can be brought to bear on theology and scripture? I will briefly outline my research design and then present the analysis which provides a basis for challenging theological discourses and practice.[4]

---

[1] Hall, T.A., 'Spiritual Effects of Childhood Sexual Abuse in Adult Christian Women', *Journal of Psychology and Theology* 23/2 (1995): 129–34; Len Hedges-Goettl, *Sexual Abuse: Pastoral Responses* (Nashville, TN, 2004), p. 12.

[2] Christie C. Neuger, 'Narratives of Harm: Setting the Developmental Context for Intimate Violence', in Jeanne Stevenson-Moessner, (ed.) *In Her Own Time: Women and Developmental Issues in Pastoral Care* (Minneapolis, MN, 2000), pp. 65–86.

[3] Ibid.

[4] For detailed rationale of methodology and theological discussion of the research, see Susan Shooter, *How Survivors of Abuse Relate to God: The Authentic Spirituality of the Annihilated Soul* (Farnham, 2012).

Research Design

In order to embody feminist methodological principles which allow the marginalized their voices, I used Glaserian grounded theory, an inductive mode of analysis,[5] and drew on oral life history ethnography to inform the interview process.[6] Considerations of power dynamics were central to criteria for sampling, so participants needed to be self-selecting volunteers, rather than referrals from someone 'in authority'. Participation was invited by advertisement in church publications and self-help websites,[7] with the definition of 'abuse' allowed a broad meaning (spiritual, physical, emotional, or sexual). I kept the research question flexible since 'the concern of the people in the substantive area' is important,[8] and because assumptions from the researcher's experience can prevent theory from being truly grounded.[9] Indeed, the volunteers brought diverse experiences of abuse, both individual instances (for example, rape) and long-term exposure to abusive environments (for example, domestic violence), or both. Participants were also from a range of denominations.[10]

I used a non-directive, open-ended style of interviewing[11] which allowed participants freedom to take the 'telling' in any direction they wished, the length of interviews depending entirely on them.[12] Transcripts of the recorded interviews were sent to participants for comment,[13] with an opportunity to withdraw from the project before analysis began. Nine participants gave permission and their interviews were coded for meaning using the NVIVO*8 software tool.[14]

---

[5] B.G. Glaser and A.L. Strauss, *The Discovery of Grounded Theory*, 4th edn (Englewood Cliffs, NJ, 2009); see B.G. Glaser, *Basics of Grounded Theory Analysis: Emergence vs Forcing* (Mill Valley, CA, 1992) on the divergence of Glaserian method from Strauss.

[6] Sherna B. Gluck and Daphne Patai, *Women's Words: The Feminist Practice of Oral History* (New York, 1991); E. Lawless, 'Women's life stories and reciprocal ethnography as feminist and emergent', *Journal of Folklore Research* 28/1 (1991): 35–60; Nicola Slee, *Women's Faith Development: Patterns and Processes* (Aldershot, 2004).

[7] For example, MACSAS (Ministry And Clergy Sexual Abuse Survivors).

[8] Glaser, *Basics of Grounded Theory Analysis*, p. 4.

[9] Ibid., p. 50.

[10] See Shooter, *Survivors of Abuse*, p. 43.

[11] Lawless, 'Women's life stories', pp. 39–40; Slee, *Women's Faith Development*, p. 54.

[12] Lawless, 'Women's life stories', p. 40.

[13] Ibid., pp. 35–60.

[14] Marketed by QSR International, NVIVO enables the systematic handling and storage of large quantities of data. The researcher categorizes sections of transcribed text which she discerns as meaningful under relevant conceptual headings. As the number of categories and coded sections of text increase, the program has cross-referencing tools that allow for easy retrieval and comparison so that the conceptual categories can be set into hierarchies of ever higher levels of meaning.

Developing a Core Category[15]

'God's timeless presence', 'Transformation' and 'Knowing ministry' were the three significant concepts which emerged from coding. I will outline these three concepts which eventually became integrated into the central, or core category, 'Knowing God's timeless presence transforms', which describes the spiritual process by which the survivors live their spiritual lives.

God's Timeless Presence

The overwhelming message from early analysis was the sense participants had of 'God's presence'. Further coding added the dimension of 'timelessness' to this concept, a modification which reveals the key to understanding how the survivors managed the dilemma of relating to a 'loving God' who did not intervene at the time of their abuse.

As a child, Esther[16] was in a concentration camp and later suffered severe domestic violence in her marriage. I coded the following incident from her interview under 'God's Presence':

> That's why that sentence we say in church nearly every week, when we were far off, God was there, when I really didn't know anything about God, he was there, I was his child. I was precious to him even then, and gradually I've seen glimpses of him. You see glimpses particularly when you go through the valleys in life. I've had some fantastic mountain-top experiences, but it's in the valley that you really meet God isn't it?

Special moments of God's presence (for example, 'in the valley') were a feature of eight interviews, and Esther's acknowledgement of God's presence throughout life, even when unaware of it, was common. This recognition of the timelessness of God's presence became significant in two ways: first, for healing past memories of abuse, and secondly, for preparing the survivor for difficulties ahead. For instance, in prayer ministry some respondents have been able to return to instances of abuse, experiencing the trauma again, but this time with the knowledge of God's loving presence; this heals the memory of abandonment and fear, because God experiences the hurt *with* the survivor, but not *for* her. Accordingly Lydia relates:

> The [minister] asked the Holy Spirit to show me where Jesus was. I was taken back to the first moment that I remembered being abused and it was just the beginning ... Jesus was stood on the stairs with me, and it was healing because it was just that sense of knowing that he was with me.

---

[15] See Keith F. Punch, *Introduction to Social Research: Quantitative and Qualitative Approaches* (London, 1998), p. 205.

[16] Participants have Biblical pseudonyms to preserve anonymity.

Recalling her sexual abuse by an uncle, Lydia later associated this experience of healing with the scripture that God is 'the same yesterday, today and forever'.[17] Because God had been there then, God could heal the past in the present.

Some respondents spoke of times when God had seemed absent, but they described later acquiring the understanding that God had been there, they just had not felt so at the time. There were only nine references across six interviews to 'God's absence', in comparison with over 150 references to the all-pervading presence of God. The significance lay not in the absence itself, rather in that these incidents were located in past spiritual struggles. These struggles involved anger about the abuse, which was aimed at God for allowing it to happen. If God is understood as being present at the scene of abuse, but did nothing to prevent it, how can survivors square this with a loving God?

The resolution of this question lay in acquiring new understanding of the God whose timeless presence is closely connected to his nature, and whose nature is integrated with his action. The women unanimously saw God as 'loving': God is 'loving' because God loves me, and God loves me so God is love, there being a certain interchangeability of verb/noun/adjective as Priscilla's interview demonstrates. She described God as 'loving father' and said: 'God's love is constant, Christ's love is constant, the Holy Spirit is constant, always constant and always there … no matter what I've been through, that has never changed, that's always been the same and always will be the same.'

Thus since God is always present and God is always love, God is always loving in every moment. Regarding her struggle with God about the incest she suffered from her grandfather, Priscilla added: 'as time went on, the more I got it off my chest, the more I felt [God's] love. I thought, he really does love me, he really does care.'

God's presence is dynamic, and the quality of the connection that exists between the respondent and God is vital.

When in the past there had been no personal connection or knowledge of who God really was, it seemed as if God 'allowed' bad things to happen. However, connection with God developed and deepened through the process of pain-sharing with God, and this close relationship changed the survivor's perception from God allowing things to happen, to an outlook of them facing the world together. The implications of this cooperation will resurface later when describing the third main concept, 'Knowing ministry'; here, I highlight that the survivor is not always at one with this joint experience of the world since the spiritual struggle goes on, but the connection with God's presence is all-important:

> the pain is [still] intense, but I choose to believe that whatever happens, Jesus is in it, and to praise God in all circumstances for whatever is happening. It's hard to do that, and we've subsequently had dark and difficult things, but I say thank you God for permitting this to happen because I know that you will use this for

---

[17] Hebrews 13:8.

> something good to come out of this. I wouldn't want you [*interviewer*] to think that it doesn't still hurt and that I float over the top. No, things hurt and hurt and hurt, but they hurt with him and not without him. (Lydia)

This quotation shows how seeing good come out of bad is crucial (a concept which I develop shortly in the next main category 'Transformation'), and that what counts is mutuality: God still allows bad things to happen, but struggle and pain are survived with God, transformed because of the active presence of the divine.

The verb 'allowing', as attributed to God, is the key to understanding the solution to the problem of non-intervention: God allows abuse to happen but also allows the survivor to be angry and have negative feelings. If God had been seen before as remote and punishing of weakness, it was now a relief to know that it was okay to feel angry and yet still be loved. Freedom to be oneself without the loss of being loved, moreover with a deepening of the faith relationship, is the other side of the coin to allowing bad things to happen. God's lack of intervention at the time of the abuse, which engendered anger for survivors, may be seen not as abandonment, but as God's commitment to humanity's freedom. God's nature and action are constant, therefore God's 'permissiveness' is a double-edged sword: God's allowance of the survivor's freedom to be angry (or whatever) also allows perpetrators to exercise their freedom to abuse. Tamar, who was sexually abused by her vicar and stepfather in collusion with each other, said:

> if [God] was to control our actions, I'm not sure I'd want to live here. So it's very awkward and very difficult. I guess the conclusion is that everyone has their own mind and their own actions. If I wanted to get up now and walk across the room, I'd get up and walk across the room. [The vicar] obviously decided, for whatever reasons, that he was going to do that to me, and he did.

This implies a view shared explicitly by others that human choices to do evil are not God's fault. In struggling with this, some have been able to discover that our human freedom, which is exactly the same freedom that abusers have, is the freedom to choose to be like God, or rather to be co-workers with God, who is present even in the hard things: precisely here *we* can allow love to work. Then transformation happens and bad things are used for good, a dynamic we now consider in the next coded category.

Transformation

Early coding suggested transformation was a strong theme, three codes coming into particular focus: transformation of self/behaviour, spiritual awakening/conversion, and transformation of evil/pain into good. First, in relation to 'transformation of self or behaviour', acknowledging the discrepancy between human choice to abuse and God's will was crucial. For Joanna, such a realization enabled the transformation of her (angry) behaviour into renewed faith: 'I was screaming at God, saying, I don't want you in my life; if you were my father you wouldn't stand there and watch somebody rape me; I was really angry with God ... then I realized that it wasn't God's fault, it was this man and not God.'

Joanna has been able to rediscover God's timeless presence: 'My feelings now, even if they've been up and down, are that Jesus is with me all the time.'

Secondly, a particular traumatic experience (for example, a humiliating court case) or life struggle (for example, depression) can precipitate a 'spiritual awakening/conversion'. This process leads to a reassessment of God's nature and to renewed spiritual commitment. A 'spiritual awakening' experienced by a survivor before she had to face a gruelling time rather than after it, revealed that God's action was not in preventing the bad experience or struggle from happening, but in providing spiritual resources to endure. For Naomi, the following experience came before a period of deep suffering, assuring her that God is committed to her even when entering the darkest places: '[I had] this overwhelming feeling of being loved ... I felt that my heart would burst. I believe that was God saying to me, "This is how much I love you." But that was before I attempted suicide. He knew all that was coming.'

Life had been very cruel for Naomi[18] and she believes that it is only because of her connection with God that she has survived: 'I know I wouldn't have got this far without God. Because that's where I get my self-worth from; that I know God loves me. I'm worth loving.'

Naomi and the other respondents still have struggles, but they now have the spiritual resource of knowing better who God really is, and the assurance of God's loving presence which positively transforms the self, as illustrated by Lydia:

> At the depths of the situation, I'd written [in my journal], OK God you're not going to bail us out, I'm sure you'll still be there for me when it's over. *When it's over*. I didn't say to him, be with me *in it*, because I hadn't learnt that. I remember saying right, I'll drown, that's it, I'll give up, the waters will go over my head, and if I'm still alive at the end of all this you can have what's left. But I did learn that he was walking along the bottom of the river with me, holding my hand. [original emphasis]

Lydia is describing the devastating period when she was healing from painful memories of her own sexual abuse, while simultaneously supporting her husband through a legal process in which he was eventually imprisoned for sexually inappropriate behaviour with children. Lydia had to confront immense loss: 'when you lose something you thought you had control over, your reputation, your significance, your status, I think you then realize that you're not controlling anything.'

---

[18] Naomi, like Joanna, has experienced multiple forms of serious abuse; both have attempted suicide.

This brought her to a 'point of no return', of being unable to turn back, of having no plans:

> You know that song, 'All I once held dear, built my life upon'? It says 'to know you in your suffering, to be like you in your death, Oh Lord?' I think at some level, that I have experienced that and I suppose in a way it's a privilege. So my relationship with God, I'm in a completely different place.

Lydia's comment about 'privilege' and earlier about thanking God for 'permitting' awful events, are not some form of masochism. She did not choose to suffer in this way, and the survivors seemingly agree that since they are involuntarily but unavoidably in this dreadful place, the only hope they have found is in God who becomes their *raison d'être*. So Lydia lives 'only for God'; Esther's relationship with God 'changed so completely, because all [she] had then was God'; and Priscilla reasoned as follows:

> If somebody said to me, you can go back and have that not happen, but not have that relationship with God, I would go through all of that again for that relationship. I wouldn't want to change that. If it was either/or, there's nothing that would make me not want to have that relationship. Although it was awful and it was horrible, I'd rather that than not have God.

Spiritual transformation via the place where there is nothing but God is dreadful, but appears irreplaceable for them.

Third, beside an incomparable and vital relationship with God, seeing evil and pain transformed for good is the one positive that participants gleaned from their difficult journey. Lydia perceived that some of the good that emerged from the terrible ordeal of her husband's imprisonment was the deepening of family relationships. She connected these blessings with the scripture someone had randomly given her years before, suggesting a further instance of the timelessness of God's presence in her life:

> 'I will show you treasures in dark places so that you will know that I am the Lord your God'.[19] Hadn't a clue what that meant. I kept it and didn't do anything with it, but I now know what God does; the treasures are the healing and goodness that's come out of all this in the way that our kids love and support each other, and respect their father, and the way as a family we've got so many blessings that other families that are fragmented and don't speak [don't have].

A problem about good coming out of evil was the question of God's part in this. While being author of spiritual transformation is seen as God's positive purpose in their lives, the implication that the experience of abuse was *worth* something

---

[19] Isaiah 45:3.

posed the dilemma about God planning such 'learning' experiences. However, this is to view things from the wrong angle. Healing and learning may indeed come as a result of the transformative struggle of dealing with abuse, but they are unequivocally not the reason for that awful experience in the first place. Miriam, survivor of clergy sexual abuse, insists that life and its traumata are no 'test': 'Even though God can make good things out of bad things, it's never God's will for people to suffer – God doesn't test us.'

Priscilla also struggled with the idea that some Christians have that God allows awful things to happen 'to make you a better person'. She insisted that a 'loving father' would not allow children to go through the terror of incest in order for them to 'be something when they grew up', and explained: 'The fact that he's used it, that it hasn't been wasted, that's a different thing. But you do hear this kind of talk that it's part of God's plan. I don't believe it was ever part of God's plan.'

For Priscilla, and others, the vital point was that God was able to *transform* what happened so that: 'out of that pain and evil, good actually came, inasmuch as I was then able to talk to other people and get close to other people ... The older I get the more I see the good that's come out of it. It took me a long time, but it wasn't all wasted.'

So how might this 'good' reveal itself?

Knowing Ministry

The most significant point about this third major category 'knowing ministry', which I will address first, is that as a result of their spiritual struggles, the respondents now appear to be active in service in a way that clearly reflects what they have experienced of God's care for them. A further observation I make in passing concerns the relationship between criteria for selection for formal ministry on the one hand, and the quality of spirituality survivors bring to their churches on the other. For while all nine respondents have, throughout their Christian lives, served in a profusion and diversity of informal ministries, none had so far succeeded in being authorized by their churches despite the majority having pursued some kind of formal ministry.[20]

Esther and Lydia have significant prayer ministries. Esther acknowledged that during her violent marriage, her faith had been her only 'secure place'. When the physical danger was over after her divorce, there was a long process of healing from psychological damage. The support she received from members of the local church now became the 'secure place', where she was allowed to cry, standing between two ladies who produced a handkerchief for her whenever she needed it. This action was a reflection of the God who allowed her to be upset and angry, and in turn Esther now provides a safe place for others who need accompaniment. When she underwent complex spinal surgery, a result of many years of physical abuse, she had been upheld in prayer by others, and was given Julian of Norwich's

---

[20] Miriam is to some extent an exception, as we will see.

prayer[21] to use for reassurance. On the interview day, she had given similar support to a young mother with spinal cancer, gently passing on Julian's prayer:

> She's having her operation today – I said, 'can you remember that?' She said, 'yes, I'll remember that. What a good idea,' she said. She's not a Christian. I didn't tell her that was Julian of Norwich. I just didn't want to; there wasn't much point in talking about that. So hopefully she'll remember to say, 'all will be well, all will be well.'

Similarly, Lydia, who found healing in knowing that God was the same yesterday, today, forever, said this about her own subsequent ministry with other people:

> That's when you can apply that truth to asking the Holy Spirit to take them back to that time, when they experience that pain that's now causing them so much trouble. The Holy Spirit gives them pictures and they have that deep sense of knowing where he was and that really does help them to let go of the past or understand that he was there with them then.

Thus 'Transformation' as described in the previous section inspires godly practice in the survivor's own ministry, that is to say, the survivor's pastoral relationship with others reflects God's healing relationship with her.

Priscilla's comments quoted earlier, suggesting the formative effect of working through the pain of incest, were preceded by her acknowledgement that her 'over-sensitivity' as an abused girl had now been transformed into a blessing by God: this sensitivity enables her to 'pick up on what other people are feeling', empathizing with them. Lydia, moreover, sees her 'Transformation' as helpful in her professional life:

> I'll sit with people at the end of their life – young people, people who are having a real shit time. I know what not to say, because no one can walk your path. No one can do your experience. When you sit alongside someone, even if it's a similar journey, it's not your journey, it's theirs and how they experience it is different, but I think that if they know that you know, they find it easier for you to sit alongside them. I still don't think that it gives you the permission to say what it's like for them. And you can't take it away either.

This is a profound reflection of what Lydia experienced in God's healing for her. God did not take the pain away; God did not 'bail' her out, and as she later commented, God does not 'answer prayer the way we want', but is 'in the business of being in it'.

Thus a grateful desire to serve God in God's way is often a consequence of a survivor's transformation. However, Naomi's story shows her experience of being

---

[21] 'All shall be well, and all shall be well, and all manner of things shall be well.'

side-lined. The women's Bible study she led was taken away from her, because the vicar had had complaints from some of the husbands (not from the women) that Naomi went 'too deeply' into things. Naomi expressed sadness that the Church discourages sharing and discussion of difficulties, and believes it must become more 'real'. She has served the Church in many practical ways when asked, supporting clergy with her secretarial skills, leading prayer groups and singing in the choir. She is very well-read and the ministry to which she feels drawn is one of spiritual leadership: 'I would love to lead quiet days, but you never get any opportunities. That's what I'd like to do more than anything – leading people into a deeper knowledge of the Lord.'

Naomi's story suggests that Christians with spiritual depth who have been making a profound spiritual journey may be finding themselves overlooked. Naomi has been to the brink of self-destruction, found God's love there, and wishes to share this knowledge, but she has been made aware by other Christians that she should keep quiet about her experiences. Joanna echoed this: 'People have said to me, "You didn't ought to tell people about things like that; you shouldn't share your experiences."'

Regarding formal ministry, four respondents met difficulties in their vocations when seeking ordination in their various denominations, due to structural discrimination (on grounds of age, gender, or theological standpoint) and/or exploitation. When Miriam sought ordination in her church, she found herself isolated and vulnerable, when the minister who had encouraged her to train instead as Pastoral Assistant used his position to exploit her sexually, emotionally and spiritually.[22] Realizing that her vocation had come long before the abusive relationship began, she found the confidence she needed to report his behaviour. This was at great cost to herself because not only did she have to leave her church and lose that community's support,[23] she also lost her own significant ministry. The minister was given ample support by the authorities, she was given none. An appraisal of recruitment for ministry and the testing of attitudes towards power and status across the denominations may be overdue, as well as a deeper scrutiny of the theology supporting ecclesiological structures, for when Tamar was reflecting on the nature of God's power and apparent non-intervention, she pinpointed the deeper dimension of a church's action as represented by its spiritual leaders:

> One of the people involved was the vicar. I feel, if he was ordained and went through the searching process and God was this almighty person, all knowing, all powerful, transcendent, how did that happen? How did he let that person

---

[22] See MACSAS leaflet, 'Clergy or Minister Sexual Exploitation of Adults in the Pastoral Relationship' <http://www.macsas.org.uk/PDFs/Homepage/sex_exploitn.pdf> accessed 28 January 13; Miriam's minister had exhibited 12 out of the 20 'warning signs'.

[23] This loss is intense because the parishioner feels as if she has lost God. See Margaret Kennedy, 'Sexual Abuse of Women by Priests and Ministers to Whom They Go for Pastoral Care and Support', *Feminist Theology Continuum* 11 (2003): 226–35.

get ordained and be in that situation to do that? Partly the reason why I feel so angry about that, is because that has caused me more damage, I feel, than what happened with my stepfather.

Consequently, if it is the Church's calling to do God's work, not least in its selection of leaders, the following question might be extrapolated from Tamar's comments in the context of the preceding incidents: when exploitative and abusive clergy are allowed through selection, yet the abused can find themselves excluded from ministry, what ideology is supporting this incongruity? Indeed, interviewee Sarah argued that the Church's true purpose is transformation, to 'turn water into wine', to turn 'something abundant, something common, something tasteless, something thin into something rich and meaningful', which involves getting dirty hands; however, her experience has been of ministers who use red tape to keep people at arm's length and questioners at bay. In contrast to such an excluding attitude, Jesus' encounter with the Samaritan woman was, according to Miriam, intimate. Moreover, he did not judge the woman's unconventional appearance; indeed, despite appearances, 'he saw what she really had, and went with it.'

To summarize, 'Knowing ministry' is a dimension of survivor spirituality because knowing from experience God's healing, transforming presence becomes the dynamic for service. Any church which reflects this transforming action of God through its members – and leaders – is a sign of divine presence.

Knowing God's Timeless Presence Transforms

Eventually the core category 'knowing God's timeless presence transforms' emerged from the data, encapsulating the dynamic process by which the survivors collectively and individually live their spiritual lives. The grammatical ambiguity of this phrase allows for two meanings: first, the survivors know God's timeless presence in their lives and this has transformed them and healed the effects of abuse, and continues to transform them; secondly, because they know and have experienced transformation through God's presence in their lives, this understanding equips and enables them to become God's agents for the transformation of others.

Thus the core category not only offers a theory about how and why survivors' spirituality might be authentic, it also raises a surprising question about who is suitable for ministry. The existing literature in the field of pastoral theology is largely concerned with ministering *to* survivors, not with what ministry might be accomplished *by* survivors. The task now is to deepen this emerging grounded theory with theological and spiritual comparisons and to allow the results to challenge the dominating theological discourses, the 'narratives of harm', which have excluded the voices of the abused.

Bibliography

Aaron, J., T. Rees, S. Betts and M. Vincentelli, *Our Sisters' Land: The Changing Identities of Women in Wales* (Cardiff: University of Wales Press, 1994).

Acker, J., K. Barry and J. Essenelt, 'Objectivity and truth: problems in doing feminist research', *Women's Studies International Forum* 6 (1983): 423–35.

Akerjordet, K., 'Being in Charge – New Mothers' Perceptions of Reflective Leadership and Motherhood', *Journal of Nursing Management* 18/4 (2010): 409–417.

Althaus-Reid, M., 'Response to Claire Herbert, "Who is God for You?"', *Feminist Theology* 23/1 (2000): 26–35.

——, *Indecent Theology* (London: Routledge, 2000).

Anderson, R., 'Introduction', in W. Braud and R. Anderson (eds), *Transpersonal Research Methods for the Social Sciences* (Thousand Oaks, CA: Sage, 1998).

Archbishops' Commission on Urban Life and Faith, *Faithful Cities: A Call for Celebration, Vision and Justice* (Peterborough: Methodist Publishing House, 2006).

Archbishops' Council, 'The Ordination of Priests' <http://www.churchofengland.org/prayer-worship/worship/texts/ordinal/priests.aspx> accessed 20 July 2012.

Arendt, H., *The Human Condition*, 2nd edn (Chicago, IL and London: University of Chicago Press, 1998).

Astley, J., *Ordinary Theology: Looking, Listening and Learning in Theology* (Aldershot: Ashgate, 2002).

—— and L.J. Francis (eds), *Exploring Ordinary Theology: Everyday Christian Believing and the Church* (Farnham: Ashgate, 2013).

Aune, K., 'Marriage in a British Evangelical Congregation: Practising Postfeminist Partnership?', *The Sociological Review* 54/4 (2006): 638–657.

Bagilhole, B., 'Prospects for Change? Structural, Cultural and Action Dimensions of the Careers of Pioneer Women Priests in the Church of England', *Gender, Work and Organization* 10/3 (2003): 361–77.

Bailey, E.K., and W.W. Wiersbe, *Preaching in Black and White: What we can learn from each other* (Grand Rapids, MI: Zondervan, 2003).

Balin, J., 'The Sacred Dimensions of Pregnancy and Birth', *Qualitative Sociology* 11/4 (1988): 275–301.

Bandura, A., *Social Learning Theory* (Englewood Cliffs, NJ: Prentice Hall, 1977).

Baraitser, L., *Maternal Encounters. An Ethic of Interruption* (London: Psychology Press, 2009).

Barlow, C., 'Mothering as a Psychological Experience: A Grounded Theory Exploration', *Canadian Journal of Counselling* 31/3 (1997): 232–7.

Barr, L., and A. Barr, *Jobs for the Boys?: Women who became Priests* (London: Hodder & Stoughton Ltd, 2001).
Barton, M., 'Gender-Bender God: Masculine or Feminine?', *Black Theology: An International Journal* 7/2 (2009): 142–66.
Baumgardner, J., and A. Richards, *Manifesta: Young Women, Feminism, and the Future* (New York: Farrar, Straus and Giroux, 2000).
Baxter, J. (ed.), *Wounds that Heal: Theology, Imagination and Health* (London: SPCK, 2007).
Beattie, T., 'Religious Identity and the Ethics of Representation', in U. King and T. Beattie (eds), *Gender, Religion and Diversity: Cross-Cultural Perspectives* (London: Continuum, 2004).
——, 'Vision and Vulnerability: The Significance of Sacramentality and the Woman Priest for Feminist Theology', in N.K. Watson and S. Burns (eds), *Exchanges of Grace: Essays in Honour of Ann Loades* (London: SCM Press, 2008).
Bebbington, D., 'Evangelical trends, 1959–2009', *Anvil* 26/2 (2009): 93–101.
Beddoe, D., *Out of the Shadows: A History of Women in Twentieth Century Wales* (Cardiff: University of Wales Press, 2000).
Belenky, M.F., B.M. Clinchy, N.R. Goldberger and J.M. Tarule, *Women's Ways of Knowing: The Development of Self, Voice and Mind* (New York: Basic Books, 1986 and 1997 edns).
Benhabib, S., 'Models of Public Space: Hannah Arendt, the Liberal Tradition and Jürgen Habermas', in S. Benhabib (ed.), *Situating the Self: Gender, Community and Postmodernism in Contemporary Ethics* (Cambridge: Polity Press, 1992).
Bennett Moore, Z., *Introducing Feminist Perspectives on Pastoral Theology* (London: Sheffield Academic Press, 2002).
Berger, T. (ed.), *Dissident Daughters: Feminist Liturgies in Global Context* (Louisville, KY: Westminster John Knox Press, 2001).
——, *Fragments of Real Presence: Liturgical Traditions in the Hands of Women* (New York: The Crossroad Publishing Company, 2005).
Berry, J., 'Transforming Rites: the practice of women's ritual making' (unpublished PhD thesis, University of Glasgow, 2006).
——, *Ritual Making Women: Shaping Rites for Changing Lives* (London: Equinox, 2009).
Bons-Storm, R., *The Incredible Woman: Listening to Women's Silences in Pastoral Care and Counseling* (Nashville, TN: Abingdon Press, 1996).
Bowie, F., *The Anthropology of Religion* (Oxford: Blackwell, 2006).
Bragdon, E., *A Sourcebook for Helping People with Spiritual Problems* (Woodstock, VT: Lightening Up Press, 2006).
Brierley, P., *Reaching and Keeping Tweenagers* (London: Christian Research, 2002).
British Social Attitudes, the 24th Report (London: Sage, 2008).
Brock, R.N., 'The Feminist Redemption of Christ' in J. Weidman, *Christian Feminism: Vision of a New Humanity* (New York: Harper and Row, 1984).

—— and R.A. Parker, *Proverbs of Ashes: Violence, Redemptive Suffering and the Search for What Saves Us* (Boston, MA: Beacon Press Books, 2001).

Brookfield, S., *The Skilful Teacher* (San Francisco, CA: Jossey Bass, 2006).

Brown Douglas, K., *The Black Christ* (Maryknoll, NY: Orbis, 1994).

Brown, B., S. Baker and G. Day, 'Lives Beyond Suspicion: Gender and the Construction of Respectability in Mid-Twentieth Century Rural North Wales', *Sociologia Ruralis* 51/4 (2011): 370–86.

Brown, C., *The Death of Christian Britain* (London: Routledge, 2001).

——, *The Death of Christian Britain, Understanding Secularisation 1800–2000* (London and New York: Routledge, 2009).

Brown, L.M., *Raising their Voices: The Politics of Girls' Anger* (Cambridge, MA: Harvard University Press, 1998).

Browning, D., *Practical Theology* (San Francisco, CA: Harper & Row, 1983).

Brueggemann, W., *The Prophetic Imagination*, 2nd edn (Minneapolis, MN: Fortress Press, 2001).

Buch, E., and K. Staller, 'The Feminist Practice of Ethnography', in S.N. Hesse-Biber and P.L. Leavy (eds), *Feminist Research Practice: A Primer* (Thousand Oaks, CA: Sage, 2007).

Butler, J., *Gender Trouble and the Subversion of Identity* (New York: Routledge, 1990).

——, *Gender Trouble: Tenth Anniversary Edition* (New York: Routledge, 1999).

Büttner, G., 'Where do children get their theology from?', in A. Dillen and D. Pollefeyt (eds), *Children's Voices: Children's Perspectives in Ethics, Theology and Religious Education* (Leuven: Peeters, 2010).

Callister, L., 'Spirituality in Childbearing Women', *Journal of Perinatal Education* 19/2 (2010): 16–24.

Cameron, H., P.J. Richter and D. Davies, *Studying Local Churches: A Handbook* (London: SCM, 2005).

Cannell, F. (ed.), *The Anthropology of Christianity* (Durham, NC and London: Duke University Press, 2007).

Carroll, R., 'At the Border between Chaos and Order', in J. Corigall and H. Wilkinson (eds), *Revolutionary Connections: Psychotherapy and Neuroscience* (New York: Karnac Books, 2003).

Chambers, P., and A. Thompson, 'Coming to Terms with the Past: Religion and Identity in Wales', *Social Compass* 52/3 (2005): 337–352.

Chodorow, N., *Feminism and Psychoanalytic Theory* (New Haven, CT: Yale University Press, 1989).

Christ, C., *Diving Deep and Surfacing: Women Writers on Spiritual Quest*, 2nd edn (Boston, MA: Beacon Press, 1986).

Christie, A., *Ordinary Christology: Who Do You Say I Am? Answers from the Pews* (Farnham: Ashgate, 2012).

Church of God of Prophecy, *Business Acts Directory 2008–2009* (Birmingham: CoGoP, 2008).

Claassens, L.J.M., 'Rupturing God-Language: The Metaphor of God as Midwife in Psalm 22', in L. Day and C. Pressler (eds), *Engaging the Bible in a Gendered World: An Introduction to Feminist Biblical Interpretation in Honor of Katharine Doob Sakenfeld* (Louisville, KY: Westminster John Knox Press, 2006).

Clanton, J.A., *In Whose Image? God and Gender* (London: SCM Press, 1991).

Clark-King, E., *Theology by Heart; Women, the Church and God* (Peterborough: Epworth, 2004).

Clements, J., D. Ettling, D. Jenett and L. Shields, 'Organic Research: Feminine Spirituality Meets Transpersonal Research', in W. Braud and R. Anderson (eds), *Transpersonal Research Methods for the Social Sciences* (Thousand Oaks, CA: Sage, 1998).

Coffey, A., *The Ethnographic Self: Fieldwork and the Representation of Identity* (London: Sage, 1999).

Collins, N.L., and S.J. Read, 'Cognitive Representations of Attachment: The Structure and Function of Working Models', in K. Bartholomew and D. Perlman (eds), *Advances in Personal Relationships* (London: Jessica Kingsley, 1994), vol. 5.

Cooper-White, P., *The Cry of Tamar: violence against women and the church's response* (Minneapolis, MN: Fortress Press, 1995).

——, 'Opening the Eyes: Understanding the Impact of Trauma on Development', in J. Stevenson-Moessner (ed.), *In Her own Time: Women and Developmental Issues in Pastoral Care* (Minneapolis, MN: Fortress Press, 2000).

Cunningham, L., and D.J. Hamilton with J. Rogers, *Why not women? A Biblical Study of Women in Missions, Ministry, and Leadership* (Seattle: YWAM, 2000).

Cusk, R., *A Life's Work: On Becoming a Mother* (London: Picador Publishers, 2001).

Daly, M., *The Church and the Second Sex* (Boston, MA: Beacon Press, 1985).

——, *Beyond God the Father: Toward a Philosophy of Women's Liberation* (London: Women's Press, 1986).

Damasio, A., *The Feeling of What Happens: Body and Emotion in the Making of Consciousness* (New York: Mariner Books, 1999).

Darvill, R., 'Psychological Factors that Impact on Women's Experiences of First Time Motherhood: a Qualitative study of the Transition', *Midwifery* 26 (2010): 357–66.

Day, A., 'Doing Theodicy: An Empirical Study of a Women's Prayer Group', *Journal of Contemporary Religion* 20/3 (2005): 343–56.

——, 'Wilfully Disempowered: A Gendered Response to a Fallen World', *European Journal of Women's Studies* 15/3 (2008): 261–76.

——, 'Researching belief without asking religious questions', *Fieldwork in Religion* 4/1 (2009): 89–106.

——, *Believing in Belonging: Belief and Social Identity in the Modern World* (Oxford: Oxford University Press, 2011).

——, 'Doing Qualitative Longitudinal Religious Research', in Linda Woodhead (ed.) *Innovative Methods in the Study of Religion* (Oxford: Oxford University Press, forthcoming).
Dierks, S.D., *WomenEucharist* (Boulder, CO: Woven Word Press, 1997).
Dowell, S. and J. Williams, *Bread, Wine and Women: The Ordination Debate in the Church of England* (London: Virago, 1994).
Downing, R.A., and F.J. Crosby, 'The Perceived Importance of Developmental Relationships on Women Undergraduates' Pursuit of Science', *Psychology of Women Quarterly* 29 (2005): 419–26.
Driscoll, C., *Girls: Feminine Adolescence in Popular Culture and Cultural Theory* (New York: Columbia University Press, 2002).
du Gay, P., J. Evans and P. Redman (eds), *Identity: A Reader* (London: Sage Publications, 2002).
Dunne, T., *Lonergan and Spirituality: Towards a Spiritual Integration* (Chicago, IL: Loyola Press, 1985).
Dyckman, K., M. Garvin and E. Liebert, *The Spiritual Exercises Reclaimed, Uncovering Liberating Possibilities for Women* (New York and Mahwah, NJ: Paulist Press, 2001).
Edwards, R., and J. Ribbens, 'Living on the Edges: Public Knowledge, Private Lives, Personal Experience', in J. Ribbens and R. Edwards (eds), *Feminist Dilemmas in Qualitative Research: Public Knowledge and Private Lives* (London: Sage, 1998).
Edwards, T., *Spiritual Director, Spiritual Companion* (New York: Paulist Press, 2001).
Elliott, J., *Using Narrative in Social Research: Qualitative and Quantitative Approaches* (London: Sage Publications, 2005).
Emond, R., 'Ethnographic research methods with children and young people', in S. Greene and D. Hogan (eds), *Researching Children's Experience* (London: Sage, 2005).
Erikson, E., *Identity: Youth and Crisis* (New York: W.W. Norton, 1968).
Estes, C.P., *Women Who Run With the Wolves* (New York: Ballantine Books, 1996).
Etherington, K., *Becoming a Reflexive Researcher: Using Our Selves in Research* (London and Philadelphia, PA: Jessica Kingsley, 2004).
Evangelical Alliance, *Ministers and Church Leaders* (4 May 2012) <http://eauk.org/church/research-and-statistics/ministers-and-church-leaders.cfm> accessed 26 January 2013.
Faludi, S., *Backlash: The Undeclared War Against American Women*, 15th anniversary edn (New York: Three Rivers Press, 2006).
Fearon, K., *Women's Work: The Story of the Northern Ireland Women's Coalition* (Belfast: The Blackstaff Press, 1999).
Feeney, J.A., and P. Noller, *Adult Attachment* (Thousand Oaks, CA: Sage, 1996).
Findlen, B., 'Introduction', in *idem* (ed.), *Listen Up: Voices from the Next Feminist Generation* (Seattle, WA: Seal Press, 1995).
Fiorenza, E.S., *In Memory of Her* (New York: Crossroad, 1983).

——, *Bread Not Stone* (Edinburgh: T&T Clark, 1984).
—— (ed.), *Searching the Scriptures* (New York, 1993) Vol. 1.
——, *Jesus: Miriam's Child, Sophia's Prophet: Critical Issues in Feminist Christology* (London: SCM, 1995).
Fischer, K., *Women at the Well: Feminist Perspectives on Spiritual Direction* (London: SPCK, 1989 and 1995 edns).
FitzGerald, C., 'Impasse and Dark Night', in J.W. Conn (ed.), *Women's Spirituality: Resources for Christian Development*, 2nd edn (Mahwah, NJ: Paulist Press, 1996).
Flax, J., 'On the Contemporary Politics of Subjectivity', *Human Studies* 16/1–2 (1993): 33–49.
Flick, U., *An Introduction to Qualitative Research*, 2nd edn (London: Sage, 2002).
Forrester, D., *Truthful Action: Explorations in Practical Theology* (Edinburgh: T&T Clark, 2000).
Foster, D., *Reading with God* (London: Continuum, 2005).
Fowler, J., *Stages of Faith: The Psychology of Human Development and the Quest for Meaning* (San Francisco, CA: Harper, 1981).
Fraser, G., *Christianity With Attitude* (London: Canterbury Press, 2007).
Friedman, A., 'Sexuality and Motherhood: Mutually Exclusive in Perception of Women', *Sex Roles: A Journal of Research* 38/20 (1998): 781–800.
Friedman, L., *Identity's Architect: A Biography of Erik H. Erikson* (New York: Scribner, 1999).
Furlong, M., 'Introduction', in M. Furlong (ed.), *Mirror to the Church: Reflections on Sexism* (London: SPCK, 1988).
Giblin, M.J., 'Empowerment', in L.M. Russell and J.S. Clarkson (eds), *Dictionary of Feminist Theologies* (London: Sheffield Academic Press, 1996).
Gibson, P.C., 'Introduction: Popular Culture', in S. Gillis, G. Howie and R. Munford (eds), *Third Wave Feminism: A Critical Exploration* (New York: Palgrave Macmillan, 2004).
Giddens, A., *Modernity and Self-Identity: Self and Society in the Late Modern Age* (Cambridge: Polity Press, 1991).
Gill, R., *Gender and the Media* (Cambridge: Polity, 2007).
—— and C. Scharff, 'Introduction', in R. Gill and C. Scharff (eds), *New Femininities: Postfeminism, Neoliberalism and Subjectivity* (Basingstoke: Palgrave Macmillan, 2011).
Gill, S., *Women and the Church of England: From the Eighteenth Century to the Present* (London: SPCK, 1994).
Gillespie, V.B., *The Experience of Faith* (Birmingham, AL: Religious Education Press, 1988).
Gilligan, A., G. Rogers and D.H. Tolman (eds), *Women, Girls and Psychotherapy: Reframing Resistance* (New York, London and Sydney: Harrington Park Press, 1991).
Gilligan, C., *In a Different Voice: Psychological Theory and Women's Development* (Cambridge, MA: Harvard University Press, 1982).

——, 'Women's Psychological Development: Implications for Psychotherapy', in B.G. Glaser, *Basics of Grounded Theory Analysis: Emergence vs Forcing* (Mill Valley, California: Sociology Press, 1992).

Glaser, B.G., and A.L. Strauss, *The Discovery of Grounded Theory*, 4th edn (New Jersey: Aldine Transaction, 2009).

Glasson, B., *The Exuberant Church: Listening to the Prophetic People of God* (London: Darton, Longman and Todd, 2011).

Glaz, M., and J. Stevenson-Moessner (eds), *Women in Travail and Transition: A New Pastoral Care* (Minneapolis, MN: Fortress Press, 1991).

Glick, P.F., S.T. Mladinic, A. Saiz, J.L. Abrams, D. Masser, B. Adetoun, B. Osagie, J.E. Akande, A. Alao, A. Annetje, B. Willemsen, T.M. Chipeta, K. Dardenne, B. Dijksterhuis, A. Wigboldus, D. Eckes, T. Six-Materna, I. Expósito, F. Moya, M. Foddy, M. Kim, H. Lameiras, M. Sotelo, M.J. Mucchi-Faina, A. Romani, M. Sakalli, N. Udegbe, B. Yamamoto, M. Ui, M. Ferreira, M.C. López, W. López, 'Beyond Prejudice as Simple Antipathy: Hostile and Benevolent Sexism across Cultures', *Journal of Personality and Social Psychology* 79/5 (2000): 763–85.

Gluck, S.B., and D. Patai, *Women's Words: The Feminist Practice of Oral History* (New York: Routledge, 1991).

Graham, E., *Making the Difference: Gender, Personhood and Theology* (London: Mowbray, 1995).

——, *Transforming Practice: Pastoral Theology in an Age of Uncertainty* (London: Mowbray, 1996).

——, *Words Made Flesh: Writings in Pastoral and Practical Theology* (London: SCM, 2009).

—— (ed.), *Grace Jantzen: Redeeming the Present* (Farnham: Ashgate, 2009).

—— and M. Halsey (eds), *Life Cycles: Women and Pastoral Care* (London: SPCK, 1993).

—— and S. Lowe, *What Makes A Good City? Public theology and the urban church* (London: Darton, Longman and Todd, 2009).

——, H. Walton and F. Ward, *Theological Reflection: Methods* (London: SCM Press, 2005).

Gramich, K., and C. Brennan, *Welsh Women's Poetry 1460–2001: An Anthology* (Dinas Powys: Honno Press, 2003).

Grant, J., *White Women's Christ and Black Women's Jesus* (Atlanta, GA: Scholar's Press, 1989).

Green, A., *A Theology of Women's Priesthood* (London: SPCK, 2009).

Grenz, S.J., 'The Social God and the Relational Self: Toward a Theology of the *Imago Dei* in a Post Modern Culture' in R. Lints, M.S. Horton and M.R. Talbot (eds), *Personal Identity in Theological Perspective* (Grand Rapids, MI: Eerdmans, 2006), pp. 70–92.

Grey, M., *Redeeming the Dream: Feminism, Redemption and Christian Tradition* (London: SPCK, 1989).

——, 'Natality and Flourishing in Contexts of Disability and Impairment', in E. Graham (ed.), *Grace Jantzen: Redeeming the Present* (Farnham: Ashgate, 2009).

Grof, S., and C. Grof, 'Spiritual Emergency: The Understanding and Treatment of Transpersonal Crises', *ReVision* 8/2 (1986): 7–20.

——, *Spiritual Emergency: When Personal Transformation Becomes a Crisis* (Los Angeles, CA: Tarcher Publishers, 1989).

Groothuis, R.M., *Women Caught in the Conflict: The Culture War between Traditionalism and Feminism* (Grand Rapids, MI: Baker Books, 1994).

——, *Good News for Women: A Biblical Picture of Gender Equality* (Grand Rapids, MI: Baker Books, 1997).

Gross, R., *A Garland of Feminist Reflections: Forty Years of Religious Exploration* (Berkeley: University of California Press, 2009).

Gunner, S., 'Learning through Liturgy' (unpublished MA dissertation, Anglia Ruskin University, 2008).

——, 'Woman-cross', in M. Rose, J. Te Paa, J. Person and A. Nelson (eds), *Lifting Women's Voices* (Norwich: Canterbury Press, 2009).

Habermas, J., *Structural Transformation of the Public Sphere*, trans. T. Burger (Boston, MA: MIT Press, 1998).

Hall, J., *Midwifery Mind and Spirit: Emerging Issues of Care* (Oxford: Books for Midwives Publishers, 2001).

——, 'Spiritual Effects of Childhood Sexual Abuse in Adult Christian Women', *Journal of Psychology and Theology* 23/2 (1995): 129–34.

Hammersley, P., 'Adult Learning Problems and the Experience of Loss: A Study of Religious Rigidity' (unpublished PhD dissertation, University of Birmingham, 1997).

Hampson, D.M., *Theology and Feminism* (Oxford: Basil Blackwell, 1990).

Hardesty, N.A., *Inclusive Language in the Church* (Atlanta, GA: John Knox Press, 1987).

Harris, M., *Teaching as Religious Imagination: An Essay in the Theology of Teaching* (San Francisco, CA: Harper Row, 1987).

Hay, D., with R. Nye, *The Spirit of the Child*, revised edn (London and Philadelphia, PA: Jessica Kingsley Publishers, 2006).

Hedges-Goettl, L., *Sexual Abuse: Pastoral Responses* (Nashville, TN: Abingdon Press, 2004).

Hedlund-de Wit, A., 'The rising culture and worldview of contemporary spirituality: A sociological study of potentials and pitfalls for sustainable development', *Ecological Economics* 70 (2011): 1057–65.

Heller, D., *The Children's God* (Chicago, IL and London: Chicago University Press, 1986).

Helminiak, D., 'Neurology, Psychology, and Extraordinary Religious Experiences', *Journal of Religion and Health* 23/1 (1984): 33–44.

Henderson, G., 'Evangelical Women Negotiating Faith in Contemporary Scotland' (unpublished PhD dissertation, University of Glasgow, 2008).

Hess, C.L., *Caretakers of our Common House: Women's Development in Communities of Faith* (Nashville, TN: Abingdon Press, 1997).

Hesse-Biber, S.N., and P. Leavy, *The Practice of Qualitative Research*, 2nd edn (Thousand Oaks, CA: Sage, 2011).

Heyward, C., *Our Passion for Justice: Images of Power, Sexuality, and Liberation* (New York: Pilgrim Press, 1984).

——, *When Boundaries Betray Us: Beyond Illusions of What is Ethical in Therapy and Life* (San Francisco, CA: HarperCollins, 1993).

—— and B.W. Harrison, 'Boundaries: Protecting the Vulnerable or Perpetuating a Bad Idea', in K.H. Ragsdale (ed.), *Boundary Wars: Intimacy and Distance in Healing Relationships* (Cleveland, OH: The Pilgrim Press, 1996).

Hillman, J., 'The Bad Mother, an Archetypal Approach', in P. Berry (ed.), *Fathers and Mothers* (Dallas, TX: Spring Publications, 1990).

Hochschild, A., and A. Machung, *The Second Shift: Working Parents and the Revolution at Home* (Berkeley and London: University of California Press, 1989).

Hogan, L., *From Women's Experience to Feminist Theology* (Sheffield: Sheffield Academic Press, 1995).

Hughes, K., '"I've Been Pondering whether You Can Be a Part-feminist": Young Australian Women's Studies Students Discuss Gender', *Women's Studies International Forum* 28 (2005): 37–49.

Hussey, E., 'Epistemology and Meaning in Heraclitus', in M. Schofield and M.C. Nussbaum (eds), *Language and Logos: Studies in Ancient Greek Philosophy presented to G.E.L. Owen* (Cambridge: Cambridge University Press, 1982).

Irigaray, L. (ed.), *Luce Irigaray: Key Writings* (London and New York: Continuum, 2004).

Isasi-Díaz, A.M., 'Experiences', in L.M. Russell and J.S. Clarkson (eds), *Dictionary of Feminist Theologies* (London/Westminster: Mowbray/John Knox, 1996).

Isherwood, L., and D. McEwan, *Introducing Feminist Theology* (Sheffield: Sheffield Academic Press, 1993).

——, *Introducing Feminist Christologies* (Sheffield: Sheffield Academic Press, 2001).

——, 'The Embodiment of Feminist Liberation Theology: The Spiralling of Incarnation' in *Embodying Feminist Liberation Theologies: A Special Edition of Feminist Theology* 12.2 (January 2004): 140–56.

Izzard, S., 'Holding Contradictions Together: an Object-relational View of Healthy Spirituality', *Contact* 140 (2003): 2–8.

Jantzen, G., *Becoming Divine: Towards a Feminist Philosophy of Religion* (Manchester: Manchester University Press, 1998, and Bloomington, IN and Manchester: Manchester University Press 1999 edn).

——, *Foundations of Violence* (London: Routledge, 2004).

——, 'The Womb and the Tomb: Health and Flourishing in Medieval Mystical Literature', in J. Baxter (ed.), *Wounds that Heal: Theology, Imagination and Health* (London: SPCK, 2007).

Jensen, D.H., *Graced Vulnerability, A Theology of Childhood* (Cleveland, OH: The Pilgrim Press, 2005).

Johnson, E., 'The maleness of Christ', in A. Carr and E.S. Fiorenza (eds), *The Special Nature of Women?* (London: SCM Press, 1991).

——, *Friends of God and Prophets: A Feminist Theological Reading of the Communion of Saints* (London: SCM, 1998).

Jones, I., *Women and Priesthood in the Church of England Ten Years On* (London: Church House Publishing, 2004).

Jones, M.R., 'Beyond Identity? The Reconstruction of the Welsh', *The Journal of British Studies* 31/4 (1992):330–57.

Jones, R., 'Sexuality and Mothering', in Andrea O'Reilly (ed.), *Encyclopedia of Motherhood* (Thousand Oaks, CA: Sage Publications, 2010).

Jones, S., *Feminist Theory and Christian Theology: Cartographies of Grace* (Minneapolis, MN: Fortress Press, 2000).

Joung, E., 'An Attachment Theoretical Approach to Women's Faith Development: A Qualitative Study' (unpublished PhD dissertation, University of Birmingham, 2007).

——, *Religious Attachment: Women's Faith Development in Psychodynamic Perspective* (Newcastle upon Tyne: Cambridge Scholars Publishing, 2008).

Juschka, D.M., 'A General Introduction to Feminism in the Study of Religion', in *idem* (ed.), *Feminism in the Study of Religion* (London: Continuum, 2001).

Kegan, R., *The Evolving Self: Problem and Process in Human Development* (Cambridge, MA: Harvard University Press, 1982).

Kennedy, M., 'Sexual Abuse of Women by Priests and Ministers to Whom They Go for Pastoral Care and Support', *Feminist Theology Continuum* 11 (2003): 226–35.

Killen, P.O., *Finding Our Voices: Women, Wisdom, and Faith* (New York: Crossroad, 1997).

King, N., and C. Horrocks, *Interviews in Qualitative Research* (London: Sage, 2010).

King, U., *The Search for Spirituality: Our Global Quest for a Spiritual Life* (New York: Bluebridge, 2011).

Kirkpatrick, L.A., 'An Attachment-theory Approach to the Psychology of Religion', *International Journal for the Psychology of Religion* 2/1 (1992): 3–28.

——, 'Attachment Theory and Religious Experience', in R.W. Hood Jr. (ed.), *Handbook of Religious Experience* (Birmingham, AL: Religious Education Press, 1995).

——, 'Attachment and Religious Representations and Behavior', in J. Cassidy and P.R. Shaver (eds), *Handbook of Attachment: Theory, Research, and Clinical Applications* (New York: The Guilford Press, 1999).

Kitcatt, C.A., 'Dancing Barefoot: An Exploration of Women's Experience of the Spiritual Accompaniment/Direction Relationship' (unpublished EdD thesis, University of East Anglia, 2010).

Klassen, C., 'Confronting the Gap: Why Religion Needs to be Given More Attention in Women's Studies', *Thirdspace* 3:1 (2003) <http://www.thirdspace.ca/journal/article/view/klassen/165> accessed 12 May 2013.

Kosttenberger, A.J., with D. Jones, *God, Marriage and Family: Rebuilding the Biblical Foundations*, 2nd edn (Wheaton, IL: Crossway Books, 2010).

Kukla, R., 'Introduction: Maternal Bodies', *Hypatia* 21/1 (2006): 7–9.

Lahood, G., 'Rumour of Angels and Heavenly Midwives: Anthropology of Transpersonal Events and Childbirth', *Women and Birth* 20/7 (2007): 3–10.

Langer, S., *Philosophy in a new key: A Study in the Symbolism of Reason, Rite, and Art* (New York: Harvard University Press, 1948).

Lanzetta, B., *Spiritual Vocations in a Multireligious World* (2008) <http://www.beverlylanzetta.net/writings/86-spiritual-vocations-multireligious-world> accessed 28 January 2013.

Lawless, E., 'Women's life stories and reciprocal ethnography as feminist and emergent', *Journal of Folklore Research* 28/1 (1991): 35–60.

Lazar, M.M., 'The Right to be Beautiful: Postfeminist Identity and Consumer Beauty Advertising', in R. Gill and C. Scharff (eds), *New Femininities: Postfeminism, Neoliberalism and Subjectivity* (Basingstoke: Palgrave Macmillan, 2011).

Lebacqz, K., and R.G. Barton, 'Boundaries, Mutuality, and Professional Ethics', in K.H. Ragsdale (ed.), *Boundary Wars: Intimacy and Distance in Healing Relationships* (Cleveland, OH: The Pilgrim Press, 1996).

Lennie, J., 'Troubling Empowerment: An Evaluation and Critique of a Feminist Action Research Project Involving Rural Women and Interactive Communication Technologies' (unpublished PhD thesis, Queensland University of Technology, 2001) <http://eprints.qut.edu.au/18365> accessed 12 May 2013.

Letherby, G., *Feminist Research in Theory and Practice* (Buckingham: Open University Press, 2003).

Liamputtong, P., 'When giving life starts to take the life out of you: Women's experiences of Depression after Childbirth', *Midwifery* 23 (2007): 77–91.

Liebert, E., 'Seasons and Stages', in J. Stevenson-Moessner (ed.), *In Her Own Time: Women and Developmental Issues in Pastoral Care* (Minneapolis, MN: Fortress Press, 2000).

Liechty, J., and C. Clegg, *Moving Beyond Sectarianism* (Dublin: The Columba Press, 2001).

Lindner, E.W., 'Children as Theologians', in P.B. Pufall and R.P. Unsworth (eds), *Rethinking Childhood* (New Brunswick, NJ: Rutgers University Press, 2004).

Llewellyn, R., *How Green Was My Valley* (London: Penguin Classic edn, 2001).

Lockwood, P., '"Someone like Me can be Successful." Do College Students need Same Gender Role Models?', *Psychology of Women Quarterly* 30/1 (2006): 36–46.

Lombardi, N., 'Dancing in the Underworld: the Quest for Wholeness', in A. Williams (ed.), *She is Everywhere! Vol. 2: An Anthology of Writings in Womanist / feminist Spirituality* (Indiana: iUniverse.com Publishers, 2008).

Lonergan, B., *Insight: A Study of Human Understanding* (Toronto: University of Toronto Press, 1957).

Looman, M., 'Reflective leadership: strategic planning from heart and soul', *Consulting Psychology Journal Practice and Research* 55/4 (2003): 215–21.

Lorde, A., 'The Master's Tools Will Never Dismantle the Master's House', *Sister Outsider*, in *The Audre Lorde Compendium: Essays, Speeches and Journals* (London: Pandora, 1996).

Loseke, D., 'The Study of Identity as Cultural, Institutional, Organizational, and Personal Narratives: Theoretical and Empirical Integrations', *The Sociological Quarterly* 48 (2007): 661–88.

Lunn, P., 'Do Women Need the GODDESS? Some Phenomenological and Sociological Reflections', *Feminist Theology* 4 (1993): 17–38.

Macquarrie, J., *Christology Revisited* (London: SCM Press, 1998).

MACSAS leaflet, 'Clergy or Minister Sexual Exploitation of Adults in the Pastoral Relationship' <http://www.macsas.org.uk/PDFs/Homepage/sex_exploitn.pdf> accessed 28 January 2013.

Maitland, S., *A Book of Silence* (London: Granta, 2009).

Manville, J., 'The Gendered Organization of an Australian Anglican Parish', *Sociology of Religion* 58/1 (1997): 25–38.

Marshall, C., and G.B. Rossman, *Designing Qualitative Research* (Thousand Oaks, CA: Sage, 2011).

Martin, C.J., 'Womanist Interpretations of the New Testament: The Quest for Holistic and Inclusive Translation and Interpretation', in J.H. Cone and G.S. Wilmore (eds), *Black Theology: A Documentary History, Volume 2: 1980–1992* (New York: Orbis Books, 1993).

Martinez Aleman, A.M., 'Understanding and Investigating Female Friendship's Educative Value', *Journal of Higher Education* 68/2 (1997): 119–59.

May, M.A., *A Body Knows: Towards a Theopoetics of Death and Resurrection* (New York: Continuum, 1995).

Mazzei, L., 'Inhabited Silences: In Pursuit of a Muffled Subtext', *Qualitative Inquiry* 9 (2003): 355–68.

McCarthy, M., 'Spirituality in a Postmodern Era', in J. Woodward and S. Pattison (eds), *The Blackwell Reader in Pastoral and Practical Theology* (Oxford: Blackwell Publishers, 2000).

McFague, S., *Metaphorical Theology: Models of God in Religious Language* (Philadelphia, PA: Fortress Press, 1982).

McGuire, M., 'Why Bodies Matter: A Sociological Reflection on Spirituality and Materiality', *Spiritus* 3 (2003): 1–18.

McKittrick, D., and D. McVea, *Making Sense of the Troubles* (London: Penguin Books, 2001).
McRobbie, A., *The Aftermath of Feminism: Gender, Culture and Social Change* (London: Sage, 2009).
——, 'Preface' in R. Gill and C. Scharff (eds), *New Femininities: Postfeminism, Neoliberalism and Subjectivity* (Basingstoke: Palgrave Macmillan, 2011).
McWhorter, L., 'Rites of passing: Foucault, power, and same-sex commitment ceremonies', in K. Schilbrack (ed.), *Thinking Through Rituals: Philosophical perspectives* (New York and London: Routledge, 2004).
Mearns, D., and B. Thorne, *Person-Centred Counselling in Action*, 3rd edn (London: Sage, 2007).
Mellott, D., 'Ethnography as Theology: Encountering the Penitentes of Arroyo Seco, New Mexico' (unpublished PhD thesis, Emory University, 2005).
Mercer, J.A., *Girl Talk, God Talk: Why Faith Matters to Teenage Girls – and Their Parents* (San Francisco, CA: Jossey Bass, 2008).
Merleau-Ponty, M., *The Phenomenology of Perception* (New York: Routledge, 1962).
Merton, T., *The Wisdom of the Desert: Sayings of the Desert Fathers of the Fourth Century* (New York: New Direction Books, 1960).
Miller-McLemore, B.J., *Death, Sin and the Moral Life* (Atlanta, GA: Scholars Press, 1988).
——, *Also A Mother: Work and Family as Theological Dilemma* (Nashville, TN: Abingdon Press, 1994).
——, 'The Living Human Web: Pastoral Theology at the Turn of the Century', in J. Stevenson-Moessner (ed.), *Through the Eyes of Women: Insights for Pastoral Care* (Minneapolis, MN: Fortress Press, 1996).
——, 'Pastoral Theology as Practical Theology' in *Christian Theology in Practice: Discovering a Discipline* (Grand Rapids, MI: Eerdmans, 2012).
—— and B.L. Gill-Austern, *Feminist and Womanist Pastoral Theology* (Nashville, TN: Abingdon Press, 1999).
Miller, A.S., and R. Stark, 'Gender and Religiousness: Can Socialization Explanations Be Saved?', *The American Journal of Sociology* 107/6 (2002): 1399–423.
Miller, J., *The Transcendent Function: Jung's Model of Psychological Growth through a Dialogue with the Unconscious* (New York: Routledge, 2004).
Miller, J.B., 'The Development of Women's Sense of Self,' in J.V. Jordan, A.G. Kaplan, I.P. Stiver, J.L. Surrey and J.B. Miller (eds), *Women's Growth in Connection: Writings from the Stone Center* (New York: Guilford Press, 1991).
Miller, L., 'Spiritual Awakening through the Motherhood Journey', *Journal of the Association for Research on Mothering* 7/1 (2005): 17–31.
Mishler, E.G., *Research Interviewing: Context and Narrative* (Cambridge, MA: Harvard University Press, 1986).
Moloney, F.J., *The Gospel of Mark, A Commentary* (Peabody: Hendrikson Publishers, 2002).

Moltmann, J., *The Trinity and the Kingdom of God: The Doctrine of God* (London: SCM Press, 1981).
Monk Kidd, S., *The Dance of the Dissident Daughter* (New York: HarperCollins, 1996).
Morley, J., *All Desires Known*, 2nd edn (London: SPCK, 1992).
Morton, N., *The Journey is Home* (Boston, MA: Beacon Press, 1985).
Moschella, M.C., *Ethnography as a Pastoral Practice: An Introduction* (Cleveland, OH: Pilgrim Press, 2008).
Nason-Clark, N., 'Ordaining Women as Priests: Religious vs. Sexist Explanations for Clerical Attitudes', *Sociology of Religion* 48/3 (1987): 259–73.
Natiello, P., *The Person-Centred Approach: A Passionate Presence* (Ross-on-Wye: PCCS Books, 2001).
Nesbitt, E., 'Researching 8 to 13-year-olds' perspectives and their experience of religion', in A. Lewis and G. Lindsay (eds), *Researching Children's Perspectives* (Buckingham and Philadelphia, PA: Open University Press, 2000).
Neu, D.L., *Women's Rites: Feminist Liturgies for Life's Journey* (Cleveland, OH: Pilgrim Press, 2003).
Neuger, C.C., 'Women and Relationality', in B.J. Miller-McLemore and B.L. Gill-Austern (eds), *Feminist and Womanist Pastoral Theology* (Nashville, TN: Abingdon Press, 1999).
——, 'Narratives of Harm: Setting the Developmental Context for Intimate Violence', in J. Stevenson-Moessner (ed.), *In Her Own Time: Women and Developmental Issues in Pastoral Care* (Minneapolis, MN: Fortress Press, 2000).
Nye, R., 'Psychological perspectives on children's spirituality' (unpublished PhD thesis, University of Nottingham, 1998).
O'Reilly, A., 'Mothering, sex and sexuality', *Journal of the Association for Research on Mothering* 4/1 (2002): 150–238.
Orevillo-Montenegro, M., *The Jesus of Asian Women* (New York: Orbis, 2006).
Ozorak, E.J., 'The Power, but Not the Glory: How Women Empower Themselves Through Religion', *Journal for the Scientific Study of Religion* 35/1 (1996): 17–29.
Page, S., 'Negotiating Sacred Roles: A Sociological Exploration of Priests who are Mothers', *Feminist Review* 97/1 (2011): 92–109.
——, 'Femmes, Mères et Prêtres dans l'Eglise d'Angleterre: Quels Sacerdoces', *Travail, Genre et Sociétés* 27 (2012): 55–71.
Painter, C.V., *Lectio Divina: The Sacred Art* (London: SPCK, 2012).
Parker, R., *The Experience of Maternal Ambivalence: Torn in two* (London: Virago Press, 1995).
Parks, S., *The Critical Years: The Young Adult Search for a Faith to Live by* (San Francisco, CA: HarperCollins, 1986).

Parrat, J., 'Territories of the Self and Spiritual Practices during Childbirth', in K. Fahy (ed.), *Birth Territory and Midwifery Guardianship* (Oxford: Books for Midwives Publishers, 2008).

——, 'A Feminist Critique of Foundational Nursing Research and Theory on Transition to Motherhood', *Midwifery* 27/4 (2010): 445–51.

Pazmiño, R.W., *Doing Theological Research: An introductory guide for survival in theological education* (Eugene, OR.: Wipf & Stock, 2009).

Pennington, B., *Lectio Divina: Renewing the Ancient Practice of Praying the Scriptures* (New York: Crossroad, 1998).

Perrin, D., *Studying Christian Spirituality* (London: Routledge, 2007).

Perrin, R., 'How Might the Evangelical Church use Neglected, Female, Biblical Role Models as a Method of Discipleship and Empowerment amongst Young Women?' (unpublished MA dissertation, University of Durham, 2007).

——, *Inspiring Women: Discovering Biblical Role Models*, Grove Biblical Series B52 (Cambridge: Grove Books 2009)

Person, E., *Feeling Strong. How Power Issues Affect our Ability to Direct our Own Lives* (New York: HarperCollins, 2002).

Phillips, A., *The Faith of Girls: Children's Spirituality and Transition to Adulthood* (Farnham: Ashgate Press, 2011).

Phillips, M., *Wales: Nation and Region* (Llandysul: Gomer Press, 1997).

Pierce, R.W., and R.M. Groothuis (eds), *Discovering Biblical Equality: Complementarity without Hierarchy* (Downers Grove, IL: IVP, 2004).

Piper, J., and D.A. Carson, *The Pastor as Scholar & The Scholar as Pastor* (Nottingham: IVP, 2011).

—— and W. Grudem (eds), *Rediscovering Biblical Manhood and Womanhood: A Response to Evangelical Feminism* (Wheaton, IL: Crossway Books, 1991);

Pitchford, S.R., 'Image Making Movements: Welsh Nationalism and Stereotype Transformation', *Sociological Perspectives* 44/1 (2001): 45–65.

Plummer, K., *Telling Sexual Stories: Power, change, and social worlds* (London and New York: Routledge, 1995).

Porter, F., *Changing Women, Changing Worlds: Evangelical Women in Church, Community and Politics* (Belfast: Blackstaff, 2002).

——, *It Will Not Be Taken Away From Her: A feminist engagement with women's Christian experience* (London: Darton, Longman and Todd, 2004).

Procter-Smith, M., 'Images of Women in the Lectionary', in E.S. Fiorenza and M. Collins (eds), *Women – Invisible In Church and Theology* (Edinburgh: T&T Clarke Ltd, 1985).

——, *In Her Own Rite: Constructing Feminist Liturgical Tradition* (Nashville, TN: Abingdon Press, 1990).

——, *Praying With Our Eyes Open: Engendering Feminist Liturgical Prayer* (Nashville, TN: Abingdon Press, 1995).

Punch, K.F., *Introduction to Social Research: Quantitative and Qualitative Approaches* (London: Sage, 1998).

Ramazanoglu, C., and J. Holland, *Feminist Methodology: Challenges and Choices* (London: Sage, 2002).
Ramshaw, E., *Ritual and Pastoral Care* (Philadelphia: Fortress Press, 1987).
Redfern, C., and K. Aune, *Reclaiming the F Word: The New Feminist Movement* (London: Zed Books, 2010).
Rees, Christina, *Voices of this Calling: Women Priests – the First Ten Years* (Norwich: Canterbury Press, 2002).
Reports of the Commissioners of Inquiry into the State of Education in Wales 1847, The National Library of Wales <http://www.llgc.org.uk/index.php?id=774> accessed 17 April 2009.
Rhys, F., 'Figure of Faith, Human Example, Secondary to God: Some Women's Understandings of Jesus Christ' (unpublished MA thesis, University of Birmingham, 2007).
Ribbens, J., 'Hearing my Feeling Voice? An Autobiographical Discussion of Motherhood', in J. Ribbens and R. Edwards (eds), *Feminist Dilemmas in Qualitative Research: Public Knowledge and Private Lives* (London: Sage, 1998).
Rich, A., *The Dream of a Common Language: Poems 1974–1977* (New York: W.W. Norton & Company, 1978).
——, *Of Woman Born* (New York: W.W. Norton & Company, 1986).
Ridgeway, C.L., and L. Smith-Lovin, 'The Gender System and Interaction', *Annual Review of Sociology* 25 (1999): 191–216.
Riessman, C.K., *Narrative Analysis* (Thousand Oaks, CA: Sage Publications, 1993).
Robson, C., *Real World Research: A Resource for Social Scientists and Practitioner-Researchers*, 2nd edn (Oxford: Blackwell, 2002).
Rogers, C.R., *Carl Rogers on Personal Power: Inner Strength and Its Revolutionary Impact* (London: Constable, 1978).
Ross, S.A., *Extravagant Affections: A Feminist Sacramental Theology* (New York: Continuum, 2001).
——, 'Church and sacrament – community and worship', in S.F. Parsons (ed.), *The Cambridge Companion to Feminist Theology* (Cambridge: Cambridge University Press, 2002).
Roth, L.M., and J.C. Kroll, 'Risky business: Assessing risk preference explanations for gender differences in religiosity', *American Sociological Review* 72/2 (2007): 205–20.
Ruether, R.R., *Sexism and God-Talk* (London: SCM Press, 1983).
——, *Women-Church: Theology and Practice of Feminist Liturgical Communities* (London: Harper & Row, 1985).
——, 'Women's Body and Blood: The Sacred and the Impure', in A. Joseph (ed.), *Through the Devil's Gateway: Women, Religion and Taboo* (London: SPCK, 1990).
Ruffing, J.K., 'Spiritual Direction: An Instance of Christian Friendship or a Therapeutic Relationship', *Studia Mystica* XII (1989): 64–73.

Russell, L.M., *Church in the Round: Feminist Interpretation of the Church* (Louisville, KY: Westminster/John Knox Press, 1993).
Said, E., *Orientalism* (London: Penguin Books, 2003).
Saunders, C.J., 'The Woman as Preacher', in D. Day, J. Astley and L. Francis (eds), *A Reader on Preaching: Making Connections* (Aldershot: Ashgate, 2005).
Scharff, C., *Repudiating Feminism: Young Women in a Neoliberal World* (Farnham: Ashgate, 2012).
Scharmer, O., *Theory U: Leading from the Future as it Emerges. Open Mind, Open Heart, Open Will. The Social Technology of Presencing* (San Francisco, CA: Berrett-Koehler, 2009).
Searles, H., *Collected Works on Schizophrenia and Related Subjects* (London: Karnac Books, 1965).
Shakespeare, S., and H. Rayment-Pickard, *The Inclusive God: Reclaiming Theology for an Inclusive Church* (Norwich: Canterbury Press, 2006).
Shapiro, L., 'Definitions of transpersonal psychology: the first twenty-three years', *Journal of Transpersonal Psychology* 24 (1992): 79–98.
Shooter, S., *The Authentic Spirituality of the Annihilated Soul: How Survivors of Abuse Relate to God* (Farnham: Ashgate, 2012).
Siegel, D., *Mindsight: The New Science of Personal Transformation* (New York: Bantam Publishers, 2010).
Silverman, D., *Qualitative Research: Theory, Method and Practice* (London: Sage, 1997).
Slee, N., 'The Holy Spirit and Spirituality', in S.F. Parsons (ed.), *The Cambridge Companion to Feminist Theology* (Cambridge: Cambridge University Press, 2002).
——, *Faith and Feminism: An Introduction to Christian Feminist Theology* (London: Darton, Longman and Todd, 2003).
——, *Praying Like a Woman* (London: SPCK, 2004).
——, *Women's Faith Development: Patterns and Processes* (Aldershot: Ashgate, 2004).
——, *Seeking the Risen Christa* (London: SPCK, 2011).
Smith, C., with M.L. Denton, *Soul Searching: The Religious and Spiritual Lives of American Teenagers* (New York: Oxford University Press, 2005).
Smith, E.J., *Bearing Fruit in Due Season: Feminist Hermeneutics and the Bible in Worship* (Collegeville, MN: The Liturgical Press, 1999).
Snorton, T., and J. Stevenson-Moessner, J. (eds), *Women Out of Order: Risking Change and Creating Care in a Multicultural World* (Minneapolis, MN: Fortress, 2009).
Stanley, L., and S. Wise, *Breaking Out Again: Feminist Ontology and Epistemology*, 2nd edn (London: Routledge, 1993).
Stevenson-Moessner, J. (ed.), *Through the Eyes of Women: Insights for Pastoral Care* (Minneapolis, MN: Fortress Press, 1996).
—— (ed.), *In Her Own Time: Women and Development Issues in Pastoral Care* (Minneapolis, MN: Fortress Press, 2000).

Stiver, I.P., 'Work Inhibitions in Women', in J.V. Jordan, A.G. Kaplan, I.P. Stiver, J.L. Surrey and J.B. Miller, *Women's Growth in Connection: Writings from the Stone Center* (New York: Guilford Press, 1991).

Storkey, E., *What's Right with Feminism?* (London: SPCK, 1985).

Strauss, A., and J. Corbin, *Basics of Qualitative Research: Techniques and Procedures for Developing Grounded Theory*, 2nd edn (Thousand Oaks: Sage Publications, 1998).

Stuart, E., 'Elizabeth Stuart Phelps: A Good Feminist Woman Doing Bad Theology?', *Feminist Theology* 9 (2001): 70–82.

——, *Gay and Lesbian Theologies: Repetitions with Critical Difference* (Aldershot: Ashgate, 2003).

——, 'Exploding Mystery: Feminist Theology and the Sacramental', *Embodying Feminist Liberation Theologies: A Special Edition of Feminist Theology* 12.2 (2004): 228–36.

Sullins, D.P., 'Gender and Religion: Deconstructing Universality, Constructing Complexity', *American Journal of Sociology* 112/3 (2006): 838–80.

Surrey, J.L., 'The Self-in-Relation: A Theory of Women's Development', in J.V. Jordan, A.G. Kaplan, I.P. Stiver, J.L. Surrey and J.B. Miller, *Women's Growth in Connection: Writings from the Stone Center* (New York: Guilford Press, 1991).

Swinton, J., *Spirituality in Mental Health Care: Rediscovering a Forgotten Dimension* (London: Kingsley Publishers, 2001).

Tamminen, K., *Religious Development in Childhood and Youth* (Helsinki: Suomalainen Tiedeakatemia, 1991).

Temple, B., *Exclusive Language – A Hindrance to Evangelism Among Women* (Nottingham: Grove Books Ltd, 1988).

Teo, H., and D. Caspersz, 'Dissenting Discourse: Exploring Alternatives to the Whistleblowing / Silence Dichotomy', *The Journal of Business Ethics* 104 (2011): 237–49.

Thorne, H., *Journey to Priesthood: An In-depth Study of the First Women Priests in the Church of England* (Bristol: Centre for Comparative Studies in Religion and Gender, 2000).

Timmerman, J., 'Body and Spirituality', in P. Sheldrake (ed.), *The New Westminster Dictionary of Christian Spirituality* (London: Westminster John Knox Press, 2005).

Tisdale, L.T., 'Women's Ways of Communicating', in J. Dempsey Douglass and J.F. Kay (eds), *Women, Gender and Christian Community* (Louisville, KY: Westminster John Knox Press, 1997).

Townsend Gilkes, C., 'Some Mother's Son and Some Father's Daughter: Gender and Biblical Language in Afro-Christian Worship Tradition', in C.W. Atkinson, C.H. Buchanan and M.R. Miles (eds), *Shaping New Vision: Gender and Values in American Culture* (Ann Arbor, MI: UMI Research Press, 1987).

Trible, P., *God and the Rhetoric of Sexuality* (Philadelphia, PA: Fortress Press, 1978).

——, *Texts of Terror: Literary-feminist Readings of Biblical Narratives* (Philadelphia, PA: Fortress Press, 1984).

——, 'Feminist Hermeneutics and Biblical Studies', in A. Loades (ed.), *Feminist Theology: A Reader* (London: SPCK, 1990).

Trzebiatowska, M., and D. Llewellyn, 'The Changing Feminist Face of Christianity', British Sociological Association's Sociology of Religion Study Group Annual Conference: 'The Changing Face of Christianity', University of Edinburgh, 6–8 April 2010.

Turner, V., *The Ritual Process: Structure and Anti-Structure* (New York: Cornell University Press, 1991).

Tyler, I., 'Reframing Pregnant Embodiment', in S. Ahmed, J. Kilby, C. Lury, M. McNeil and B. Skeggs (eds), *Transformations: Thinking through Feminism* (London: Routledge, 2000).

Van Gennep, A., *The Rites of Passage* (London: Routledge, 2004).

Vaughan, F., 'What is Spiritual Intelligence?', *Journal of Humanistic Psychology* 42/2 (2002): 16–33.

Walby, S. *Theorizing Patriarchy* (Oxford: Blackwell, 1990).

——, *The Future of Feminism* (Cambridge: Polity Press, 2011).

Walsh, C., 'Speaking in Different Tongues? A Case Study of Women Priests in the Church of England', *Sheffield Hallam Working Papers on the Web* 1 (2000).

——, *Gender and Discourse: Language and Power in Politics, the Church and Organisations* (Harlow: Longman, 2001).

Walter, T., and G. Davie, 'The Religiosity of Women in the Modern West', *The British Journal of Sociology* 49/4 (1998): 640–60.

Walton, H., *Imagining Theology: Women, Writing and God* (Edinburgh: T&T Clark, 2007).

Ward, F., *Lifelong Learning: Theological Education and Supervision* (London: SCM, 2005).

Wasey, K., 'Being in Communion: A Qualitative Study of Young Lay Women's Experience of the Eucharist' (unpublished ThD thesis, University of Birmingham, 2012).

Watson, N.K., *Introducing Feminist Ecclesiology* (Sheffield: Sheffield Academic Press, 2002).

Watts, F., R. Nye and S. Savage, *Psychology for Christian Ministry* (London and New York: Routledge, 2002).

Webster, A.R., *Found Wanting: Women, Christianity and Sexuality* (London and New York: Cassell, 1995).

Webster, M., *A New Strength, A New Song: The Journey to Women's Priesthood* (London: Mowbray, 1994).

Weil, S. 'Reflections on the right use of school studies with a view to the love of God', in *idem*, *Waiting on God* (Glasgow: Fount, 1977).

West, C., and D.H. Zimmerman, 'Doing Gender', *Gender and Society* 1 (1987): 125–51.

Whitney, D.S., 'Teaching Scripture Intake', in K.O. Gangel and J.C. Wilhoit (eds), *The Christian Educator's Handbook on Spiritual Formation* (Grand Rapids, MI: Baker Publishing Group, 1994).

Wilber, K., *The Atman Project: A Transpersonal view of Human Development* (Wheaton, IL: The Theosophical Publishing House, 1980).

——, *Sex, Ecology, Spirituality: The Spirit of Evolution* (Boston, MA: Shambhala, 2011).

Wiles, M., *Archetypal Heresy, Arianism Through the Centuries* (Oxford: Oxford University Press, 1996).

Wilson, B., 'Salvation, Secularization, and De-moralization', in R.K. Fenn (ed.), *The Blackwell Companion to Sociology of Religion* (Oxford: Blackwell, 2001).

Wolter-Gustafson, C., 'Women's Lived Experience of Wholeness' (unpublished EdD dissertation, Boston University, 1984).

——, 'How Person-Centered Theory Informed My Qualitative Research on Women's Lived-Experience of Wholeness', *Person-Centered Review* 5 (1990): 221–32.

Woodhead, L., 'Feminism and the sociology of religion: from gender-blindness to gendered difference', in R.K. Fenn (ed.), *The Blackwell Companion to Sociology of Religion* (Oxford: Blackwell, 2001).

Wootton, J.H., *Introducing a Practical Feminist Theology of Worship* (Sheffield: Sheffield Academic Press, 2000).

Wren, B., *What Language Shall I Borrow? God-Talk in Worship: A Male Response to Feminist Theology* (London: SCM Press, 1989).

Wuthnow, R., *Sharing the Journey: Support Groups and America's New Quest for Community* (New York: Free Press, 1994).

Wynn, F., 'The Embodied Chiasmic Relationship of Mother and Infant', *Human Studies* 19 (1997): 253–70.

Young, I.M., *Justice and the Politics of Difference* (Princeton, NJ: Princeton University Press, 1990).

Young, M., and M. Cullen, *A Good Death: Conversations with East Londoners* (London: Routledge, 1996).

Young, P.D., 'Experience', in L. Isherwood and D. McEwan (eds), *An A–Z of Feminist Theology* (Sheffield: Sheffield Academic Press, 1996).

Index

Names in the index refer to authors cited in the main body of the text and in substantive footnotes. Authors only referenced in footnotes do not appear in the index.

Aaron, Jane 104–6
absence 117, 136, 143, 149, 158, 224
abuse 2, 6, 9, 29–32, 34, 87, 99, 125, 126, 134, 135, 180, 221–31
Acker, J. 17–18
accountability in research 22–3, 28, 30, 31
action research 2, 5, 9, 18, 131–7, 139–46
age cohorts 3–4, 37–88
agency, *see* women's agency
alienation 16, 68–9, 72–5, 95, 104, 107, 132, 164, 189
Althaus-Reid, Marcella 104, 186
Anderson, Rosemarie 174
'angel in the home' 30
Anglican church, *see* church, churches
anthropology 40, 41, 208–9
apophatic faith, *see* faith, faithing
Arendt, Hannah 27–9, 32, 196–7
attachment 4, 5, 129, 161–71
    attachment figures 162–7
    attachment, religious 161–71
    attachment systems 162–3
    attachment theory 5, 162–3, 168–70
Aune, Kristin 51, 52, 53, 58
authority, *see* church authority and women's authority
auto-ethnography 14, 33
autonomy, *see* women's agency

backlash, *see* feminist
Baker, Sally 105
Bandura, Albert 114
baptism 67–8, 108, 121
Baptist churches, *see* church, churches
Barry, K. 17–18
Barton, Mukti 125–6
Barton, Ronald G. 180

Baumgardner, Jennifer 60
Beattie, Tina 52, 75
beauty 137, 196, 197, 200
belief 3, 4, 39–49, 60, 70, 73, 75, 82, 83, 92, 97, 98, 103, 107, 117, 129, 162, 163, 164, 168, 185–92, 195, 198, 204, 205, 207, 209, 217–18
belonging 20, 28–31, 39–49, 65–76
Benhabib, Seyla 29–30
Bennett [Moore], Zoë 1, 2, 32, 103, 131, 133, 136, 198
bereavement 6, 9, 81, 91–2, 134, 195–205
Berger, Teresa 140, 141, 146
Berry, Jan 2, 3, 8, 25–35, 145–6
Bible, biblical 4, 9, 52, 56, 60, 61, 62, 77–88, 111–19, 121–8, 139–46, 169, 188, 216, 223, 230
biblical feminism, *see* feminism
biblical women, *see* women
birth, birthing 6, 9, 85–6, 87, 88, 124, 131–7, 142–3, 195–205, 207–20
Black women, *see* women
body, bodies, *see* women's bodies
Boisen, Anton 32
Bons-Storm, Riet 32, 131
boundary, boundaries 5, 35, 65–76, 81, 82, 100, 107, 165, 173–84, 215
Brennan, Catherine 105
Brown, Brian 105
Brown, Callum 42, 186
Brown, Lyn Mikel 82
Browning, Don 147
Brueggemann, Walter 35
Buch, Elena 33
Butler, Judith 34, 103
Büttner, Gerhard 84

case studies 2, 55, 145, 121–8
Catholic church, *see* church, churches
charismatic tradition 111–19
childbearing, *see* motherhood
childhood, theologies of 77–88
Christ, Carol 164, 167
Christ, Jesus 5, 6, 9, 20, 34, 68, 71–2, 75, 77, 84–5, 87, 98, 99, 112, 113, 116, 125, 126, 136, 139–46, 185–92, 196, 223, 224, 226, 231
Christa 24, 136, 188
Christie, Ann 5, 186, 189
Christology 5, 6, 9, 20, 75, 185–92
church, churches 1, 4–6, 9, 15, 16, 24, 30, 32, 33, 41, 46–7, 51–63, 65–76, 77–8, 80, 82, 85–6, 103, 107–9, 111–19, 121–8, 131–7, 139–46, 151, 176, 185–6, 191–2, 195, 199, 204, 205, 222, 223, 228–31
   Anglican church 40, 46, 51–63, 65–76, 131–7
   Baptist churches 4, 77–88, 122–3
   Catholic church 4, 66, 68–9, 70, 91–101, 107, 148, 186
   Evangelical churches 111–19
   Free churches 66, 78, 106
   Methodist church 185, 195
   Nonconformist churches 103–9
   Pentecostal churches 121–8
      Church of God of Prophecy 121–8
   Protestant churches 4, 91–101, 103–9, 148
   Quaker tradition 148, 155, 189
church authority 40, 60, 66, 68, 70–71, 74–5, 117, 222, 229–31
Clanton, Jann Aldredge 122–3, 127
Clark-King, Ellen 186
class, *see* social class
Clegg, Cecelia 91, 93
Clements, Jennifer 174–5
'coercive space' 72–4
Coffey, Amanda 26
Collins, Nancy 162–3, 170
communion, *see* Eucharist
communion of saints 17, 155, 195
community 15, 20, 22, 29, 32, 33, 41, 46–8, 57, 65–76, 83, 91–101, 103, 108, 111, 123, 131–7, 139–46, 163, 169, 171, 190
confidentiality 26, 79, 82, 177
conflict 4, 54, 81, 86, 91–101, 115, 135, 154, 157, 169, 176, 210, 212, 213, 216, 219–20
control, *see* church authority, 'coercive space', women's agency
Cooper-White, Pamela 31, 166
counselling 32, 175, 176, 181, 207
creativity 6, 35, 79–80, 88, 142–3, 174, 197, 199–200
creeds, credal language 44, 73, 185, 186, 188, 191
crisis, spiritual/psychological 6, 21, 46, 81, 208, 210–13, 217
cross-cultural research, *see* research
culture 4, 7, 9, 31, 52, 53–4, 59, 62–3, 71, 86, 91, 104, 108, 115, 123, 209, 215, 217
   church culture 4, 9, 71, 108
   consumer culture 52
   patriarchal culture 53–4, 217
   popular culture 52, 59, 80
   research culture 7, 141
   secular culture 63

Daly, Mary 51, 52, 61
data 6, 33, 40, 43, 54, 66, 77–80, 87, 107, 113, 133–4, 196, 198–9, 200–205, 208, 222
   data analysis 18, 20, 21–2, 77–81, 196, 200–205, 222
   data collection 43, 54–5, 66, 78–9, 107, 113, 133–4, 198–9
Davis, Deseta 4, 9, 16, 121–8
Day, Abby 3, 8, 9, 16, 39–49
Day, Graham 105
De Beavoir, Simone 51
death and dying 6, 9, 42, 87, 92, 131, 135, 136, 195–205, 210–11
Denton, Melinda Lundquist 82
Dickinson, Emily 79
Dierks, Sheila 65
dissent 66, 72–4, 108, 198
Divine, the 6, 17, 34, 43, 69, 84, 87, 88, 98, 99, 137, 145, 149, 150, 156,

158, 174, 188–9, 190–2, 197, 203, 204–5, 225, 231
doctrine(s), *see* creeds, credal language
Douglas, Kelly Brown 187
Downing, Roberta 112
dualism 27–30, 34, 35, 75, 99
Dyckman, Katherine 186
dying process, *see* death and dying

Edwards, Rosalind 16, 19, 25
Edwards, Tilden 179
egalitarianism 58, 61, 62, 63, 66, 112, 119, 139, 180
embodiment 6, 34, 65, 66, 80, 140, 190, 199–203, 204, 208, 214–17
empowerment, *see* power
equality 52–63, 70, 75, 79, 108, 112, 123, 197
Erikson, Erik 81–2
Essenelt, J. 17–18
Etherington, Kim 14, 19
ethics, *see* research ethics
ethnic minorities 16, 121–28, 161–71
ethnography 2, 14, 15, 17, 18, 26, 33, 78, 131, 207, 222
Ettling, Dorothy 174
Eucharist 3–4, 20, 46, 65–76, 188
Evangelical churches, *see* church, churches
exclusion 3, 28, 31, 57, 63, 65–76, 97

faith, faithing
　apophatic faith/faithing 144, 166
　faith as habitus, practice 39–49, 204–5
　faith development 2, 4, 7, 83, 84–5, 111, 113, 141, 171, 197
　faith journey 5, 26, 54, 67–9, 74, 88, 111, 113, 117, 118, 131–7, 141–6, 148, 161, 164, 168, 171, 173, 220, 230
　faith of girls 77–88, 197
　faith of women 14–15, 16, 22, 25–35, 39–49, 51–63, 91–101, 103–109, 131–7, 139–46, 147–59, 161–71, 173–84, 185–92, 195–205, 207–220, 221–31
　faith of young women 60–63, 65–76, 111–119
　faith stages 3–4, 9–10, 37, 39–88, 117

faith styles 3–4, 37, 39–88, especially 84–5
faithing 4, 5, 82, 83, 84–5, 141, 144–5, 166
　ritual faithing 5, 26–7, 35, 67–72, 139–46
Faludi, Susan 52, 56
family 29, 30, 35, 42, 43, 48, 65–6, 69, 78, 85, 92, 93, 97, 103, 108, 112, 115, 126, 132, 164, 165, 190, 200–201, 203–4, 227
fatherhood of God, *see* God
fear 59, 66, 68, 74, 75, 80, 82, 95, 97, 131, 212, 213, 223
feminism 1, 3, 17, 24, 40, 51–63, 118, 123, 135, 161
　attitudes to feminism 3, 51–63
　biblical feminism 118
　definitions of feminism 51–3, 56–9, 61, 62, 123
　postfeminism 52, 53, 62
　secondwave feminism 51, 135
　strategic feminism 17
　thirdwave feminism 59
feminist
　feminist backlash 52, 56, 59
　feminist ecclesiology 20, 66
　feminist liturgy 26–7, 65–6, 139–140, 144–6
　feminist research methodology 1–2, 6–8, 9–10, 13, 78–80, 133, 141, 163–4, 174–5, 198–9
　feminist theology 1–2, 6, 16, 18, 27, 30–32, 34–5, 58, 77, 147–8, 185–6, 199
Fiorenza, Elizabeth Schüssler 20, 35, 111
Fischer, Kathleen 167, 169, 173–4
Flax, Jane 149
Forrester, Duncan 30, 31
Foster, David 21
Foucault, Michel 33
Fowler, James 82, 83, 117
Fraser, Giles 196
Free churches, *see* church, churches
friendship 5, 35, 46, 59, 118, 173, 177–84
Furlong, Monica 53

Garvin, Mary 186

Generation 'A' 3, 39
gender
    concepts of gender 34–5, 51–63
    construction of gender 40–42, 46–8, 51–4, 69–71, 151, 162, 199, 200. 203
    gender awareness 121
    gender bias/inequality 3, 51, 53–4, 60–63, 69, 221, 230
    gender critique 31, 40–41
    gender differences 29, 31, 40–41
    gender equality 53–5, 58–9, 60–63, 197
    gender hierarchy 164
    gender identity 69, 71, 79, 103–104, 113, 115
    gender imagery 4, 43–4, 46–8, 124–7, 185–7, 190
    gender issues 3, 7, 17, 96, 121, 184
    gender theory 34–5, 41
    gender and language, *see* language
Gilligan, Carol 81, 82, 150, 162
girls 3, 4, 9, 16, 47, 77–88, 117, 118, 126, 136, 197, 221, 229
Glasson, Barbara 151, 158
Glick, Peter 117
God
    fatherhood of God 83, 125–6, 136–7, 163, 165, 167, 188, 190, 191, 224, 226, 228
    girls'/women's beliefs, concepts, models and images of God 4, 40, 43–8, 58, 68, 73, 82, 83–5, 92, 97–101, 117–18, 126, 133, 134, 135, 136, 155, 163, 162–71, 189–180
    girls'/women's lives as sources for knowledge of God 17, 87–8
    girls'/women's relationship to God 5, 6, 14, 15, 24, 97–101, 108, 150–51, 152, 153, 156, 157, 158, 162–71, 176, 182, 203–5, 221–31
Goddess 27
Graham, Elaine 1, 2, 15, 30, 31, 134, 145, 197, 198
Gramich, Katie 105
Grant, Jacquelyn 185
Grenz, Stanley 104
Grey, Mary 24, 197
Grof, Christina 211, 213
Grof, Stanislav 211, 213

Groothuis, Rebecca M. 112, 115
grounded theory, *see* theory
groups, use of in research 5, 9, 26, 27, 39, 41, 78–9, 92, 112–13, 114, 115, 116, 118, 133–6, 137, 140–41
Gunner, Susanna 5, 9, 139–46

Habermas, Jürgen 29
habitus, *see* faith as habitus
Halsey, Margaret 2
Hammersley, Peter 163
Hampson, Daphne 51, 190
Hardesty, Nancy 127
Harris, Maria 19
Harrison, Beverly Wildung 179–80
Hay, David 80, 82
Heller, David 82
Helminiak, Daniel 209
Henderson, Gwen 16
Heraclitus 219–20
Hess, Carol Lakey 82, 86
heuristic research 14
Heyward, Carter 34, 179–80
Hillman, James 213
Hochschild, Arlie 42
holiness, the holy 15, 17–18, 19–20, 20–21, 68–72, 74–5, 82, 98–9, 136–7, 145, 157, 169, 174–6, 207, 210
Holland, Janet 25, 26
Hughes, Katie 62
Hunt, Mary 139
Hurd, Jennifer 6, 9, 195–205
humour 108–9

identity 4, 27, 33, 34–5, 45, 55, 75, 77, 79, 88, 94, 101, 103–9, 112, 118, 134, 151, 153, 157, 158, 161–2, 165, 210–11, 214, 216, 217, 218, 219
images of God, *see* God
inclusion, women's and girls' 3, 53–4, 55, 56, 59, 62, 63, 65–76
inclusive language, *see* language
initiation rites, *see* baptism, rites of initiation
interconnectedness, *see* relationality
interviews 2, 6, 18, 20, 26, 42, 43, 54, 55, 59, 60, 61, 63, 66, 67, 78–9, 82,

84, 92, 105, 106–7, 134, 144, 148, 164, 173, 200, 207, 222
invisibility of women's lives 4, 25, 48, 80, 124, 173
Irigaray, Luce 82, 87, 203
Isay, Dave 18
Isherwood, Lisa 34, 123, 139, 186
Izzard, Susannah 170, 171

Jantzen, Grace 6, 87, 88, 195–205
Jenett, Diane 174
Johnson, Elizabeth 17, 186
Jones, Serena 51
Joung, Eun Sim 5, 9, 16, 161–71

Kegan, Robert 81, 82, 85, 86
Kennedy, Margaret 230
Kidd, Sue Monk 164
Killen, Patricia 167, 169
Kirkpatrick, Lee 163, 168
Kitcatt, Caroline 5, 9, 173–84
Klassen, Chris 51
Korean women, *see* women

language 61, 67, 69, 83, 84, 105, 140, 142, 145, 153, 168, 185, 186, 187, 188, 191
 body language 19, 148
 exclusive language 28, 121–8, 133, 136
 inclusive language 56, 127–8, 187
Lanzetta, Beverly 174
Lebacqz, Karen 180
lectio divina 20, 21
Lennie, June 18
liberation 1, 5, 24, 26, 31, 66, 76, 121–2, 126, 133, 135, 153, 185, 188–91, 192
Liebert, Elizabeth 117, 186
Liechty, Joseph 91, 93
liminal, liminality 6, 16, 81, 86, 133, 137, 158, 193–231
listening 18–20, 26, 32, 99, 121, 123, 131, 134, 142, 144, 148–9, 151, 156–9, 167–9, 181, 192
liturgy, *see also* feminist liturgy 27, 65–76, 139–46, 147, 191, 192
 liturgical robes/vestments 67, 70–71, 74–5

liturgical space 66, 67, 71, 74
Llewellyn, Dawn 51, 52
Lonergan, Bernard 209, 219
longitudinal research 39, 41
Lorde, Audre 13
Lunn, Pam 27

McEwan, Dorothea 123, 139,
McKittrick, David 91
McRobbie, Angela 52, 53
McVea, David 91
McWhorter, Ladelle 33
Machung, Anne 42
marginalization 16, 25, 28, 30, 41, 69, 75, 95, 111, 124, 191, 208, 222
Mearns, Dave 175
Mechain, Gwerful 105, 109
meaning, search for 3, 145, 165, 166, 201, 208, 211, 213, 219
Mellott, David 15
mentoring 5, 9, 22, 85, 86, 112, 119
Mercer, Joyce Ann 80
Methodist church, *see* church, churches
methods, *see* research methods
midwife, midwifery 86, 207, 208, 210, 211
Miller, Jean Baker 161, 165
Miller-McLemore, Bonnie 30, 32, 132, 151, 198, 199
ministry, Christian 1, 2, 3, 6 , 9, 54, 55, 65, 66, 75, 112, 131, 195, 196, 203, 221, 223, 224, 228–31
misogyny 53, 108
models of God, Christ, *see* Christ & God
Molina, Noelia 6, 9, 207-220
Moltmann, Jürgen 190
morality 4, 29, 41–3, 46–8, 105–9, 118, 161–2, 199
Morley, Janet 26
Morton, Nelle 18, 141, 147
Moschella, Mary Clark 14, 15, 17, 18, 19
motherhood 6, 47–8, 54, 55, 63, 81, 87–8, 125–6, 131, 134, 135, 136, 137, 167–8, 207–20
 mother-daughter relationship 47, 74, 168, 201, 202, 203
MOW (Movement for the Ordination of Women) 56, 57, 59
Muslim women, *see* women

narrative
- biblical/patriarchal/religious narrative 61, 85, 87, 106, 112, 113, 115, 116, 118, 125, 128, 140, 221
- narrative analysis/research 14, 49, 54, 151–3, 158, 164, 167, 171, 207
- narrative faith/identity 107, 144–5, 186
- 'narratives of harm' 221, 231
- women's narratives 5, 6, 32, 52, 59, 61, 87, 106, 123, 150, 152, 168, 212, 221

natal, natality 6, 87–8, 195–205
Natiello, Peggy 180
necrophilia 196–7, 199, 202
Nesbitt, Eleanor 78
Neu, Diann 26
Neuger, Christie 151, 221
nonconformist tradition, *see* church, churches
nonverbal communication 19, 148, 157–8
NVIVO 222
Nye, Rebecca 79, 80, 82, 86

oral history 2, 222
'ordinary Christology' 5, 186, 189
'ordinary theology' 4
ordination, women's 8, 53–4, 56–60, 61, 63, 75, 136, 178, 197, 230
organic research 14, 174, 175

Page, Sarah-Jane 3, 9, 51–63
pain, *see* suffering
Painter, Christine Valters 21
pastoral care 2, 6, 15, 31–2, 85–6, 108–9, 117, 131, 135–6, 145, 147, 166, 195–205, 207, 208, 221, 230
pastoral theology 1, 2, 13–14, 15, 18, 19, 30, 32, 131, 198, 221, 231
Pazmiňo, Robert 14, 15
Pennington, Basil 21
Pentecostal churches, *see* church, churches
Perrin, Ruth 4, 9, 111–19
person-centred psychology 174, 175, 176, 180, 245
Phillips, Anne 1–10, 16, 77–88, 197
pilot study 6, 196, 200–205, 207–8, 220
Plummer, Ken 31
poetry 4, 14, 24, 105, 109, 134, 140, 149

Porter, Fran 1–10, 62, 91–101
power 23, 26, 27, 28, 31, 32, 33, 34, 40, 41, 56, 66, 67, 70, 72, 73, 74, 75, 76, 79, 91, 107, 122, 133, 144–6, 147, 157, 168, 169, 176, 180, 181, 183, 184, 185, 214, 217, 230
- disempowerment/powerlessness 5, 27, 62, 66, 74, 75, 94–6, 97, 104, 106, 127, 135, 137, 139, 185, 188, 217
- empowerment 1, 8, 9, 17–18, 24, 26, 33, 86, 94–6, 97–9, 100–101, 106, 112, 115, 128, 132, 139, 169, 185, 191, 214, 217, 219
- power dynamics 29, 32, 70, 78, 141, 146, 173, 176, 222

practical theology 1–2, 16, 30, 31, 32, 132, 147, 198–9
prayer 5, 18–19, 22, 39, 43, 45, 72, 85, 93, 108, 139, 140, 144, 155, 169, 170, 188, 204, 223, 228–30
praxis 1, 15, 17, 22, 123, 132, 198
preaching 4, 21, 22, 58, 59, 62, 108, 116, 121–8, 192
presence 5, 6, 17, 46, 80, 83, 84, 87, 96, 140, 143, 145, 149–50, 151, 155, 156, 157, 158, 161, 173, 180, 181, 188, 189, 205, 223–5, 226, 227
priesthood, *see* ministry, sacraments, women – ordained/clergy women
private, privacy 3, 8, 16, 19, 23, 25–35, 108, 109, 133, 146, 166
Procter-Smith, Marjorie 65, 72, 122, 127, 139
prophecy, prophetic 15, 17, 25–35, 87, 100, 151
Protestant churches, *see* church, churches
psychology 32, 81, 82, 86, 111, 112, 117, 163, 174, 208, 209
- transpersonal psychology 174, 208, 209, 210, 211, 213

psychotherapy 32, 81, 176, 180, 183, 210
puberty 77, 81, 82, 86
public theology 3, 8, 30–35
purity 71, 87

Quaker tradition, *see* church, churches
qualitative research, *see* research
quantitative research, *see* research

Ramazanoglu, Caroline 25, 26
rape 31, 222, 226; *see also* abuse
Read, Stephen 162, 163, 170
Redfern, Catherine 51
reflexivity, *see* research
relationality 4, 5, 34, 83, 84, 85, 111, 112, 144, 147–59, 161–71, 197, 199, 200, 201, 202, 203, 205
relationship/s
  abusive relationships, *see* abuse
  family relationships 93, 200–201, 203, 218, 227
  parental relationships 6, 23, 161–71, 215
  relationship with God/Jesus 5, 15, 44, 69, 82–3, 84, 85, 97, 98, 101, 116, 162, 163, 165, 167, 170, 174, 176, 182, 224, 225, 227, 229
  relationship with others, general 6, 26, 35, 66, 80, 81, 83, 85, 135, 153–6, 157, 161, 162, 163, 165, 169, 170, 221, 229
  relationship with research participants 25, 26, 78, 134, 141
  relationship with self 69, 151–3
  relationship with spiritual director 5, 173–184
  relationships between women 57, 113
  same-sex relationships 31, 33–35, 108–9
  social relationships 39, 44, 46, 66, 92, 93, 200, 219
religion/religiosity 3, 4, 5, 8, 13, 14, 34, 39–49, 51–4, 55, 62, 69, 71, 84, 91, 93, 94, 96, 103–9, 123, 147, 176, 189, 209, 214
  definitions of religion/religiosity 29, 39–41, 91–2
  religion and feminism/gender 1, 3, 4, 5, 8, 39–49, 51–4, 55, 60, 61, 62–3, 103–9, 173
  religious attachment, *see* attachment
  religious experience 3, 5, 77, 80, 162, 163, 174
  study of religion 1, 3
research
  cross-cultural research 207, 209
  qualitative research 1–2, 3, 6–7, 9, 13–24, 25, 26, 39, 41, 65, 78–9, 82, 113, 132–4, 141, 161, 164, 185–6, 198, 221
  quantitative research 2, 40, 48, 54–5, 113
  reflexivity in research 9, 14, 26, 132–3, 142, 198–9, 200
  research ethics 13, 78–9
  research journal 9, 21, 131, 132–3, 226
  research methods 2, 14, 16, 19, 21, 54–5, 78–9, 113, 133–4, 141–2, 198–9
  research process 1, 3, 4, 5, 9, 13–24, 26, 33, 78–9, 118, 132–4, 136–7, 141–2, 145, 164, 174–5, 198, 200, 222
  research proposal 18
  research supervision 7, 8–9, 18, 22
resistance 73–4, 81, 86, 165, 169, 171, 181, 221
responsibility in research, *see* accountability
Rhys, Francesca 5, 9, 185–92
Ribbens, Jane 16, 19, 25
Rich, Adrienne 24, 149, 216, 217
Richards, Amy 60
rite(s), ritual 5, 26–7, 33, 35, 65–75, 139–46, 209
  rites of initiation 67–8
  rites of passage 135–6, 195, 209
  ritual faithing, *see* faith
Rogers, Carl 176
role models 4, 9, 60, 61, 111–19, 125
  biblical role models 111–19, 125
Ross, Susan 65, 66, 139
Rothwell, Emma 5, 9, 131–7
Ruether, Rosemary Radford 59, 65, 69, 186
Ruffing, Janet 181

sacraments 65, 66, 145; *see also* baptism, Eucharist
sacred, *see* holy, holiness
same-sex relationships, *see* relationship/s
Saunders, Cheryl 124, 127
Savage, Sara 86
Scharff, Christina 52, 53, 56, 59, 61, 62, 63

sectarianism 91–101
seeker, spiritual 173–84
self
　concepts of the self 6, 20, 32, 47, 81–2, 103–4, 106, 149
　relationship to self, *see* relationship
　self acceptance 152, 158, 211, 214, 217, 220
　self awareness 80, 152, 157, 158, 181, 182, 183, 211, 217, 218
　self belief/esteem/worth 16, 26, 71, 74, 82, 85, 103, 104, 108, 123, 127, 133, 154, 158, 169, 171, 214
　self criticism 104, 114
　self determination/ownership 74, 79, 96, 132, 176, 191, 209, 219
　self-discipline 48
　self disclosure 177, 178
　self harming/destruction 108, 230
　self identity/perception/understanding 69, 70, 71, 73, 92, 115, 150, 151–3, 154, 155–7, 210, 214
　self image/representation 163, 164, 165, 166, 167, 170, 171
　self sacrifice 82, 134, 135
　self transcendence/transformation 208–9, 211, 219, 225–228
　use of self in research, *see* reflexivity in research
sermons, *see* preaching
sexuality 29, 31, 33, 34, 35, 42, 54, 55, 105, 108, 196, 214, 215, 216
　desexualization 215–16
　sexualization 52, 80–81, 85
Shakespeare, Steven 71
Shields, Lisa 174
Shooter, Susan 2, 6, 9, 221–31
silence 5, 8, 19, 32, 131–7, 147–59, 166, 168
　practices of silence 9, 147–59
　silencing 5, 18, 30, 131–7
Slee, Nicola 1–10, 13–24, 26, 79, 80, 85, 107, 111, 124, 131, 136, 141, 144, 145, 162, 164, 166, 169, 186, 188, 190, 222
Smith, Christian 82
Smith, Elizabeth 127, 128
social action 15, 31, 39

social class 35, 39, 55, 62, 101, 104, 105, 107, 115, 123, 131
social sciences 8, 16, 174, 198
socialization 40, 41, 48, 82
sociology 41, 80, 82, 111, 208
sociology of religion 3, 40, 52
spiritual accompaniment/direction 5, 9, 157, 169, 173–184
spiritual practice 3, 4, 10, 13–24, 129–192
spirituality 6, 13–24, 25–35, 40–41, 43, 46, 77–8, 79, 80, 82, 83–5, 109, 132, 136, 137, 170–71, 207–20, 221, 223–31
Staller, Karen 33
Stanley, Liz 26
Stations of the cross 5, 139–46
stereotypes 56, 93, 106–7, 125, 143
Stevenson-Moessner, Jeanne 2, 32, 117, 131, 166, 221
Stiver, Irene 161, 168
stories, *see* narrative
Stuart, Elizabeth 33, 34, 35, 199
suffering/pain 6, 20, 24, 34, 46, 47, 66, 87, 91, 94, 98, 99, 100, 133, 134, 135, 136, 139, 153, 165, 169, 171, 188, 200, 201, 202, 205, 210, 212, 214, 221, 224, 225, 226, 227, 228, 229
survivor 6, 47, 221–31
symbols, the symbolic 27, 70, 74, 75, 84, 87, 133–4, 140, 143, 144, 145, 162, 166, 196, 197, 201, 210, 211, 213
Symposium on the Faith Lives of Women and Girls 6–8, 15

taboo 68, 75, 190
Tamminen, Kalevi 79, 82
Temple, Barbara 122, 123
theory
　attachment theory, *see* attachment
　discourse theory 29
　faith development theory 83
　grounded theory 79, 207, 222, 231
　person-centred theory 176, 180
　political theory 28
　social learning theory 114
Thorne, Brian 175
Thorne, Helen 54, 55, 57

transcendence 34, 68, 83, 84, 98, 100, 155, 168, 208, 209, 211, 217, 230
transcripts, transcription 18, 19–21, 26, 43, 79, 124, 134, 148, 164, 200, 222
transference 180
transformation 6, 13, 14, 23, 65, 66, 75, 122, 132, 133, 137, 140, 147, 151, 158, 199, 207, 208, 211, 216, 217, 218, 220, 223, 225–8, 229, 231
transitions 23, 67, 77, 80, 82, 86, 117, 133, 145, 151, 152, 207, 208, 209, 211, 212, 213, 214, 215, 216, 219, 220
transpersonal psychology, *see* psychology
trauma 97, 98, 135, 136, 166, 202, 223, 226, 228
Trible, Phyllis 52, 85, 86, 87, 118
Troubles, the 4, 91. 92–4, 95, 97, 98, 99, 100
Trzebiatowska, Marta 51, 52
Tyler, Imogen 214

Van Gennep, Arnold 209
violence 29, 31–2, 42, 91, 92, 93, 98, 100, 133, 134, 136, 196, 222, 223; *see also* abuse, rape
vocation, *see* ministry
voice, voices
    children's/girl's voices 84
    women's voices 18, 19, 20, 23, 26, 30–31, 32, 34, 35, 57, 65, 66, 71, 73, 79, 81, 82, 96, 106, 107, 114, 117, 128, 131–7, 147, 148, 152, 158, 162, 166, 167, 173, 174, 176, 214, 221, 222, 231
    young adult voices 117

Walby, Sylvia 42, 60, 62
Walton, Heather 1, 2, 134, 145, 198
Ward, Frances 32, 134, 145, 198
Wasey, Kim 3, 8, 9, 65–76
WATCH (Women and the Church) 59
Watson, Natalie 20, 66, 75
Watts, Fraser 86
Weil, Simone 18
West, Candace 42
Wiles, Maurice 189
Wilson, Bryan 47

Wise, Sue 26
Wolter-Gustafson, Carol 174
Woman-Cross 5, 139–46
womanist 123, 124, 148, 151, 186, 198, 213
womb 4, 85–6, 87, 196, 203
women
    biblical women 4, 9, 61, 87–8, 111–19, 124–6, 140–44
    Black and ethnic minority women 4, 9, 16, 121–8
    Korean women 5, 161–71
    lay women 3, 5, 6, 8, 55, 60–62, 65–76, 91–101, 103–9, 111–19, 121–8, 131–7, 139–46, 161–71, 173–84, 185–92
    mothers 6, 54, 207–20
    Muslim women 53
    old women 3, 9, 16, 39–49
    ordained/clergy women 3, 54, 55–60, 62, 75
    young women 3, 4, 9, 52, 53, 55, 60–62, 63, 65–76, 111–19
    Welsh women 4, 103–9
    women researchers 7, 10, 14, 16, 18
    women survivors 221–231
Womenchurch 20, 139
women's agency 23, 41, 68, 72–4, 94–5, 97–8, 101, 103, 108
women's authority 24, 60, 66, 75, 78, 85
women's bodies 20, 26, 34, 35, 52, 66, 75–6, 80, 87, 106, 124, 144, 196–7, 202, 214–17
women's experience(s) 3, 17, 25, 74, 77, 80, 126, 131, 132, 148, 158, 161–2, 187, 209
women's faith, *see* faith/faithing
women's leadership 53, 54, 63, 112, 185, 218, 230
worship, *see* liturgy and feminist liturgy
Woolley, Alison 5, 8, 9, 147–59
Wootton, Janet 143, 144
Wuthnow, Robert 41

Young, Iris 28–9

Zimmerman, Don H. 42